MW01118442

LEADING IT PROJECTS

The IT Manager's Guide

LEADING IT PROJECTS

The IT Manager's Guide

Jessica Keyes

CRC Press
Taylor & Francis Group
Boca Raton   London   New York

CRC Press is an imprint of the
Taylor & Francis Group, an **informa** business

AN AUERBACH BOOK

Auerbach Publications
Taylor & Francis Group
6000 Broken Sound Parkway NW, Suite 300
Boca Raton, FL 33487-2742

© 2009 by Taylor & Francis Group, LLC
Auerbach is an imprint of Taylor & Francis Group, an Informa business

No claim to original U.S. Government works
Printed in the United States of America on acid-free paper
10 9 8 7 6 5 4 3 2 1

International Standard Book Number-13: 978-1-4200-7082-8 (Softcover)

This book contains information obtained from authentic and highly regarded sources. Reasonable efforts have been made to publish reliable data and information, but the author and publisher cannot assume responsibility for the validity of all materials or the consequences of their use. The authors and publishers have attempted to trace the copyright holders of all material reproduced in this publication and apologize to copyright holders if permission to publish in this form has not been obtained. If any copyright material has not been acknowledged please write and let us know so we may rectify in any future reprint.

Except as permitted under U.S. Copyright Law, no part of this book may be reprinted, reproduced, transmitted, or utilized in any form by any electronic, mechanical, or other means, now known or hereafter invented, including photocopying, microfilming, and recording, or in any information storage or retrieval system, without written permission from the publishers.

For permission to photocopy or use material electronically from this work, please access www.copyright.com (http://www.copyright.com/) or contact the Copyright Clearance Center, Inc. (CCC), 222 Rosewood Drive, Danvers, MA 01923, 978-750-8400. CCC is a not-for-profit organization that provides licenses and registration for a variety of users. For organizations that have been granted a photocopy license by the CCC, a separate system of payment has been arranged.

Trademark Notice: Product or corporate names may be trademarks or registered trademarks, and are used only for identification and explanation without intent to infringe.

Library of Congress Cataloging-in-Publication Data

Keyes, Jessica, 1950-
    Leading IT projects : the IT manager's guide / author, Jessica Keyes.
        p. cm.
    Includes bibliographical references and index.
    ISBN 978-1-4200-7082-8 (hardback : alk. paper) 1. Project management. 2. Information
technology--Management. 3. Strategic planning. I. Title.

HD69.P75K512 2008
004.068'4--dc22   2008014380

Visit the Taylor & Francis Web site at
http://www.taylorandfrancis.com

and the Auerbach Web site at
http://www.auerbach-publications.com

Dedication

This book is dedicated to my family and friends.

Contents

Chapter 5

Project Critical Success Factors

PART II: BASICS OF PROJECT MANAGEMENT

Chapter 6

Project Scope Management and System Requirements

Chapter 7

Project Scheduling

Chapter 8

Project Estimation

Chapter 9

PART IV: INDEX

Foreword

In Tracy Kidder's book *Soul of a New Machine*, he details the riveting story of a project conducted at breakneck speed, and under incredible pressure. Driven by pure adrenaline, the team members soon became obsessed with trying to achieve the impossible. For more than a year, they gave up their nights and weekends—in the end logging nearly 100 hours a week each! Somewhere buried in the midst of Kidder's prose we find that at the end of this project the entire staff quit. Not just one or two of them, but every single one!

The information technology field is ripe with stories such as this one. Software development projects are usually complex and often mission critical. As a result the pressure on staff to produce is great. And sometimes, as in the Kidder example, even with success comes failure. The purpose of *Leading IT Projects: The IT Manager's Guide* is to provide a detailed roadmap for project success that project and senior managers can use right off the shelf. Although *Leading IT Projects* does indeed provide detailed information about the technical aspects of project management, most importantly it also focuses on the human side of project management—e.g., leadership skills, team building, promoting creativity, etc.

Part One focuses on the principles of strategic project management—i.e., the "soft skills." Here, we cover such topics as fundamentals of project management, project management skill sets, managing the team, critical success factors, and tracking and control of the project. Part Two delves into the nitty-gritty technical aspects of project management, including scope management, scheduling, estimation, budgeting, risk management, procurement management, and project termination. All 11 chapters in Parts One and Two are written in a "hands-on," "roll up those sleeves" style, providing numerous examples and checklists.

Part Three provides eight reference guides, including a complete IT metrics reference, complete sample project plan, and even an introduction to software engineering for those project managers who have sidled into the department without hands-on software development experience.

Leading IT Projects: The IT Manager's Guide finishes up in Part Four, located on the CD, with a set of appendices that provide a complete project managers compendium of tools and techniques; 61 project management forms, 9 Excel spreadsheets, and 3 Microsoft project templates are provided for immediate use. I would like to thank the City of Raleigh, North Carolina, and Enterprise PMO for many of the templates in this section.

About the Author

Jessica Keyes is president of New Art Technologies, Inc., a high-technology and management consultancy and development firm started in New York in 1989. She is also a founding partner of New York City-based Manhattan Technology Group. Keyes is a member of the Beta Gamma Sigma and Delta Mu Delta honorary societies.

Keyes has given seminars for such prestigious universities as Carnegie Mellon, Boston University, University of Illinois, James Madison University, and San Francisco State University. She is a frequent keynote speaker on the topics of competitive strategy, and productivity and quality. She is former advisor for DataPro, McGraw-Hill's computer research arm, as well as a member of the Sprint Business Council. Keyes is also a founding board of director member of the New York Software Industry Association. She has recently completed a two-year term on the mayor of New York City's Small Business Advisory Council. She is currently a professor of computer science at Fairleigh Dickinson University's graduate center as well as the University of Phoenix, where she is a member of the College Advisory Council. She has been the editor for WGL's *Handbook of eBusiness* and CRC Press' *Systems Development Management* and *Information Management*.

Prior to founding New Art, Keyes was managing director of R&D for the New York Stock Exchange and has been an officer with Swiss Bank Co. and Banker's Trust, both in New York City. She holds a master of business administration degree from New York University where she did her research in the area of artificial intelligence.

A noted columnist and correspondent with over 200 articles published, Keyes is the author of 24 books, including Auerbach's *Knowledge Management, Business Intelligence, and Content Management* and *X Internet: The Executable and Extendable Internet*.

Permissions Notice

The following, which appear in the appendices, are used with permission and were developed by Covansys for the City of Raleigh Enterprise PMO with generic format by CVR-IT (www.cvr-it.com):

Consultant Evaluation Form
Cost Benefit Analysis
Customer Reference Rating Form
Enterprise Project Management Office Charter
Exit Plan Form
Meeting Minutes
Monthly Status Report
Planning Risk Evaluation Checklist
Project Change Management Plan Template
Project Change Request Form
Project Charter Form
Project Charter Form Deliverables
Project Charter Form Milestones
Project Close Out
Project Commitments Agreement Form
Project Issue Document Form
Project Plan
Project Procurement Plan
Project Quality Plan
Project Resource Plan
Project Risk Management Plan
Project Scope Statement
Project Use Case Template
Risk Assessment Questionnaire
Risk Assessment SOW
Service Level Agreement
Statement of Work for Services

PRINCIPLES OF STRATEGIC PROJECT MANAGEMENT

Chapter 1

Fundamentals of Project Management

Our first chapter will examine the fundamentals of project management. Readers will examine project management in an organizational context and identify the people, processes, technologies, and products involved. Project management will be examined within the context of the systems development life cycle (SDLC).

Why Is Project Planning Important?

The Standish Group published their landmark Chaos Report in 1995. It included statistics such as "84 percent of projects fail or are significantly challenged" and "45 percent of developed features are never used," and is among the most oft-quoted reports in the industry. A decade later there seems to be some improvement. Most of the troublesome projects in the 2004 Chaos Survey had a cost overrun of under 20 percent of the budget, a threefold improvement over the first 1994 study. Of all projects with cost overruns, including failed projects, the average project cost overrun in 2004 was found to be 43 percent against an average cost overrun of 180 percent in 1994. Of the projects studied, 53 percent were deemed challenged, 18 percent failed and the rest were successful.

Although project planning will never eliminate all over-budget and over-schedule situations, the systematic methodology that project planners should utilize will certainly reduce the likelihood of problems.

Similar to all other aspects of systems development, the development of a project plan (i.e., project planning) cannot be done in a vacuum. A wide variety of people (i.e., stakeholders) need to be involved for the plan to be accurate and workable. Once the project plan is developed, it is used to systemize the ideas presented in the plan (i.e., manage the project). The plan itself is never "cast in concrete." What this means is that a project plan is often modified as constraints and assumptions, and even risks, change during the life cycle of the systems development effort.

Project Management and SDLC

To understand IT project management, one must first understand where project planning fits within the SDLC. As shown in Figure 1.1, the SDLC is a set of phased processes that guide a systems development effort from its inception through its implementation.

Projects are similar to living entities: they are conceived, they live, and then they die. This is why the term *life cycle* is used. A system starts out as someone's idea, i.e., *a concept*. For example, someone in Finance might have an idea to build an accounts payable system that processes payments through the Internet. If the idea is deemed feasible, it is placed in development, i.e., systems development and design. Once the system has been designed, it can be coded and then implemented, i.e., placed in production for end users to use. Eventually, however, systems outlive their usefulness. At this point, they are either retired or replaced. We can then say that the system is "closed out."

Thus, the four generic stages of the project life cycle can be said to be:

1. Concept (i.e., feasibility, project planning)
2. Development (i.e., analysis, design, code, test)
3. Implementation (i.e., conversion, maintenance)
4. Closeout

This is the macro view of the project life cycle. As is often the case, there are variations on this theme, as shown in Table 1.1.

Concept

The *idea* phase of the SDLC is when the end users, systems analyst, and various managers meet for the first time, although the systems analyst might not actually be involved at this point. This is where the scope and objectives of the system are fleshed out in a very-high-level document.

Next, a team composed of one or more systems analysts and end users tries to determine whether the system is feasible. There are many reasons why systems are not feasible: expense overrun, unavailability of technology, and insufficient experience to create the system are just some of the reasons why a system will not be undertaken.

Many metrics are used to determine feasibility. One of the most popular is return on investment (ROI), which we will discuss in Chapter 8. However, be forewarned, some in the IT field find ROI determination an inexact science.

Once the system is deemed feasible, a project plan is completed that details the project's scope, costs, schedule, and resource requirements.

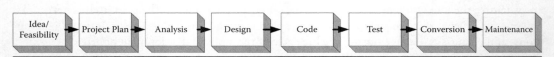

Figure 1.1   How the project plan fits within the systems development life cycle (SDLC).

Table 1.1 Project Life Cycle

Discovery	Initiation	Study	Design, Build, and Test	Operate
Project value and prioritization	Project approach (build/buy, phases)	Project charter	High-level design	Business build
Feasibility study	(RFI) request for information	Project kickoff	Low-level design	Human resources (HR) build
Estimation	Business case	Business requirements	Product build	Transition to operations
IT budget	RFP (request for proposal) for study	System requirements	User procedures	Post implementation review
IT roadmap revision	Source selection	Update business case	Training	Customer satisfaction survey
Demand assessed	Contract for study	RFP for build	Acceptance testing	Project closure
	Costs/benefits identified	Source selection	Finished product	Support
		Contract for build		Maintenance requests
		Requirements scoped/cost benefits updated		Steady requests

Development

Systems analysis can now be initiated using software engineering methodologies. This is when the analysts determine the rules and regulations of the system. For example:

What are the inputs?
What are the outputs?
What kind of online screens will there be?
What kind of reports should there be?
Will paper forms be required?
Will any hookups to external files or companies be required?
How will this information be processed?

In general, methodologies can be categorized as follows (it should be noted that a methodology can be used in conjunction with another methodology):

Systems development life cycle (SDLC): This is a phased, structured approach to systems development. The phases include requirements feasibility, analysis, systems design, coding, testing, implementation, and postimplementation testing. Variations of these stated phases are possible. Usually, phases are executed sequentially, although there is some potential for overlap. This is the methodology that is used most often in industry.

Iterative (prototyping) model: Most often, this approach is used to replace several of the phases in the SDLC. In the SDLC approach, the "time to market" can be several months (sometimes years). During this time, requirements (scope) may change and the final deliverable, therefore, might become obsolete. To prevent this from happening, it is a good idea to try and compress the development cycle, shortening the time to market, and providing interim results to the end user. The iterative model consists of three steps: (1) listen to customer, (2) build or revise a mock-up, (3) the customer test-drives the mock-up; then, return to the first step.

Rapid application development (RAD): This is a type of iterative model. The key word here is "rapid." Development teams try to get a first pass of the system out to the end user within 60–90 days. To accomplish this, the normal seven-step SDLC is compressed into the following steps: business modeling, data modeling, process modeling, application generation, and testing and turnover. Note the term *application generation*. RAD makes use of application generators, formerly called CASE (computer-assisted software engineering) tools.

Incremental model: The four main phases of SDLC are analysis, design, coding, and testing. If we break a business problem into chunks (or increments), we can use an overlapping, phased approach to software development. For example, we can start the analysis of Increment 1 in January, Increment 2 in June, and Increment 3 in September. Just when Increment 3 starts up, we will be at the testing stage of Increment 1 and coding stage of Increment 2.

Joint application development (JAD): JAD is more of a technique than a complete methodology. It can be utilized as part of any of the other methodologies discussed here. In this technique, one or more end users are "folded" into the software development team. Instead of an adversarial software developer–end-user dynamic, the effect is to have the continued, uninterrupted attention of the persons who will ultimately be using the system.

Reverse engineering: This technique is used to first understand a system from its code, generate documentation based on that code, and then make desired changes to the system. Competitive software companies often try to reverse-engineer their competitors' software.

Reengineering: Business goals change over time. Software must also change to be consistent with these goals. Instead of building a system from scratch, the goal of reengineering is to retrofit an existing system to new business functionality.

Object-oriented (OO) methods: Object-oriented analysis (OOA), object-oriented design (OOD), and object-oriented programming (OOP) are very different from what has been already discussed. In fact, you will need to learn a whole new vocabulary as well as new diagramming techniques.

As you can see, there is much work to be done and many questions to be answered. All of the answers to these questions will be fully documented in a requirements document.

There are a wide variety of software engineering methodologies, including the traditional linear (or waterfall method), OO, RAD, JAD, and the newer agile methods. The Agile Project Management (APM) Tooling Survey Results (Behrens, 2006) found that there was a rise in the number of large enterprises using agile methods. The survey also found that new (and perhaps more prescriptive) agile processes were created, including Extreme Programming (http://www.extremeprogramming.org/), Enterprise Scrum (http://www.scrumalliance.org/), and Microsoft for Agile Software Development (http://msdn2.microsoft.com/en-us/teamsystem/aa718801.aspx).

Implementation

Upon delivery of a systems specification to programmers, implementation can get under way. The systems analyst, project leader (PL), and project manager (PM) are all responsible for making sure that the implementation effort goes smoothly. Programmers write code and then test their code. This first level (unit testing) of testing is followed by several other phases of testing, including systems testing (putting all of the programs in the system together to see how they work as a group), parallel testing (testing the old system versus the new one), and integration testing (testing program-to-program interfaces).

Once the system has been fully tested, it is turned over to production (changeover). Usually, just prior to this, the end-user departments (not just the team working on the project) are trained and manuals distributed. The entire team is usually on call during the first few weeks of the system after changeover, as errors often crop up and it can take several weeks for the system to stabilize.

If the development is not targeted for in-house consumption (that is, it is meant to be sold to external customers), another setup is needed for the testing. In many cases, trusted customers of the developing company are approached with the offer to become the testers of the "beta" (a version released for testing before its final wrap-up) version.

Once the system has been stabilized, it is evaluated for correctness. At this point, a list of faults to be corrected as well as a "wish list" of features that were not included in the first phase of the system are created and prioritized. The team, which consists of technical and end-user staff, usually is retained and works on the future versions of the system. This phase of the SDLC is referred to as *maintenance*.

Closeout

Eventually, all systems reach the end of their utility. They must be either retired or replaced. There are many reasons for closeout, such as,

1. Requirements have changed.
2. Regulations have changed.
3. New technologies are introduced.
4. Technologies in use are deemed obsolete.
5. Functionality has been outsourced.
6. Functionality has been incorporated into another system.

The Project Planning Document

The project planning document articulates what the system will do. Some developers are troubled by the fact that the project planning process is usually undertaken prior to the stages of systems analysis and design, where end-user requirements are typically captured. Whereas the systems analysis and design stages capture a "micro" view of the system, the project planning process captures a "macro" view of the system. This is usually sufficient for the purposes of planning, resource allocation, and budgeting.

The project plan consists of the following functions:

Defines what will be done: The goals and objectives section of the project plan provides a general statement of the scope of the project as well as a more detailed list of requirements, interfaces (e.g., EDI, database, etc.), and constraints (e.g., the system must have a response time of <1 s).

Clearly defines when it will be done: Most organizations permit only the most experienced of personnel to tackle the difficult task of scheduling. These professionals utilize a variety of methodologies (e.g., deterministic approach, stochastic approach, etc.) and toolsets (e.g., Microsoft Project) to apportion tasks to available personnel in the most optimal manner, as shown in Figure 1.2.

Clearly defines how much it will cost: The project plan is bottom-line oriented and therefore must include the estimated costs of the project for review and approval by the various stakeholders.

Estimators may use a wide variety of techniques to perform the project cost effort. It is customary, in fact, for the estimator to use at least two techniques and then "triangulate" the two (i.e., discuss the reasons why the two estimates have differences). Often, the "true" estimate is the average of the results of the various estimation methods used.

One of the more popular estimation methodologies is COCOMO (Cost Construction Model II), devised by Dr. Barry Boehm in 1981 (see http://sunset.usc.edu/Research_Group/barry.html), which is both a formula and a software tool (http://sunset.usc.edu/research/COCOMOII/). Figure 1.3 shows its application to cost estimation in project planning.

The true cost of a project must also include software and hardware required, time expended by outside personnel such as trainers, end users, and managers, as well as administrative overhead.

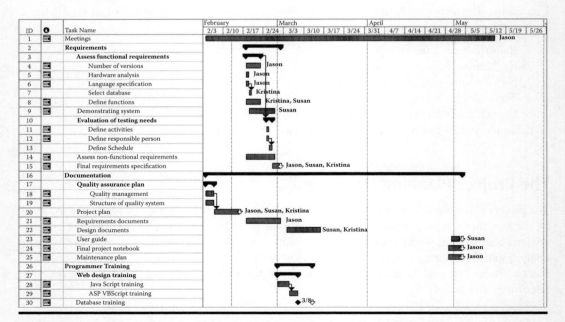

Figure 1.2   A typical schedule. This one was created using Microsoft Project.

File Edit View Parameters Calibrate Phase Maintenance Help

Project Name: Project DeDS

Scale Factor   Schedule

Development Model: Early Design

X	Module Name	Module Size	LABOR Rate ($/month)	EAF	NOM Effort DEV	EST Effort DEV	PROD	COST	INST COST	Staff	RISK
	Website Desing F	S:2246	10032.00	1.00	8.2	8.2	275.0	81922.53	36.5	0.7	0.0
	System Administr	S:702	10032.00	1.00	2.6	2.6	275.0	25605.35	36.5	0.2	0.0
	User Administrat	S:561	10032.00	1.00	2.0	2.0	275.0	20462.40	36.5	0.2	0.0
	Search Engine	S:421	10032.00	1.00	1.5	1.5	275.0	15355.92	36.5	0.1	0.0
	e-Payment	S:1404	10032.00	1.00	5.1	5.1	275.0	51210.70	36.5	0.5	0.0
	Marketing	S:1263	10032.00	1.00	4.6	4.6	275.0	46067.75	36.5	0.4	0.0
	Discussion Forum	S:702	10032.00	1.00	2.6	2.6	275.0	25605.35	36.5	0.2	0.0
	Communications	S:421	10032.00	1.00	1.5	1.5	275.0	15355.92	36.5	0.1	0.0
	Report	S:421	10032.00	1.00	1.5	1.5	275.0	15355.92	36.5	0.1	0.0
	Authentication	S:280	10032.00	1.00	1.0	1.0	275.0	10212.96	36.5	0.1	0.0

	Estimated	Effort	Sched	PROD	COST	INST	Staff	RISK
Total Lines of Code: 8421	Optimistic	20.5	9.6	410.5	205793.70	24.4	2.1	
	Most Likely	30.6	10.9	275.0	307154.78	36.5	2.8	0.0
	Pessimistic	45.9	12.4	183.4	460732.17	54.7	3.7	

Figure 1.3   Using COCOMO to estimate a project's cost.

Clearly defines what resources (people and other) will be needed: The reader of the project plan should be able to easily ascertain

1. How much the project will cost?
2. How long it will take?
3. How many people are needed?
4. What these people will do?
5. What kinds of people (e.g., programmers, trainers, etc.) are needed?
6. What, if any, software will be required to be purchased?
7. What, if any, hardware will be required to be purchased?
8. What, if any, outside services will be required to be secured?
9. What business, project, or product risks might be encountered, and the resources required to counter these risks?

Roles in Project Management

The people involved in the creation, implementation, and subsequent running of a computer system are called *stakeholders*. Stakeholders are interrelated. The best way to get a "bird's-eye view" of how your stakeholders are organized is to request or build an organization chart for the company. This will provide you with a veritable who's who in your organization.

From a PM perspective, three stakeholder groups are relevant:

1. The PM
2. The management
3. The project team

The Project Manager

There are several categories of IT managers. Starting from the top, you have the chief information officer (CIO). This person is usually a senior officer of the company and might report directly to the president or chairman. Sometimes the CIO is called the chief technical officer (CTO). Some organizations have both a CIO and a CTO.

Reporting to the CIO are a number of PMs. The PM is usually responsible for one or more systems. Reporting to the PM may be one or more PLs.

A PL is responsible for a specific project. Reporting to the PL may be one or more systems analysts and programmers (see Figure 1.4). The project might also require the services of a graphic designer, Web designer, database administrator (DBA), and quality assurance (QA) person. Usually these additional people do not actually work for the PL but are merely assigned to him or her for a specific purpose according to a project plan.

The PM's responsibilities include the following:

1. Interfacing with other stakeholder groups, including end users and senior management
2. Interfacing with technology staff, including PLs, systems analysts, programmers, etc.
3. Developing or aiding in developing the project plan
4. Overseeing the feasibility study
5. Managing one or more projects
6. Maintaining the schedule (i.e., allocating and reallocating resources as necessary)
7. Keeping the project on budget
8. Overseeing project tracking and control

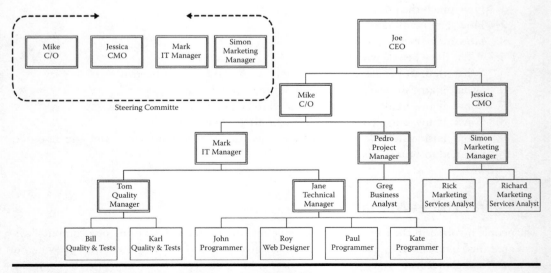

Figure 1.4   A typical IT organization and staff breakdown.

Management Layers

There are several layers of management that PMs need to be concerned with:

1. Senior managers—The chief executive officer (CEO), president, senior vice presidents, and chief financial officer (CFO) are usually only peripherally involved in a particular project. However, without their initial support, the project will never be funded. Without their continued support, the project will never be successfully implemented.
2. Business managers—These are the line managers who oversee the departments that the end users work for. These managers are instrumental in getting the project proposal elevated and prioritized. In addition, these managers often act as "champions," cajoling reluctant end users into cooperating with the project team and reluctant senior management into funding the project.
3. IT managers—IT managers work with both senior managers and business managers to determine project priorities. In addition to this responsibility, they (a) oversee all project development efforts; (b) champion new technologies and methodologies, securing funding from senior management; and (c) act as a liaison to corporate senior managers as well as business managers.

Without management support and involvement, a project will certainly fail.

The Project Team

A wide variety of people other than managers are involved in the process of systems development. The highest-level goal of the project team is to successfully implement the system as specified in the project plan. This section discusses the makeup of a typical project team.

The systems analyst: Today's systems analysts need to know the end users' business; they should also be technically proficient (e.g., know accounting and Java or human resources and C++). It is the systems analyst who is responsible for working with the end users to determine system feasibility and then develop the scope, requirements, design, and other documents. He or she is then responsible for implementing, testing, and then turning over a completed, working system.

Programmer: The programmer is usually the most technical person on the systems team. It is this person who knows all of the buzzwords that you see in help-wanted ads: Java, C++, Oracle, Sybase, etc. The role of the programmer is to take the specifications handed to him or her by the systems analyst and turn these specifications into working programs, and ultimately, complete systems.

End users: The end-user department is composed of experts who do a particular task. Maybe they are accountants or maybe they are in marketing—they still are experts in what they do. A single system may have many end users who hail from many different departments. Some end users might not work for the company at all.

Each end user will have a different set of requirements. It is the role of the end user to work with the systems analyst to uncover and then document these requirements. It is also the job of the end user to assist in other phases of the SDLC such as the testing component of the implementation stage.

Other roles: There are other people involved in the systems development effort. Systems organizations have many departments. Systems analysts and programmers generally work for the application development department. Other departments reporting to the CIO might include the Web development department (home to graphic designers and those who can program using HTML), QA department (home to people responsible for rigorously testing your system), technical writing department (home to people who might write your policies and procedures, guides, and other manuals), database administration (home to the DBA), networking department (home to the folks who administer your network), and help desk (home to the people who support your end users).

Other roles include clients and partners of your company. Many companies partner with organizations and, thus, share data. Electronic data interchange (EDI) is an example of this. For example, a jewelry manufacturer will use EDI to process orders from major clients, such as department stores, that purchase its jewelry.

Project Management Office

As we've learned, project management is a set of discrete steps that sees a project from inception to closure, as shown in Figure 1.5.

However, project management should not be performed in a vacuum. A particular project is just one of many projects that will be implemented at any given time. A particular project might be one of many projects for a specific program. A program is related to a corporate strategy—e.g., become an E-book publisher. In this E-book example, multiple projects may be related to this goal. One project might be to develop a Web site where E-books could be sold. Another project could be to develop the software that converts print books into E-books.

Most organizations will have several ongoing programs in play at once—all related to one or more business strategies. It is conceivable that hundreds of projects are in operation, all in various

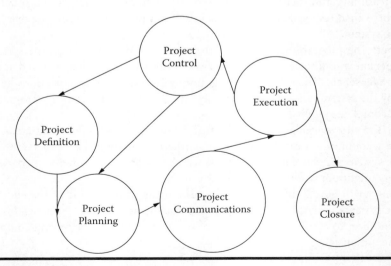

Figure 1.5 Project management perspectives.

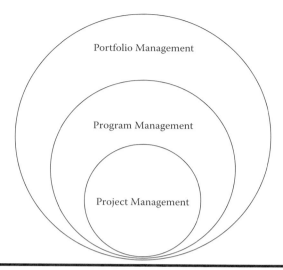

Figure 1.6 Portfolio management.

stages of execution. Portfolio management is needed to provide the business and technical stewardship of all of these programs and their projects, as shown in Figure 1.6.

Portfolio management is often performed by the project management office (PMO). This is the department or group that defines and maintains the standards of process, generally related to project management, within the organization. The PMO strives to standardize and introduce economies of repetition in the execution of projects. The PMO is the source of documentation, guidance, and metrics on the practice of project management and execution.

A good PMO will base project management principles on accepted, industry-standard methodologies, such as Project Management Body of Knowledge (PMBOK) or Projects in Controlled Environments (PRINCE2), which are discussed later on in this chapter. Increasingly influential industry certification programs such as ISO 9000 and the Malcolm Baldrige National Quality Award (MBNQA), government regulatory requirements such as Sarbanes–Oxley, and business process management (BPM) techniques such as balanced scorecard spurred have organizations to standardize processes.

Balanced Scorecard

Over the past decade, many CIOs have realized that it is not sufficient to manage merely the IT end of the business. The integration of IT strategy with business strategy must be managed as well. As mentioned in the last section, one tool chosen for this task is the balanced scorecard, as shown in Figure 1.7.

Robert S. Kaplan and David P. Norton developed the balanced scorecard approach in the early 1990s to compensate for the shortcomings of using only financial metrics to judge corporate performance. They recognized that in this new economy it was also necessary to value intangible assets. Because of this, they urged companies to measure such esoteric factors as quality and customer satisfaction. By the middle 1990s, balanced scorecard became the hallmark of a well-run company. Kaplan and Norton often compare their approach for managing a company to that of

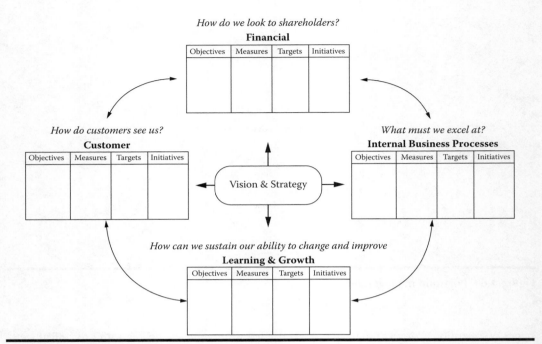

Figure 1.7   The balanced scorecard.

pilots viewing assorted instrument panels in an airplane cockpit—both need to monitor multiple aspects of their working environment.

In the scorecard scenario, a company organizes its business goals into discrete, all-encompassing perspectives: financial, customer, internal process, and learning or growth. The company then determines cause–effect relationships—for example, satisfied customers buy more goods, which increases revenue. Next, the company lists measures for each goal, pinpoints targets, and identifies projects and other initiatives that help reach those targets.

Departments create scorecards tied to the company's targets, and employees and projects have scorecards tied to their department's targets. This cascading nature provides a line of sight between individuals, what they're working on, the unit they support, and how that impacts the strategy of the whole enterprise.

For IT managers, the balanced scorecard is an invaluable tool that will finally permit IT to link to the business side of the organization using a cause-and-effect approach. Some have likened balanced scorecard to a new language, which enables IT and business line managers to think together about what IT can do to support business performance. A beneficial side effect of the use of the balanced scorecard is that when all measures are reported one can calculate the strength of relations between the various value drivers.

The Portfolio Perspective

Kutnick and Cearley (2002) of the META Group found that if companies manage IT from an investment perspective—with a continuing focus on value, risk, cost, and benefits—it would help businesses reduce IT costs by up to 30 percent with a two to three times increase in value. This is often referred to as portfolio management.

Freedman (2003) provides a stepwise plan for implementation:

1. Take inventory: A complete inventory of all IT initiatives should be compiled. Information such as the project's sponsors and champion, stakeholder list, strategic alignment with corporate objectives, estimated costs, and project benefits should be collected.
2. Analyze: Once the inventory is completed and validated, all projects on the list should be analyzed. A steering committee should be formed that has enough insight into the organization's strategic goals and priorities to place IT projects in the overall strategic landscape.
3. Prioritize: The output of the analysis step is a prioritized project list. The order of prioritization is based on criteria that the steering committee selects. This is different for different organizations. Some companies might consider strategic alignment to be the most important, whereas other companies might decide that cost–benefit ratio is the better criterion for prioritization.
4. Manage: Portfolio management is not a one-time event. It is a constant process that must be managed. Projects must be continually evaluated on the basis of changing priorities and market conditions.

Project Management Methodologies

There are two major project management methodologies. The PMBOK, which is most popular in the United States, recognizes five basic process groups typical of almost all projects: initiating, planning, executing, controlling and monitoring, and closing. PRINCE2, which is the de facto standard for project management in the United Kingdom and is popular in more than 50 other countries, defines a wide variety of subprocesses and organizes them into eight major processes: starting a project, planning, initiating a project, directing a project, controlling a stage, managing product delivery, managing stage boundaries, and closing a project.

PMBOK

PMBOK is an IEEE standard (1490-2003). It provides a methodology for a wide range of project categories: i.e., software, engineering, construction, and automotive. The five basic process groups and nine knowledge areas are typical of most projects, programs, and operations. Processes overlap and interact throughout a project or phase and are described in terms of inputs (e.g., documents, plans, and designs), tools and techniques, and outputs (e.g., documents, products, etc.).

The nine knowledge areas are project integration management, project scope management, project time management, project cost management, project quality management, project human resource management, project communications management, project risk management, and project procurement management.

PRINCE2

PRINCE is the United Kingdom government's standard for IT project management. The latest version, PRINCE2, was designed for all types of management projects.

PRINCE provides a structured approach (i.e., method) to project management, within a clearly defined framework.

Similar to PMBOK, PRINCE2 is a process-driven method. It defines 45 separate subprocesses organized into eight major processes:

Starting Up a Project (SU)
    SU1: Appointing a project board executive and PM
    SU2: Designing a project management team
    SU3: Appointing a project management team
    SU4: Preparing a project brief
    SU5: Defining project approach
    SU6: Planning an initiation stage
Planning (PL)
    PL1: Designing a plan
    PL2: Defining and analyzing products
    PL3: Identifying activities and dependencies
    PL4: Estimating
    PL5: Scheduling
    PL6: Analyzing risks
    PL7: Completing a plan
Initiating a Project (IP)
    IP1: Planning quality
    IP2: Planning a project
    IP3: Refining the business case and risks
    IP4: Setting up project controls
    IP5: Setting up project files
    IP6: Assembling a project initiation document
Directing a Project (DP)
    DP1: Authorizing initiation
    DP2: Authorizing a project
    DP3: Authorizing a stage or exception plan
    DP4: Giving ad hoc direction
    DP5: Confirming project closure
Controlling a Stage (CS) (Projects should be broken down into stages and these subprocesses dictate how each individual stage should be controlled.)
    CS1: Authorizing work package
    CS2: Assessing progress
    CS3: Capturing project issues
    CS4: Examining project issues
    CS5: Reviewing stage status
    CS6: Reporting highlights
    CS7: Taking corrective action
    CS8: Escalating project issues
    CS9: Receiving completed work package
Managing Product Delivery (MP)
    MP1: Accepting a work package
    MP2: Executing a work package
    MP3: Delivering a work package

Managing Stage Boundaries (SB)
   SB1: Planning a stage
   SB2: Updating a project plan
   SB3: Updating a project business case
   SB4: Updating the risk log
   SB5: Reporting stage end
   SB6: Producing an exception plan
Closing a Project (CP)
   CP1: Decommissioning a project
   CP2: Identifying follow-on actions
   CP3: Project evaluation review

PRINCE2 comprises a number of components, including the business case (justification of the project), plans, controls, management of risk, quality, configuration management, and change control.

The business case is a crucial element of the PRINCE2 methodology, but is surprisingly absent from PMBOK. However, if one adopts a software engineering approach to project management, as recommended in this chapter, then the omission of the business case within PMBOK itself should present no problem.

Project Management Process Maturity Model

The Project Management Process Maturity (PM²) model determines and positions an organization's relative project management level with other organizations (Kwak and Ibbs, 2002). There are a variety of PM² models, all based on work done by the Software Engineering Institute (SEI) at Carnegie Mellon on improving the quality of the software development process.

The PM² model defines five steps, as shown in Figure 1.8.

Key processes, organizational characteristics, and key focus areas are defined in Table 1.2.

PM² serves to motivate organizations and people to accomplish more sophisticated levels of project management maturity by using a systematic and incremental approach. Essentially, it's a reference point or yardstick for project management practices and processes.

Conclusion

Projects operate in an environment much broader than the project itself. This means that the PM needs to understand not only the intricacies of the particular project, but also the greater organizational context in which its stakeholders exist. PMs must identify and understand the needs of all the stakeholders (i.e., project team, management, end users, etc.), while delivering a quality product on time and within budget.

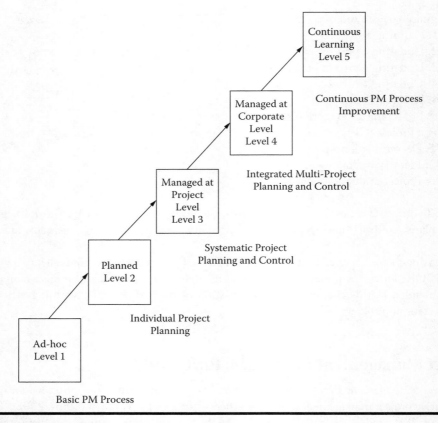

Figure 1.8   The PM² model.

Table 1.2   Key Components of the PM² Model

Maturity Level	Key Project Management Processes	Major Organizational Characteristics	Key Focus Areas
Level 5 (continuous learning)	Project management processes are continuously improved	Project-driven organization	Innovative ideas to improve project management processes and practices
	Project management processes are fully understood	Dynamic, energetic, and fluid organization	
	Project management data is optimized and sustained	Continuous improvement of project management processes and practices	

Table 1.2   Key Components of the PM² Model (Continued)

Maturity Level	Key Project Management Processes	Major Organizational Characteristics	Key Focus Areas
Level 4 (managed at corporate level)	Multiple program managements	Strong teamwork	Planning and controlling multiple projects in a professional manner
	Project management data and processes are integrated	Formal project management training for project team	
	Project management data is quantitatively analyzed, measured, and stored		
Level 3 (managed at project level)	Formal project planning and control systems are managed	Team orientation (medium)	Systematic and structured project planning and control for individual project
	Formal project management data is managed	Informal training of project management skills and practices	
Level 2 (planned)	Informal project management processes are defined	Team orientation (weak)	Individual project planning
	Informal project management problems are identified	Organizations possess strengths in doing similar work	
	Informal project management data is collected		
Level 1 (ad hoc)	No project management processes or practices are consistently available	Functionally isolated	Understand and establish basic project management processes
	No project management data is consistently collected or analyzed	Lack of senior management support	
		Project success depends on individual efforts	

Links

http://www.dmh.cahwnet.gov/Admin/regulations/docs/GuideProjectManagement_old.pdf   Guide   to   PMBOK.

www.pmi.org The Project Management Institute (PMI) Web site. Lots of information here. Go here to join PMI, get updated PMP certification information, etc.

http://www.pmi-issig.org/ PMI Information Systems Specific Interest Group (ISSIG) Web site. If you are interested in IT project management, you should join this group.

http://www.studentsofpm.org/ Students of project management Web site.

http://sunset.usc.edu/Research_Group/barry.html and http://sunset.usc.edu/research/COCOMOII/. Two sites about COCOMO (Cost Construction Model II).

http://people.msoe.edu/~peck/EM-795/Skills%20Assessment%20Worksheet.doc PM skills assessment worksheet.

http://www.openworkbench.org/index.php?option=com_docman&task=cat_view&gid=12&Itemid=26 Open Workbench.

http://www.prince2.org.uk/home/home.asp PRINCE2 Web site.

References

Behrens, P. (2006). Agile Project Management (APL) Tooling Survey Results. Retrieved from http://www.trailridgeconsulting.com/files/2006AgileToolingSurveyResults.pdf.

Freedman, R. (September 2003). Helping clients value IT investments. *Consulting to Management*. Vol. 14, No. 3.

Kutnick, D. and Cearley, D. (January/February 2002). *The Business of IT Portfolio Management*. META Group white paper.

Kwak, Y. H. and Ibbs, C. W. (July 2002). Project management process maturity (PM²) model. *Journal of Management in Engineering, 18*(3).

Chapter 2

Project Management Skill Sets

A common cause of project failure is assigning under-skilled project managers (PMs) to complex projects. Projects vary widely in their complexity because of differences in business and technical environments. Project sponsors and PMs need to clearly understand the complexities of their projects (Chief Financial Officers Council, 2001). The PM really does need to be a jack of all trades in addition to being a master of all—to twist an old adage. In this chapter, we will discuss exactly what it is a PM needs to know.

Role of the Project Manager

The PM needs to satisfy his or her managers, end users, and staff members while making sure that projects are delivered on time and on or under budget. Aside from technical skills, the PM needs to be a "people's person." More specifically, the PM should be able to perform the following functions.

Manage Expectations

Each set of stakeholders will have their own expectations about the outcome of the project:

1. End users will have expectations about what the system will be able to do. End users should not be told that features will be implemented in a particular phase, if it is uncertain that they will be. This will surely lead to disappointment and possibly even project failure.
2. IT staff will have expectations about what role they will play in the development of the project. They are usually quite excited to be involved in a new development effort. Promising them a role in the new development effort and then not delivering on that promise will lead to disappointment, a loss of productivity, and sometimes even the loss of the team member.

3. Senior management will have expectations about the project cost and resource utilization. It is critically important that the PM always provide a complete picture of the status and current expenses of the project.

Resolve Conflict

Whenever two or more people are put together, there is room for conflict. The PM needs to be both cheerleader and referee during the lengthy project development process. Types of conflict can include the following:

1. Developer to developer
2. End user to end user
3. Developer to end user
4. Department to department
5. Manager to manager
6. Customer to employee

Overcome Fears

Over time, end users develop a level of comfort with the systems and practices that they already have in place. Therefore, some might feel threatened by change. If not handled properly, this fear of the unknown can lead to project failure, which actually happened during the systemization of the U.S. Post Office. When more sophisticated technologies were implemented about a decade ago, the employees were not involved in any of the meetings. Hence, change was foisted upon them suddenly and dramatically. Employees, motivated by the fear of losing their jobs to this new technology, sabotaged the system.

This expensive problem could have been easily avoided if the PM had considered the effect of technological change on these employees and had spent some time overcoming their fears. Such a challenge could easily be met by taking the following steps:

1. Involving end users in the process of technology change from the beginning.
2. Keeping all employees informed about what is going on. This can be done via newsletter, e-mail, public meetings, systems demonstrations, etc.
3. Actively listening to employees about their fears and acting to alleviate them.

Facilitate Meetings

What does it mean to facilitate a meeting? Meetings do not run well on their own; instead, a meeting must be "managed." The steps for effective meeting facilitation include the following:

1. The PM acts as chairperson. He or she schedules the meeting, invites appropriate staff, and sets the agenda.
2. The agenda is sent out to attendees in advance.
3. The chairperson moderates the meeting, moving through each item on the agenda.
4. The chairperson appoints a secretary to take notes.
5. The chairperson ensures that all items on the agenda are covered and that the meeting adjourns on time.

6. The chairperson ensures that everyone is permitted to voice his or her opinion.
7. The chairperson resolves all disagreements.
8. After the meeting, the chairperson makes sure that the meeting notes are distributed to the attendees.
9. The chairperson schedules a follow-up meeting, if necessary.

Motivate Team Members

Perhaps the most important responsibility of the PM is to motivate team members. This means that he or she must wear many hats:

1. The PM must motivate senior management such that they retain interest in funding and supporting the project.
2. The PM must motivate end users and end-user management so that they support the project and cooperate in its development.
3. The PM must motivate development staff so that the effort is completed on time, on budget, and with high quality.

How does one go about motivating people? Some of the methods have already been discussed in this paper: (1) managing expectations, (2) resolving conflict, and (3) active listening.

The PM must be all things to all people involved in the project. He or she needs to be a constant presence in the lives of all team members, congratulating their successes as well as supporting and consoling them in the face of failures.

Organizational Values

Every organization promotes a set of values that guide people in their work. This can be done consciously, as in cases where specific values are promoted in policy statements, or unconsciously, by values conveyed through the actions and examples of PMs.

Honesty and integrity are the cornerstones of the project management process. Quality, flexibility, and innovation require wholesale involvement by organizational members and a willingness to work together, which depend on mutual trust. Some ways to promote this attitude are the following:

1. Make only those commitments you can live up to.
2. Put ethics policy in writing. Try to keep gray areas to a minimum.
3. Demand total integrity—both inside and outside the organization.

People are the most basic project factor in any organization. The attitudes and morale of the workforce are important determinants of successful project management. Motivation underlies every person's performance. Motivation is affected by quality of leadership, job fulfillment, personal recognition, and the overall support present in the working environment. To improve employee morale, make sure that complaints are resolved quickly. It is also a good idea to assign jobs in an equitable manner so that everyone has a sense of fair play. Finally, recognize top performance in your staff and provide training to make sure that as many staff as possible do become top performers.

Interpersonal Skill Sets

For a PM, the ability to manage people is critical. They need to navigate their way through an organization, replete with politics and conflict, to usher their projects to successful completion. Because PMs are responsible for a team of people, understanding how to motivate and lead these people is a skill that must be learned. A great story about motivating staff comes from Oren Harari (1993), a professor at the University of San Francisco and a management consultant. While he was waiting for an appointment with a manager, he overheard two of the manager's clerical assistants calling customers and asking them how they liked the company's product. Professor Harari reflected that it was no wonder this manager had such a good reputation. When he finally met with her, he offered his congratulations on her ability to delegate the customer service task to her staff. "What you talking about?" she asked, bewildered. "Why, your secretaries are calling up customers on their own," Harari replied. "Oh, really? Is that what they're doing?" she laughed. "You mean you didn't delegate that task to them?" asked Harari. "No," she said, "I didn't even know they were doing it. Listen, Oren, my job is to get everyone on my team to think creatively in pursuit of the same goal. So what I do is talk to people regularly about why we exist as a company and as a team. That means we talk straight about our common purpose and the high standards we want to achieve. I call these our goal lines. Then we talk regularly about some broad constraints we have to work with, like budgets, ethics, policies, and legalities. Those are our sidelines.

"It's like a sport. Once we agree on the goal lines and sidelines, I leave it to my people to figure out how to best get from here to there. I'm available and attentive when they need feedback. Sometimes I praise; sometimes I criticize—but always constructively, I hope. We get together periodically and talk about who's been trying what, and we give constructive feedback to one another. I know that sounds overly simplistic, but I assure you that is my basic management philosophy.

"And that's why I don't know what my assistants are doing, because it's obviously something they decided to try for the first time this week. I happen to think it's a great idea, because it's within the playing field and helps keep high standards for being number one in our industry. I will tell you something else: I don't even know what they intend to do with the data they're collecting, but I know they'll do the right thing.

"Here's my secret: I don't know what my people are doing, but because I work face to face with them as a coach, I know that whatever it is they're doing is exactly what I'd want them to be doing if I knew what they were doing!"

Business Skill Sets

The PM should have a general understanding of accounting practices, operations, and procedures. This includes an understanding and knowledge of the methods of accounting such as accrual, obligation, and cost methods.

Financial management controls are vital to the usefulness and integrity of the data in a system. The manager must understand the requirements and the importance of a strong system of management controls. This includes the ability to establish management controls by identifying and implementing appropriate general and application controls. It is also important that the manager be able to understand and implement management controls that reasonably ensure that financial integrity is maintained for the recording of transactions and the reporting of results. Understanding and implementing management controls also include the ability to assess, improve, and correct them by monitoring and evaluating systems and identifying deficiencies.

Implementation of systems invariably includes a need to analyze and redesign business processes. The need for redesign can arise from a variety of reasons including the introduction of new technologies or regulations. To properly handle business process analysis, the PM must understand the business domain in question.

Leadership Skills

The PM must have experience in managing, and communicating effectively with, a wide variety of people. In offshore outsourcing, communication skills become even more critical. Key human resources competencies for a PM are leadership, change management, communication, negotiating, team building, decision making, and problem solving.

An ability to lead is clearly one of the most important competencies a PM must have. An absence of leadership qualities can readily result in the failure or delay of the financial system implementation. Therefore, the PM must be able to set goals and objectives. The manager must then be able to identify and implement the steps necessary to achieve them. Working closely with the customer, the PM must have the skill necessary to translate the customer's expectations into a practical vision.

In many cases, the PM is responsible for identifying, training, and retaining team members. He or she must be able to assess the mix of knowledge and skills needed, and match them to the individual team members. The PM must be able to influence and motivate team members, and to change leadership styles depending upon the situation.

Important leadership qualities include drive, the ability to take risks, experience with the type of project at hand, and a sense of the "big picture." A PM must also be attentive to details. Without the ability to think through the details, the feasibility of achieving the big picture may not be fully considered.

Organizational Skills

A PM must have strong organizational skills, be able to manage change, communicate effectively, build consensus using influencing or negotiating skills and team-building skills, solve problems, and make decisions.

The PM must also have the ability to guide and handle change. Frequently, the systems implementation will affect and change existing procedures and methods of accomplishing various tasks. The PM must be able to identify how the users of the system will react to the changes, and must be able to effectively inform the principal how the implementation will impact the organization. Change must involve the end users. Even the best-managed project can fail without their support. The PM must be able to explain to end users how the changes will affect them and, more importantly, how the changes will benefit the organization. In addition, the PM must anticipate changes and plan accordingly.

It is important to ensure that a training plan is developed and implemented so that users and those charged with maintaining the system have the necessary skills and knowledge of the new system to use it efficiently.

Communicating with project stakeholders (including team members, sponsors, and end users) is a necessary skill. The PM must be proficient in different types of communication. A key component of this skill is the ability to recognize each individual's communication style and adapt to it easily. This ability enables the PM to influence different types of individuals, which in turn

Table 2.1 Communication Styles

Style	Content (the speaker talks about ...)	Process (the speaker is ...)
Action	Results, objectives, performance	Down to earth, direct, impatient
Process	Facts, procedures, planning	Factual, systemic, logical
People	People, communication, feeling	Spontaneous, warm, empathetic
Idea	Concepts, possibilities, issues	Imaginative, unrealistic, full of ideas

makes getting the job done much easier. All individuals fall within four communication styles: action, process, people, and idea, as shown in Table 2.1. Effective speakers know their personal communication style as well as that of their audience. The most effective way to communicate is to recognize other people's styles and talk to them on their own level. For example, people with an "action" communication style will talk about results and objectives. They are down-to-earth, direct, and impatient. Table 2.1 summarizes the different communication styles and their associated "content" and "process" characteristics for the manager to recognize when speaking or listening to others.

A PM must also exhibit active listening skills and be able to communicate effectively, both orally and in writing, at all organizational levels. Finally, the PM must be able to prepare reports, documenting achievements and providing options to alleviate any problems, for presentation to management.

The ability to negotiate and, when necessary, act as a coach is an important competency. This role includes providing feedback to the team and stakeholders. The PM must be able to learn the strengths and weaknesses of individual team members by observing them as they work together, and he or she must be able to use them to complement and support each other. The PM must be able to identify and define customer requirements, manage customer expectations, and orchestrate customer relations.

Leading a team also requires the ability to gain a consensus. Not all team members will necessarily be in complete agreement, so the PM must be able to persuade all team members to cooperate and accept the recommendations of others. In other words, the PM must be able to negotiate to reach mutually agreeable solutions.

The PM must be a leader handing out orders to the team, but must also work alongside the team and participate actively in it. One key aspect of this participation is encouraging and facilitating a cooperative environment. To ensure a cooperative environment, the manager should work with the team as a whole to achieve its goals and objectives.

A complex array of outside contractors may be on the team. The PM must be actively involved with the contract PM to set clear goals and objectives, develop project schedules, negotiate and agree to cost estimates, and allocate human resources.

The PM needs to ensure that the integrated team works cohesively. Teams, by their very nature, tend to be heterogeneous. Working with a diverse group of people is challenging and can be difficult. The PM must therefore be able to integrate individuals from many disciplines into an efficient team, coach it, and lead brainstorming sessions.

During a system implementation, problems will inevitably surface. These problems can range from basic staffing decisions to major vendor disagreements over a contract and resolving problems with end users. The PM must be able to identify the specific problem and to use sound judgment to develop alternative solutions and make recommendations. To do this, the PM must be able to distinguish between needs and wants, and prioritize items based on how critical they are to the success of the project.

Making sound, well-informed decisions is a key competency in this regard. The PM must determine the scope and boundaries on which decisions should be made. Decisions must be made, and frequently they are not major enough to require a principal. Therefore, the PM must be able to make them. Making such decisions requires that the manager be able to determine the impact and implications of the decision, and commit to the necessary actions to accomplish the project goals and objectives.

Further, the PM must have the ability to admit mistakes. A PM who will continue to follow a wrong path rather than admit a mistake will ultimately cost an agency time, money, and credibility with the users.

Technical Competencies

Key technical competencies for PMs are project integration management, information technology management, scope management, time management, cost management, quality management, risk management, and procurement management skills. The PM must be able to understand technical language and tasks that need to be performed to manage quality and risk.

Project Integration Management

At the start of any large system implementation, the PM must be able to develop a comprehensive project plan that integrates all the objectives necessary to complete the task. Project integration management seeks to ensure that the various elements of the project are properly coordinated. It involves making trade-offs among competing objectives and alternatives to meet or exceed stakeholder needs and expectations. Project integration management includes the following:

1. Taking the results of other planning processes and putting them into a consistent, coherent document
2. Carrying out the project plan by performing the activities included in it
3. Coordinating changes across the entire project

The PM can develop a project plan using a variety of methods, but to prepare the detailed project schedule, the manager should be familiar with tools such as project management software. The project schedule must include all necessary details for project tracking.

As part of project integration, the manager must define the project's strategic direction, business objectives, goals, deliverables, assumptions, constraints, and implementation phases. The manager must be able to recognize and obtain the resources necessary to complete the implementation. The manager must also be able to evaluate performance and provide the necessary feedback to team members and managers. The PM should identify any training needed to support the project and obtain the appropriate resources.

Although developing the project plan is an important aspect of project integration, the manager must also be able to fully coordinate the implementation with all the program offices that are affected. In addition, because project plans may be written and then ignored, an important competency is the ability to manage the execution of tasks in accordance with the project plan.

Managing the execution of tasks also includes the ability to measure progress against the plan and coordinate changes that may occur. Without this ability, project integration can fail.

Information Technology Management

A PM needs to have knowledge of the software development life cycle, including requirements analysis, design, development, data conversion, and testing. Even when off-the-shelf products are used, ancillary software is normally required to be developed for interfaces, reporting, and data conversion. It is critical that a PM have the expertise to manage this part of the overall project effectively.

Configuration management is a critical core competency. One of the key tenets to success with the use of commercial off-the-shelf (COTS) products is to avoid making changes to the baseline COTS software. This requires an understanding of the configuration management process and associated software baseline management. A PM should have an understanding of the time and level of skill it takes to perform each conversion, upgrade, programming modification, etc.

PMs must have enough knowledge about computer security to ensure that appropriate implementation decisions are made to adequately protect critical financial data.

Scope Management

A clear understanding of project scope, its definition, and the manner in which scope changes would be implemented into the project is key to project success. The PM must have the ability to manage scope throughout the lifetime of the project. One of the most complicated challenges a PM must deal with is keeping the project scope contained to the level that was originally defined in the project initiation phase and that satisfies the project objectives as originally defined—i.e., avoiding "scope creep." It is a natural tendency of stakeholders (and sometimes developers) to pile on additional requirements and bells and whistles that often substantially increase project risk, time, or cost.

Time Management

Without proper time management, a system implementation can easily take much longer than initially estimated. When this occurs, the risk of project failure increases dramatically. The PM must be able to ensure that the project is completed on time. The PM must have the ability to identify the human resources needed to support the project, and be able to allocate the resources as needed to support the plan or schedule. Project time management includes the following:

1. Identifying the specific activities that must be performed to produce the various project deliverables
2. Identifying and documenting interactivity dependencies
3. Estimating the number of work periods needed to complete individual activities
4. Analyzing activity sequences, activity durations, and resource requirements to create the project schedule
5. Controlling changes to the project schedule

To keep the project on time, the manager must ensure that all of the project tasks identified in the project plan are implemented and completed on time and within acceptable variances from original estimates. When necessary, the PM must update the project schedule to reflect new task completion time estimates. In addition, the manager needs to develop a schedule control change system and take the actions necessary to ensure that all commitments are completed as planned or are rescheduled.

Cost Management

Frequently cited problems in systems implementations are related to costs. Project costs may be underestimated or the project may go over budget. The PM must be able to ensure that the project is completed within the approved budget. Project cost management includes the following:

1. Determining what resources (people, equipment, materials) and what quantities of each resource should be used to perform project activities
2. Developing an approximation (estimate) of the costs of the resources needed to complete project activities
3. Allocating the overall cost estimate to individual work items
4. Controlling and managing changes to the project budget

The PM is responsible for preparation of a cost–benefit analysis (or a return on investment computation). In developing the initial budget, the manager must be able to provide the supporting detail for the cost justifications and the timing for project-fund expenditures.

When the manager finds that the cost schedule is not being followed, he or she must be able to take the necessary action to maintain the agreed-upon cost schedule, and document all cost changes that occur during the project. In addition, several competencies are related to keeping the project within budget, including the ability to perform resource planning, cost estimation, and cost control. The PM must also have a strategy to deal with the need to ensure adequate funding over a number of years if the project is to be funded from annual or multiple appropriations.

Quality Management

The PM must be able to manage the quality of the project to ensure that it satisfies the needs and objectives for which it was undertaken. Project quality management includes the following:

1. Identifying the quality standards that are relevant to the project and determining how to satisfy them
2. Regularly evaluating overall project performance to provide confidence to the stake holders that the project will satisfy the relevant quality standards
3. Monitoring specific project results to determine if they comply with relevant quality standards, and identifying ways to eliminate causes of unsatisfactory performance

The manager must develop and implement a quality assurance program based on a series of plans covering quality management (which should identify the quality standards), quality assurance, and quality control. After the plans are developed, he or she must be able to implement the quality assurance program as a means of measuring the project quality against defined standards. The managers must be able to provide management reports on quality, and more importantly, they must take the necessary action when quality performance is below the standards.

Risk Management

The PM must thoroughly understand the various risks that may affect the implementation and must be prepared to manage them. Risks may be internal or external. Internal risks are those that the project team can control or influence, such as staff assignments and cost estimates. External risks are things beyond the control or influence of the project team, such as market shifts or failure to perform by outside vendors.

Project risk management comprises the processes concerned with identifying, analyzing, and responding to project risk. It includes maximizing the results of positive events and minimizing the consequences of adverse events. The processes include the following:

1. Determining which risks are likely to affect the project and documenting the characteristics of each
2. Evaluating the risks and risk interactions to assess the range of possible project outcomes
3. Defining enhancement steps for opportunities, and responses to threats
4. Responding to changes in risk over the course of the project

To mitigate possible risks, the PM must be able to develop a risk management plan as a subset of the project plan. The plan must identify and document the risks that are likely to affect the outcome of the project. Managers must also be able to evaluate and quantify each risk, and assess the range of possible outcomes. In other words, they must be able to distinguish between high risk and low risk. In many cases the risk may not warrant a response, but when the risk is significant, the manager must be able to develop a risk response plan and take the necessary actions to mitigate the risk in accordance with the risk management plan.

Procurement Management

Procurement management is another core competency for the PM. Project procurement management comprises the processes required to acquire goods and services from outside the performing organization. The processes include the following:

1. Determining what to procure and when
2. Documenting product requirements and identifying potential sources
3. Obtaining quotations, bids, offers, or proposals as appropriate
4. Choosing from among potential sellers
5. Managing the relationship with the seller
6. Completing and settling the contract, including resolution of any open items

The PM must be able to determine and justify the need for goods and services required by the project, work with appropriate contract personnel, develop an acquisition plan, solicit competition, and select sources. The acquisition plan documents what goods and services are needed, and when they are needed, during the project life cycle. The manager needs to be able to develop solicitation materials including statements of work and evaluation criteria to ensure that goods and services are procured by the most effective and efficient means, and are available when needed.

The PM must organize a competent and knowledgeable project team of functional and technical subject matter experts to participate in the contractual process (such as vendor analysis, vendor demonstrations, and evaluation of proposals). For many large systems, one or more contractors may be providing support in the systems design and implementation effort. The PM must work closely with acquisition staff to ensure that each contractor provides services and work products that are consistent with contractual obligations.

Conclusion

The technology manager needs to satisfy his or her managers, end users, and staff members while making sure that projects are delivered on time and on or under budget.

Aside from technical skills, the manager needs to be a "people person." He or she needs to be able to do the following:

1. Talk the language of the end users
2. Talk the language of the tech gurus
3. Understand and deal with corporate and departmental politics
4. Cajole reluctant end users into doing something new
5. Resolve problems
6. Manage expectations
7. Motivate staff and end users
8. Resolve conflict
9. Overcome fears

Links

http://www.gantthead.com/ The online community for PMs.
http://searchcio.techtarget.com/originalContent/0,289142,sid19_gci1047064,00.html CIO articles on PM skill sets.
http://www.pmforum.org/viewpoints/2007/PDFs/Young-4-07.pdf Article on PM skills shortage.
http://www.pmboulevard.com/Default.aspx?page=2409 Resource for PMs.
http://www.management-hub.com/project-manager-skills.html Management Hub.
http://search.techrepublic.com.com/search/Project+Manager+and+leadership.html Tech Republic resources for PMs.

References

Chief Financial Officers Council and Joint Financial Management Improvement Program (April 2001). *Core Competencies for Project Managers Implementing Financial Systems in the Federal Government.* Retrieved from fsio.gov/fsio/download/jfmip/CoreComps/CoreCompetenciesForProjectManagers-Final-April2001.doc.
Harari, O. (November 1993). Stop Empowering Your People. *Management Review.* 26–29.

Chapter 3

Managing the Project Team

An accurate estimate and effective schedule is only one part of the equation. The project will not be successful unless the right people are on the team and the team is effectively managed.

Team Dynamics

A team goes through several stages before it reaches its optimal level of performance. When a team is first assembled, it goes through the stage referred to as **forming**. At this point, team members do not yet know one another or what their role in the team will be. The project manager can expedite this stage by having one or more introductory meetings, where team members can meet for the first time. Off-site, or social-themed meetings, can also be valuable team-forming techniques. The second stage of team development is called **storming** for a good reason. Although team members now accept the members in their group, individual roles have yet to be determined. The project manager will no doubt assign job- or task-oriented roles within the group (i.e., project leader, analyst, programmer), but the social aspects of the team are still very much in play. This can cause turmoil, to which the project manager needs to be attuned. Once the team finds its inner dynamic, or balance, the team can get down to business in the **norming** phase of team development. When a team has been together for some time, it achieves its optimal level of performance. This is referred to as the **performing phase**. As we will see in Chapter 11, there will come a time when the project is complete and the team might be disbanded. This is the **adjourning** phase of team development.

Teams become more effective as they move through the phases discussed earlier. These five steps can be followed out of sequence, or even simultaneously, and still be effective.

The project manager should keep in mind that there are a variety of teaming problems to be aware of. One problem is that a team might never move past the forming or storming stages. It is entirely possible for a team to experience such dysfunction that the project manager should consider transfers or replacements as a resolution. Another common problem is groupthink. This is defined as rationalized conformity. Certo (2000) explains that groupthink is a mode of thinking that group members engage in when the desire for agreement so dominates the group that it overrides the need to realistically appraise the alternatives. Janis (1977) identified eight symptoms of groupthink:

1. Illusions of invulnerability, thereby creating excessive optimism and encouraging excessive risk taking
2. Rationalizing warnings that might challenge the group's assumptions
3. Unquestioned belief in the morality of the group, causing members to ignore the consequences of their actions
4. Stereotyping those who are opposed to the group as weak, evil, or stupid
5. Direct pressure to conform on any member who questions the group, couched in terms of "disloyalty"
6. Self-censorship of ideas that deviate from the apparent group consensus
7. Illusions of unanimity among group members; silence is viewed as agreement
8. Mindguards—self-appointed members who shield the group from information contradicting the group consensus.

Janis also devised some techniques for preventing groupthink:

1. Leaders should assign each member the role of "critical evaluator." This allows each member to freely air objections and doubts.
2. Higher-ups should not express an opinion when assigning a task to a group.
3. The organization should set up several independent groups and assign them to the same problem.
4. All effective alternatives should be examined.
5. Each member should discuss the group's ideas with trusted people outside the group.
6. The group should invite outside experts into meetings. Group members should be allowed to discuss with and question the outside experts.
7. At least one group member should be assigned the role of devil's advocate. This role should be assigned to a different person for each meeting.

The Healthy Team

As mentioned, there are a variety of teaming problems the project manager needs to be on the lookout for. Aside from groupthink and improper team development, team members might harbor hidden or individual agendas, make decisions in secret, show competitive behaviors, or not take responsibility for their behavior or that of the team.

Healthy teamwork is characterized by individuals who do the following:

1. Contribute at their highest level of experience and expertise.
2. Demonstrate good faith and goodwill, focusing on what is best for the team.
3. Willingly subordinate their personal agendas to the will of the majority.
4. Honor individual diversity and contributions.
5. Demonstrate open, honest, and respectful communication and confidentiality.
6. Demonstrate trustworthiness in word and deed while extending trust to others.
7. Consciously relinquish the need to control all decisions.
8. Listen well, seeking first to understand rather than to be understood.

Team Building

The team unit is the fundamental component of any project. Building a successful team requires more than just randomly assigning "bodies" to a group. The psychological and sociological aspects of team dynamics must be considered and steps taken to ease team members' induction into a new team. A variety of studies attest to the wisdom of this. Most recently, Harvard's Robert Putnam studied 30,000 Americans. He found a strong positive relationship between interracial trust and ethnic homogeneity. What this translates to is that the more ethnically diverse the people around you, the less you trust them. Although his treatise was addressing neighborhoods, his study points to the fact that the ramifications of team diversity need to be addressed as well.

Team building is a process of developing and maintaining a group of people who are working toward a common goal. The process of team building usually focuses on one or more of the following objectives: (1) clarifying role expectations and obligations of team members; (2) improving superior–subordinate or peer relationships; (3) improving problem-solving, decision making, resource utilization, or planning activities; (4) reducing conflict; and (5) improving the organizational climate.

Teams must be supported at the departmental as well as at the organizational level, as shown in Figure 3.1. Sydenham (2003) discusses several layers or supports for project teams. The external environmental layer greatly influences how an organization operates. This impacts projects and the teams working on them. The enterprise environment is the layer in which all projects of the enterprise are sited. This layer comprises the set of software engineering methodologies, tools, policies, etc. These impact how the project, and hence the team, operates. Supporting layers include organizational (i.e., stakeholder) support for the specific project.

Social interactions may not appear to be related to successful project deployment at first glance. However, in most organizations, people need to work together toward a common goal to accomplish their work successfully. It is certainly easier and more enjoyable to work together in a friendly atmosphere and, most likely, more productive as well. To promote a friendly work environment, you may wish to do the following:

1. Encourage after-work recreational activities.
2. Encourage fair treatment of all organizational members.
3. Make sure work is assigned equitably.

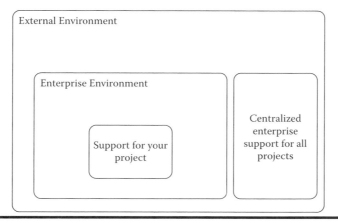

Figure 3.1   Project environmental layers.

4. Ensure that work goals and standards are reasonable.
5. Discourage favoritism.

It is important that a spirit of cooperation and teamwork exist in all areas of the organization. When individuals are rewarded only for their own accomplishments, team efforts may suffer. Some actions to improve team spirit include the following:

1. Reward team accomplishments by utilizing recognition, increased responsibilities, and some time off.
2. Set aside a few hours every few months for team members to sit down together to discuss how they are working together or any problems they may be having.
3. Encourage teams to develop group identities (a logo, team name). Locate members in the same area if possible.
4. Establish cross-functional quality teams.

The U.S. Department of State Foreign Affairs Handbook (2006) on team building and communication suggests the following teaming techniques to encourage high team productivity:

1. Focus on "ends" (what we are here to accomplish).
2. Involve each team member in a decision that impacts him or her.
3. Set agendas and schedules as a team.
4. Set high standards and high expectations, and encourage achievement.
5. Openly support the senior service providers in actions consistent with expectations.
6. Provide formative and summative assessments. Recognize and reward achievement. Cite areas for improvement fairly, tactfully, and in private.
7. Maintain an effective flow of two-way communication with all team members.
8. Avoid imposing individual direction or personal standards.
9. Be sensitive to factors that cause dissatisfaction and frustration and resolve conflicts in a timely manner.
10. Avoid surprises.
11. Forgive and forget small offenses.
12. Celebrate even small successes.

Teaming Tools

Some tools involving group participation that can be utilized to define missions, goals, and objectives are as follows:

Nominal Group Technique (NGT)—A tool for idea generation, problem solving, mission and key result area definition, and goals or objectives definition. The group should include participants from all levels (i.e., workers, supervisors, managers). A group leader addresses the subject and presents the problem or issue to be dealt with by the group. Participants spend a few minutes writing down their ideas. The leader conducts a round-robin listing of the ideas by asking each participant in turn for one idea. All ideas are written on a flip chart as stated, and no judgments or evaluations are made at this time. Each item is then discussed in turn. Some ideas are combined, some discarded, and some new ideas are added. The leader then asks participants to vote for the top three, five, or seven priority items. The results are tallied, and the top five priority items (on the basis of the voting results) are discussed. For example, as applied to key result area definition, the top five priority items would be the five key result areas chosen by the group as most important for mission accomplishment.

Roadblock Identification Analysis—A tool that focuses on identifying problems that are causing the group to be less productive than it could be. This tool utilizes NGT to identify and prioritize performance roadblocks. Action teams are formed to analyze barriers and develop proposals to remove these roadblocks. The proposals are implemented, tracked, and evaluated.

Productivity by Objectives—A systematic process for involving everyone in a comprehensive plan to achieve selected goals and objectives. This process involves a hierarchical system with councils, teams, and coordinators.

Management by Objectives—An approach that stresses mutual goal setting by managers and subordinates, clarity and specificity in the statement of goals, and frequent feedback concerning progress toward goals. Goals should be couched in terms of specific measurable outcomes (such as units produced or product quality). Goals should be realistic and attainable.

Force Field Analysis—A technique involving the identification of forces "for" and "against" a certain course of action. NGT could be used in conjunction with this technique. The group might prioritize the forces for and against by assessing their magnitude and probability of occurrence. The group might then develop an action plan to minimize the forces against and maximize the forces for.

Team communications—Modern project teams are often widely dispersed and global. Table 3.1 presents some alternatives to the standard face-to-face meeting.

A poll conducted by Harris Interactive on team (i.e., peers, partners, customers) collaboration (Aragon, 2006) found the following:

1. More than 65 percent of the respondents regularly use e-mail, fax, and audio conferencing.
2. In-person meetings are common, requiring more than 50 percent of the respondents to travel for business each month.
3. Almost 33 percent say that they would like to conduct more meetings via Web conferencing to reduce travel costs and time out of office as well as to better allocate already limited project budgets.
4. Only 16 percent currently use Web conferencing to facilitate meetings.

Table 3.1 Information Dissemination Techniques

	Same Place	Different Place
Same time	• Conversations • Meetings	• Teleconferences • Videoconferences • Web-based meetings • Telephone calls
Different time	• Reports • Newsletters • Videotapes • Audiotapes • Yellow sticky notes • Intranet • Memos	• Voice mail • E-mail • Fax • Web sites • Network-based tools • Interoffice mail • Other mail • Intranet

According to Aragon (2006), a constant theme of this 2006 Harris Interactive study was the importance of improving project collaboration and document exchange, the chief complaints being as follows:

1. Delays receiving input
2. Challenges communicating across time zones
3. People using incompatible software applications
4. Difficulty interpreting feedback

Team Effectiveness Leadership Model

Dr. Robert Ginnett, when a senior fellow at the Center for Creative Leadership (http://www.ccl.org/leadership/index.aspx), developed the Team Effectiveness Leadership Model, which can be used to identify what is required for a team to be effective and point the leader either toward the roadblocks that are hindering the team or toward ways to make the team even more effective. The U.S. Office of Personnel Management uses this technique and finds it invaluable (1996). Their experience is the basis for the following discussion.

The model uses a systems theory approach that includes inputs (i.e., individual, team, and organizational factors), processes (i.e., what one can tell about the team by observing team members), and outputs (i.e., how well the team fared in accomplishing its objectives).

Inputs are what are available to teams as they go about their work. There are multiple levels in the input stage. Input factors at both the individual and organizational levels, affect the team design level, as indicated by the direction of the arrows between these levels.

Outputs are the results of the team's work. A team is effective if (1) the team's product or service meets its stakeholders' standards for quantity, quality, and timeliness; and (2) if the group process that occurs while the group is performing its task enhances its members' ability to work together as a team in the future. Also, an equally important result of effective teamwork is the satisfaction its members derive from that work as individuals. Those team results depend on the group process and the inputs available to the team.

The model identifies four Process Criteria yardsticks managers can use to examine the ways in which teams work, as shown in Figure 3.2. If a team is to perform effectively, it must do the following:

1. Work hard enough (Effort (P-1)).
2. Acquire sufficient knowledge and skills to perform the task (Knowledge and skills (P-2)).
3. Devise a strategy to accomplish its work or ways to approach the task at hand (Strategy (P-3)).
4. Ensure constructive and positive group dynamics among its members (Group dynamics (P-4)).

Research has shown consistently that effective group dynamics is the foundation on which other teamwork proceeds. If the team is ultimately to achieve the valued outcome measures of effectiveness, a firm foundation of effective group process is critical.

Suppose a manager discovers that a team's members are not working very hard. Looking at the model's Process Criteria, an initial diagnosis would suggest a problem of effort (P-1). Instead of either encouraging or threatening the team members to get them to work harder, the manager could first consider the model's inputs to see if an underlying problem can be identified. The component in each input section with the number that corresponds to the initial problem offers

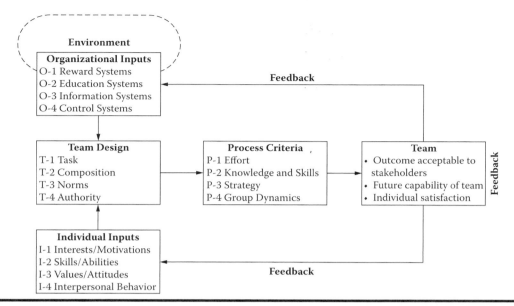

Figure 3.2   Team Effectiveness Leadership Model.

a natural starting point because the items have been numbered systematically to align related concepts.

The Individual Inputs (I in Figure 3.2) piece of the model asks managers to look at the interests and motivations of the individual team members (Level I-1, corresponding to a P-1 diagnosis), because team members who are interested in the group's task will be more likely to succeed at it. If the manager finds that the team members do in fact have an interest in the task, the model then leads the manager to consider another possibility.

The model emphasizes the way teams are influenced by both individual and organizational level inputs. So, the next step is to look at the Organizational Input (O in Figure 3.2) level. At the organizational level, the model suggests the manager examine the system of rewards (or disincentives to teamwork; O-1) that may be impacting the team. If the organization has not provided incentives to individuals for putting forth effort, they might not be very inclined to work hard, or they might not work at all. Also, the reward system may have been structured to promote only individual performance. Such reward structures are inconsistent with team tasks, where interdependence and cooperation among members is necessary.

If the manager concludes that both the individual- and organizational-level factors do support the team's ability to perform the task, the model offers yet another area to explore. Problems can also occur at the Team Design (T) level. Here, it is likely that a poorly designed task (T-1) is the culprit. If a job is meaningless, provides insufficient autonomy, or gives no knowledge of results, team members may not put forth much effort.

Using this model, a manager can find key points at various levels of the input stage that would impact the way the team goes about its work. In this example, a process-level problem with effort was diagnosed, and the model led the manager to the "1" level factors at the individual, organizational, and team levels as being the most likely sources of input problems. Ginette (2005) indicates that Process Criteria leverage points can be plotted against corresponding solutions, as shown in Table 3.2.

Table 3.2 Problems and Solutions

Problem	Review Inputs		
	Organizational Inputs (O)	Team Design (T)	Individual Inputs (I)
Effort (P-1)	**Reward Systems (O-1)**	**Tasks (T-1)**	**Interests/Motivation(I-1)**
Knowledge and Skills (P-2)	Education Systems (O-2)	Design Composition (T-2)	Skills/Abilities (I-2)
Strategy (P-3)	Information Systems (O-3)	Norms (T-3)	Values/Attitudes (I-3)
Critical foundation blocks			
Group Dynamics (P-4)	**Control Systems (O-4)**	**Authority (T-4)**	**Interpersonal Behaviors (I-4)**

Of course, additional factors impact teams and team effectiveness, including complex interactions among the variables described in this model. Even so, this model can be useful to understand how teams operate and can help managers analyze problems and lead more effectively.

The Virtual Team

Many modern organizations have gone virtual. Team members are dispersed across departments, campuses, states, and even countries. Virtual teams have some different requirements in terms of communication, working collaboratively, sharing information, and mutually supporting other team members. Naturally, in an information technology (IT) environment, these problems are usually overcome with the use of technology: e-mail, instant messaging, faxing, wikis, telephony, common whiteboard, application sharing, electronic meeting systems, project management software, electronic calendars, intranets and extranets, and knowledge management systems.

One of the more popular collaborative software solutions is Microsoft's Sharepoint (http://www. microsoft.com/sharepoint/capabilities/collaboration/overview.mspx), as shown in Figure 3.3.

Thompson (2005) lists the ten key issues that must be addressed to create a successful virtual team:

1. Trust building
2. Open communications
3. Accountability
4. Conflict management
5. Virtual decision-making process
6. Virtual meeting practices
7. Personal collaboration strategy
8. Collaborative document editing—techniques for planning, developing, and reviewing collaborative documents
9. Multicultural integration—tools and methods for harnessing the different cultures (business, ethnic, social) within a team as an asset rather than a weakness
10. Virtual brainstorming workflow
11. Self-managed teams—techniques for creating a "self-managed team" style

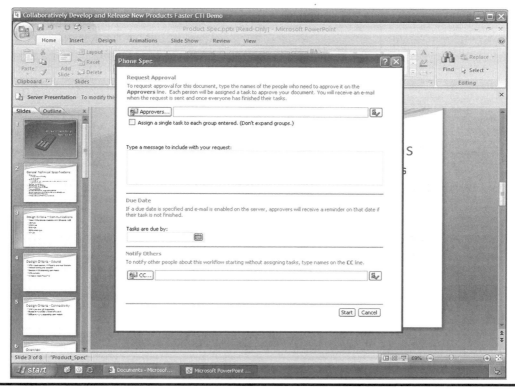

Figure 3.3 Microsoft's Sharepoint permits the collaborative use of Microsoft Office products. With permission.

Motivational Techniques

Many say chief information officers (CIOs) live by the 10 percent rule: The greatest productivity you can get comes from hiring within the top ten percentile. The easiest approach to developing an efficient technology department is to bring in better people. Because there is a 25 to 1 differential between the best and worst people and a 4 to 1 differential between the best and worst teams, maybe the best way to improve productivity and quality is just to improve hiring practices.

In addition to hiring, "peopleware" techniques could go a long way toward increasing productivity. Studies have shown that the productivity of people with adequate office space is substantially higher than people with traditionally allocated smaller amounts of space. Training also makes a difference, particularly if workers can accrue their training days the way they accrue their vacation time.

Productivity can also be improved in many other ways, such as by training managers to develop more skills in handling employee performance reviews or even by focusing on the psychological makeup of the development team. Much work has been done in recent years on team dynamics. For a team to work together successfully, team members must complement one another. Each team needs a distribution of leaders, followers, idea people, testers, problem solvers, and so on. Even in an industry where personality profiles are skewed toward introversion, it is still possible to build an effective working team. All it needs is some good management.

Table 3.3 What Do Employees Really Want?

What Employees Want In Priority Order	Items	What Employers Think Employees Want
1	Interesting work	Good wages
2	Appreciation of work	Personal loyalty
3	Feeling "in on things"	Sympathetic help with problems
4	Job security	Appreciation of work
5	Good wages	Interesting work
6	Promotion/growth	Feeling "in on things"
7	Good working conditions	Job security
8	Personal loyalty	Promotion/growth
9	Tactful discipline	Good working conditions
10	Sympathetic help with problems	Tactful discipline

Source: **Kovach, K.** (1999). *Employee Motivation: Addressing a Crucial Factor in your Organization's Performance. Human Resource Development.* Ann Arbor, MI: University of Michigan Press.

Creating a better workforce means understanding how to work with people. You'd be surprised (or maybe not) at how differently bosses and their staff look at the same things, as shown in Table 3.3. The object, clearly, is to narrow the gap. One way to do so is through motivating the workforce. Now, this doesn't mean taking up the pom-poms and giving the old college cheer. It does mean taking some specific steps.

One technique that many managers pay only lip service to can really make the difference between having a motivated employee and one who feels that he or she is just another number. Take the time to learn about your employees and their families. What are their dreams? Then, ask yourself how you, as a manager, can fulfill these dreams from a business perspective.

Perhaps the best way to learn about your employees is to meet with them outside the office, over lunch or on a company outing. As you learn more about your employees' motives, you can help each one develop a personalized strategic plan and vision. Ultimately, you could convert those painful yearly performance reviews into goal-setting sessions and progress reports.

Generating a positive attitude is also very important. Studies show that a very high percentage of all management feedback is negative, and that traditional management theory has done little to correct the situation. Your goal should be to reverse this trend.

Respect for and sensitivity toward others remains essential in developing positive attitudes. Ask employees' opinions regarding problems on the job and treat their suggestions and ideas as priceless treasures.

The partner of positive attitude in the motivational game is shared goals. A motivated workforce needs well-defined objectives that address both individual and organizational goals. This means that you should include all your employees in the strategic planning process. Getting them involved leads to increased motivation. It also acts as a quality check on whether or not you are doing the right thing. And, you'll close the communication gap at the same time.

Just setting a goal is insufficient. You have to monitor progress. The goal-setting process should include preparation of a detailed road map that shows the specific path each person is going to take to meet that goal. One of the things that IT professionals dislike the most is the feeling that they're left out of the business cycle. In essence, IT is just one facet of a grand strategic plan. IT staffers frequently complain that they rarely get to see the fruits of their labor. Distributing the IT function into the business unit mitigates this problem somewhat, but it is still up to the manager to put technologists into the thick of things—make them feel as though they are a part of the entire organization.

Finally, recognizing employee or team achievement is the most powerful tool in the motivating manager's toolbox. Appreciation for a job well done consistently appears at the top of employee wish lists. So, hire a band, have a party, send a card, or call in a clown— but thank that person or that team.

Some studies find that the top five motivating techniques are the following:

1. Manager personally congratulates the employee who does a good job.
2. Manager writes personal notes about good performance.
3. Organization uses performance as basis for promotion.
4. Manager publicly acknowledges an employee's good performance.
5. Manager holds morale-building meetings to celebrate successes.

One doesn't have to actually give an award for recognition to happen. Giving your attention is just as effective. The Hawthorne effect states that the act of measuring behavior (paying attention) will itself change it.

Nelson and Blanchard (1994) suggest the following low-cost rewards or recognition techniques:

1. Make a photo collage about a successful project that shows the people who worked on it, its stages of development, and its completion and presentation.
2. Create a "yearbook" to be displayed in the lobby that contains each employee's photograph, along with his or her best achievement of the year.
3. Establish a place to display memos, posters, photos, and so on, recognizing progress toward goals and thanking individual employees for their help.
4. Develop a "Behind the Scenes Award" specifically for those whose actions do not usually come into the limelight.
5. Thank your boss, your peers, and your employees when they have performed a task well or have done something to help you.
6. Make a thank-you card by hand.
7. Cover the person's desk with balloons.
8. Bake a batch of chocolate-chip cookies for the person.
9. Make and deliver a fruit basket to the person.
10. Tape a candy bar on delivery of an interim milestone with a note saying, "Halfway there."
11. Give a person a candle with a note saying, "No one can hold a candle to you."
12. Give a person a heart sticker with a note saying, "Thanks for caring."
13. Purchase a plaque, stuffed animal, or anything fun or meaningful, and give it to an employee at a staff meeting, specifically praising him or her. That employee keeps it for some time and then gives it to another employee at a staff meeting in recognition of some other accomplishment.
14. Call an employee into your office (or stop by his or her office) just to thank him or her; don't discuss any other issue.
15. Post a thank-you note on the employee's office door.
16. Send an e-mail thank-you card.

17. Praise people immediately. Encourage them to do more of the same good work.
18. Greet employees by name when you pass them in the hall.
19. Make sure you give credit to the employee or group that came up with an idea that is being used.
20. Acknowledge individual achievements by using employees' names when preparing status reports.

McCarthy and Allen (2000) suggest that you set up your employees for success. When you give someone a new assignment, tell the employee why you trust him or her with this new challenge. "I want you to handle this because I like the way you handled _____ last week." McCarthy and Allen also suggest that you never steal the stage. When an employee tells you about an accomplishment, don't steal his or her thunder by narrating a similar accomplishment of yours. They also suggest that you never use sarcasm, even in a teasing way. Resist the temptation to say something such as, "It's about time you gave me this report." Deal with the "late" problem by setting a specific time the report is due. If it's done on time, make a positive comment.

Conclusion

Most IT project managers have never studied team management techniques. That's a crucial omission. In this chapter, we've delved into a variety of techniques for effective management of teams and the individuals in those teams.

Links

http://wilderdom.com/games/TeamBuildingExercisesWebsites.html Team building exercises.
http://www.projectsmart.co.uk/helping-project-teams-succeed.html Helping project teams succeed.
http://www.asme.org/Communities/EarlyCareer/Five_Simple_Strategies.cfm Unifying project teams.
http://www.ibm.com/developerworks/rational/library/content/RationalEdge/jul02/TopTenWaysJul02.pdf
    Teams and use cases.
http://www.gembapantarei.com/2005/12/kaizen_blitz_for_project_teams_1.html Kaizen blitz for project
    teams.
http://jobfunctions.bnet.com/whitepaper.aspx?docid=298520 Building effective project teams (from
    Microsoft).
http://www.onlamp.com/pub/a/onlamp/2004/11/04/which_wiki.html List of wiki software.

References

Aragon, P. (September 14, 2006). Reinventing Collaboration Across Internal and External Project Teams. Retrieved from http://www.aecbytes.com/viewpoint/2006/issue_28.html.
Certo, C.C. (2000). *Modern Management*. Upper Saddle River, NJ: Prentice Hall.
Ginette, R. (April 2005). Leading a Great Team: Building Them from the Ground Up, Fixing Them on the Fly. Retrieved from http://www.executiveforum.com/PDFs/GinnettSummary.pdf.
Janis, I.L. (1972). *Victims of Groupthink*. Boston: Houghton Mifflin Company.
Kovach, K (1999). *Employee Motivation: Addressing a Crucial Factor in your Organization's Performance. Human Resource Development*. Ann Arbor, MI: University of Michigan Press.

McCarthy, M. and J. Allen. (2000). *You Made My Day: Creating Co-Worker Recognition and Relationships.* New York: L-F Books.

Nelson, B. and K. Blanchard. (1994). *1001 Ways to Reward Employees.* New York: Workman Publishing Co.

Sydenham, P. (2003). *Systems Approach to Engineering Design.* Norwood, MA: Artech House.

The U.S. Department of State Foreign Affairs (2006). Team Building and Communications. Retrieved from http://www.state.gov/documents/organization/89191.pdf.

Thompson, K. (April 6, 2005). Bioteaming: A manifesto for networked business teams. The Bumble Bee. Retrieved from http://www.bioteams.com/2005/04/06/bioteaming_a_manifesto.html.

U.S. Office of Personnel Management (1996). Model Leads to More Effective Teams. Retrieved from http://www.opm.gov/perform/articles/077.asp.

ID	❶	Task Name	Duration	Start	Finish	Pred
1		Develop Feature Requirements Statement	10 days	Tue 11/4/03	Mon 11/17/03	
2	▦	Complete Market Research	7 days	Mon 11/10/03	Tue 11/18/03	
3	▦	Develop Management Business Case	5 days	Thu 11/20/03	Wed 11/26/03	
4	▦	Present Business Case for Approval	1 day	Fri 11/28/03	Fri 11/28/03	3
5	▦	Management Approval of Business Case	1 day	Mon 12/1/03	Mon 12/1/03	4
6		Develop Feature Design Document	8.33 days	Tue 12/2/03	Fri 12/12/03	5
7		Complete Design Review	2.17 days	Fri 12/12/03	Tue 12/16/03	6
8		Complete Design Approval	1 day	Tue 12/16/03	Wed 12/17/03	7
9		Develop Technical Specifications	1 day	Wed 12/17/03	Thu 12/18/03	8
10	▦	Complete Approval of Technical Specifications	1 day	Tue 1/6/04	Tue 1/6/04	9
11	▦	Develop Server Code	39.38 days	Wed 1/7/04	Tue 3/2/04	10
12	▦	Develop GUI Code	39.38 days	Wed 1/7/04	Tue 3/2/04	
13	▦	System Testing	10 days	Fri 3/12/04	Thu 3/25/04	12
14		Integration Testing	7 days	Mon 3/29/04	Tue 4/6/04	13
15	▦	Regression Testing	5 days	Wed 4/7/04	Tue 4/13/04	14
16		Feature Documentation Developed	68 days	Wed 1/7/04	Fri 4/9/04	
17		Operational Packaging	5 days	Wed 4/14/04	Tue 4/20/04	15
18		QA Acceptance Testing	4 days	Wed 4/21/04	Mon 4/26/04	17
19		QA Acceptance	2 days	Tue 4/27/04	Wed 4/28/04	18

Figure 4.1 Using Microsoft Project to manage a project's schedule.

ID	Task Name	Work	Baseline	Variance	Actual	Remaining	% W. Comp.
1	Develop Feature Requirements Statement	196 hrs	196 hrs	0 hrs	0 hrs	196 hrs	0%
2	Complete Market Research	42 hrs	42 hrs	0 hrs	0 hrs	42 hrs	0%
3	Develop Management Business Case	30 hrs	30 hrs	0 hrs	0 hrs	30 hrs	0%
4	Present Business Case for Approval	4 hrs	4 hrs	0 hrs	0 hrs	4 hrs	0%
5	Management Approval of Business Case	3.6 hrs	3.6 hrs	0 hrs	0 hrs	3.6 hrs	0%
6	Develop Feature Design Document	400 hrs	400 hrs	0 hrs	0 hrs	400 hrs	0%
7	Complete Design Review	126 hrs	126 hrs	0 hrs	0 hrs	126 hrs	0%
8	Complete Design Approval	8 hrs	8 hrs	0 hrs	0 hrs	8 hrs	0%
9	Develop Technical Specifications	56 hrs	56 hrs	0 hrs	0 hrs	56 hrs	0%
10	Complete Approval of Technical Specifications	16 hrs	16 hrs	0 hrs	0 hrs	16 hrs	0%
11	Develop Server Code	1,260 hrs	1,260 hrs	0 hrs	0 hrs	1,260 hrs	0%
12	Develop GUI Code	1,260 hrs	1,260 hrs	0 hrs	0 hrs	1,260 hrs	0%
13	System Testing	320 hrs	320 hrs	0 hrs	0 hrs	320 hrs	0%
14	Integration Testing	168 hrs	168 hrs	0 hrs	0 hrs	168 hrs	0%
15	Regression Testing	120 hrs	120 hrs	0 hrs	0 hrs	120 hrs	0%
16	Feature Documentation Developed	680 hrs	680 hrs	0 hrs	0 hrs	680 hrs	0%
17	Operational Packaging	50 hrs	50 hrs	0 hrs	0 hrs	50 hrs	0%
18	QA Acceptance Testing	96 hrs	96 hrs	0 hrs	0 hrs	96 hrs	0%
19	QA Acceptance	96 hrs	96 hrs	0 hrs	0 hrs	96 hrs	0%

Figure 4.2   Tracking variances to the baseline.

Technology Metrics

Just as there is an abundance of business metrics, there is also an abundance of technology metrics. Some of the most common include the following:

1. Lines of code
2. Pages of documentation
3. Number and size of tests
4. Function count
5. Variable count
7. Number of modules
8. Depth of nesting
9. Count of changes required
10. Count of discovered defects
11. Count of changed lines of code
12. Time to design, code, and test
13. Defect discovery rate by phase of development
14. Cost to develop
15. Number of external interfaces
16. Number of tools used and why
17. Reusability percentage
18. Variance of schedule
19. Staff years of experience with team
20. Staff years of experience with language
21. Software years of experience with software tools
22. MIPS (million instructions per second) per person
23. Support-to-development-personnel ratio
24. Nonproject-to-project-time ratio

ID	Task Name	Fixed Cost	Fixed Cost Accrual	Total Cost	Baseline	Variance	Actual	Remaining
1	Develop Feature Requirements Statement	$0.00	Prorated	$12,700.00	$12,700.00	$0.00	$0.00	$12,700.00
2	Complete Market Research	$10,000.00	Prorated	$13,500.00	$13,500.00	$0.00	$0.00	$13,500.00
3	Develop Management Business Case	$0.00	Prorated	$2,350.00	$2,350.00	$0.00	$0.00	$2,350.00
4	Present Business Case for Approval	$0.00	Prorated	$400.00	$400.00	$0.00	$0.00	$400.00
5	Management Approval of Business Case	$0.00	Prorated	$320.00	$320.00	$0.00	$0.00	$320.00
6	Develop Feature Design Document	$0.00	Prorated	$22,333.33	$22,333.33	$0.00	$0.00	$22,333.33
7	Complete Design Review	$0.00	Prorated	$7,342.76	$7,342.76	$0.00	$0.00	$7,342.76
8	Complete Design Approval	$0.00	Prorated	$700.00	$700.00	$0.00	$0.00	$700.00
9	Develop Technical Specifications	$0.00	Prorated	$3,120.00	$3,120.00	$0.00	$0.00	$3,120.00
10	Complete Approval of Technical Specifications	$0.00	Prorated	$1,400.00	$1,400.00	$0.00	$0.00	$1,400.00
11	Develop Server Code	$15,000.00	Prorated	$86,662.50	$86,662.50	$0.00	$0.00	$86,662.50
12	Develop GUI Code	$5,000.00	Prorated	$76,662.50	$76,662.50	$0.00	$0.00	$76,662.50
13	System Testing	$2,500.00	Prorated	$18,900.00	$18,900.00	$0.00	$0.00	$18,900.00
14	Integration Testing	$0.00	Prorated	$8,960.00	$8,960.00	$0.00	$0.00	$8,960.00
15	Regression Testing	$0.00	Prorated	$6,400.00	$6,400.00	$0.00	$0.00	$6,400.00
16	Feature Documentation Developed	$0.00	Prorated	$58,400.00	$58,400.00	$0.00	$0.00	$58,400.00
17	Operational Packaging	$5,000.00	Prorated	$7,800.00	$7,800.00	$0.00	$0.00	$7,800.00
18	QA Acceptance Testing	$0.00	Prorated	$5,120.00	$5,120.00	$0.00	$0.00	$5,120.00
19	QA Acceptance	$0.00	Prorated	$6,320.00	$6,320.00	$0.00	$0.00	$6,320.00

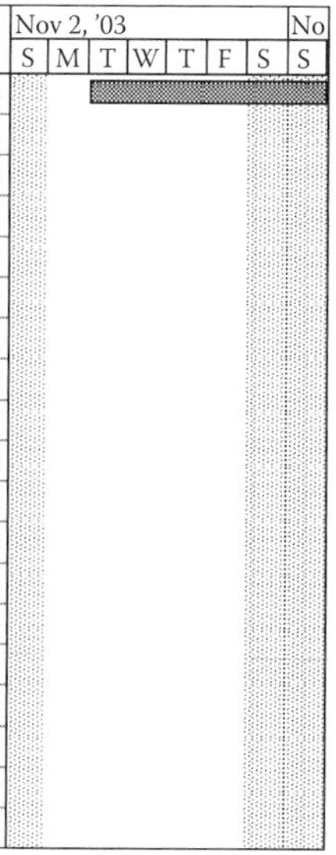

Figure 4.3 Tracking project costs.

Table 4.1 Popular Business Metrics

Category	Metric
Cost	• Actual cost versus budget (variance)
	• Total cost per transaction
	• Labor costs versus nonlabor costs
	• Staff costs versus consultant costs
Duration	• Actual time expended versus budget (variance)
Productivity	• Effort hours per unit of work
	• Effort hours reduced from standard project processes
	• Effort hours saved through reuse
	• Number of process improvement ideas implemented
	• Number of hours/dollars saved from process improvements
Quality of deliverables	• Percentage of deliverables going through quality reviews
	• Percentage of deliverable reviews resulting in acceptance the first time
	• Number of defects discovered after initial acceptance
	• Percentage of deliverables that comply with organization standards
	• Number of hours to rework previously completed deliverables
	• Number of best practices identified and applied on the project
Client satisfaction	• Overall client satisfaction
	• Number of approved business requirements satisfied by the project

Technology metrics measure both productivity as well as quality. The following checklist measures a variety of quality attributes of the technology used:

Rate 1 to 5 (1 being the worst, 5 being the best)

1. How easy is it to use? 1 2 3 4 5
2. How secure is it? 1 2 3 4 5
3. Level of confidence in it? 1 2 3 4 5
4. How well does it conform to requirements? 1 2 3 4 5
5. How easy is it to upgrade? 1 2 3 4 5
6. How easy is it to change? 1 2 3 4 5
7. How portable is it? 1 2 3 4 5
8. How easy is it to locate a problem and fix it? 1 2 3 4 5
9. Is the response time fast enough? 1 2 3 4 5
10. How easy is it to train staff? 1 2 3 4 5
11. How easy is it to test? 1 2 3 4 5
12. How easy is it to couple this system to another system? 1 2 3 4 5
13. Does the system utilize the minimum storage possible? 1 2 3 4 5
14. Is the system self-descriptive? 1 2 3 4 5
15. Is there a program for ongoing quality awareness for all employees? 1 2 3 4 5
16. Is this the right system to be developed? 1 2 3 4 5

Sample Project Plan Metrics Section

The project plan will describe appropriate metrics that will be used to track the progress of the project, as shown in the following sample. Comments are in italic.

Metrics

As part of our company's metrics program, the project team used the **function points metric** to gauge the relative size of the ACME Library Management System. The function points metric is suitable for GUI-based client/server systems, and provides valuable information for the ongoing measurement of productivity within the organization. The function point (FP) value for the system can be compared with FP values of previous projects to gain an estimate of the relative size of the system.

Function points are a measure of the size of computer applications and the projects that build them. The size is measured from a functional, or user, point of view. It is independent of the computer language, development methodology, technology, or capability of the project team used to develop the application.

The function point value is calculated in three steps:

1. Complete the function point table.
2. Calculate the value adjustment factor (VAF).
3. Compute the final function points (FP) value.

Each of these steps is described in the following sections and a conclusion is drawn in the final section.

Function Point Metric

Completing the Function Point Table

The completed function point table for the ACME Library Management System is as follows.

Measurement Parameter	Count	Weighting Factor			Total Count
		Simple	Average	Complex	
Number of user inputs	55	3	4	6	165
Number of user outputs	60	4	5	7	240
Number of user enquiries	55	3	4	6	220
Number of files	30	7	10	15	210
Number of external interfaces	80	5	7	10	400
Count total					**1235**

The weighting factor selected depends on the type of system being developed. In this case, Simple was the weighted factor most often selected.

Calculating the Value Adjustment Factor (VAF)

The Total Degree of Influence (TDI) factor, an interim factor necessary for the calculation of the Value Adjustment Factor (VAF), is calculated by answering the questions in the following table. The options for the degree of influence range from Not Applicable (0) to Absolutely Essential (5). The total value is calculated by summing up the values in the rows.

General System Characteristic	Degree of Influence
1. Does the system require reliable backup and recovery?	4
2. Are data communications required?	1
3. Are there distributed processing functions?	3
4. Is performance critical?	2
5. Will the system run in an existing heavily utilized operational environment?	1
6. Does the system require online data entry?	3
7. Does the online entry require the input transaction to be built over multiple screens or operations?	2
8. Are the master files updated online?	0
9. Are the inputs, outputs, files, or enquires complex?	2
10. Is the internal processing complex?	2
11. Is the code designed to be reusable?	3
12. Are conversion and installation included in the design?	2
13. Is the system designed for multiple installations in different organizations?	1
14. Is the application designed to facilitate change and ease of use?	5
Total Degree of Influence (TDI)	**31**

These 14 questions are the ones asked in all FP calculations. Each question is answered using a scale that ranges from 0 (not important or applicable) to 5 (essential or critical).

Using the TDI factor, the VAF can be calculated using the following formula:

$$\text{VAF} = (\text{TDI} \times 0.01) + 0.65 \text{ //This is the standard FP formula}$$
$$\textbf{VAF} = (31 \times 0.01) + 0.65 = \textbf{0.96}$$

Computing the Final FP Value

The FP value can be calculated using the formula:

$$\text{FP} = \text{Count Total} \times \text{VAF}$$
$$\textbf{FP} = 1235 \times 0.96 = \textbf{1186}$$

Conclusion

An FP value of 1186, when compared with the historical data maintained for other projects, does not indicate a very large or complex system. The data for this project will be captured so that they can be used for comparison with other projects.

Other Metrics

Our company employs other metrics to assess the quality of the software product. Metrics are used to measure the quantity and quality of the source code by measuring various aspects of the code and the lines of code (LOC). The metrics are described in the following categories:

- Source code size metrics
- Code understandability metrics
- Function metrics

There are a wide variety of other metrics. Which metrics are selected is dependent upon the type of system and the standards of the organization.

Source Code Size Metrics
Lines of Code (LOC) Metric

One of the common bases on which to estimate a software project is the lines of code (LOC) metric. LOC is used to determine time and cost estimates. The LOC estimate becomes the baseline to measure the amount of work performed on a project. Once a project is under way, the LOC becomes a tracking tool that can measure the degree of progress on a project. Experienced developers can gauge a LOC estimate using prior knowledge of previous projects.

Effective Lines of Code

An effective line of code is the measurement of all lines that are not comments, blank lines, standalone braces, or parenthesis. This measurement more closely represents the quantity of work performed. It is common for programmers to use a single brace or parenthesis on a line to denote a specific block of code. A single character on a line should not really count as a line of code. This type of coding style can therefore increase the LOC metric by 20 to 40 percent.

Code Understandability Metrics
Comment Line Metric

The number of comments in a source program is a measure of the care taken by the programmer to make the source code and algorithms understandable. Code that is not well commented is very difficult to maintain.

Comments can occur by themselves on a physical line or be commingled with source code. A line is considered a comment line if the physical line contains a comment.

Blank Line and White Space Metric

The number of blank lines within a program determines the readability. White space highlights the logical grouping of constructs and variables. Programs that use few blank lines are difficult to read and more expensive to maintain.

Function Metrics

Function Count Metric

The total number of functions within a program determines the degree of modularity. This metric is used to quantify the average LOC per function, the maximum LOC per function, and the minimum LOC per function.

Average LOC per Function Metric

The average LOC per function indicates how the code meets the accepted standard. The accepted industry standard of 200 LOC/function is the desired average. Functions that have a larger number of LOC per function are difficult to understand and maintain. They provide a good indication that a function should be broken into smaller functions.

Maximum LOC per Function Metric

Although the average LOC per function gives an interesting source code trend, the maximum LOC per function gives an indication of the largest function in the system.

Minimum LOC per Function Metric

A LOC value of 2 may indicate that functions are just prototypes; they will need to be completed later.

Methods for Assessment

Linkman (1991) outlined a methodology for establishing targets and means for assessment. The procedure is not focused on any particular set of metrics; rather, it stresses that metrics should be selected on the basis of goals. This procedure is suitable for setting up goals for either the entire project deliverables or for any partial product created in the software life cycle. The procedure is as follows:

1. Define measurable goals: The project goals establishment process is similar to the development process for project deliverables. Software projects usually start with abstract problem concepts, and the final project deliverables are obtained by continuously partitioning and refining the problem into tangible and manageable pieces. Final quantified goals can be transformed from initial intangible goals by following the same divide-and-conquer method for software deliverables. Three sources of information are helpful in establishing the targets:

- Historical data under the assumptions that data is available, development environment is stable, and projects are similar in terms of type, size, and complexity.
- Synthetic data such as modeling results, is useful if models used are calibrated to the specific development environment.
- Expert opinions.

2. Maintain balanced goals: The measurable goals are usually established on the basis of the following four factors—cost, schedule, effort, and quality. It is feasible to achieve just a single goal, but it is always a challenge to deliver a project with the minimum staff and resources on time and within budget. It needs to be kept in mind that trade-off is always involved, and all issues should be addressed to reach a set of balanced goals.

3. Set up intermediate goals: A project should never be measured at its endpoint only. Checkpoints should be set up to provide confidence that the project is running on course. The common practice involves setting up quantifiable targets for each phase, measuring the actual values against the targets, and establishing a plan to make corrections for any deviations. All four earlier-mentioned factors (cost, schedule, effort, quality) should be broken down into phases or activities for setting up intermediate targets. Measurements for cost and effort can be divided into machine and human resources according to the software life-cycle phase so that expenditures can be monitored, to ensure that the project is running within budget. Schedules should always be defined in terms of milestones or checkpoints to ensure that intermediate products will be evaluated and final product can be delivered on time. The quality of intermediate products should always be measured to guarantee that the final deliverable will meet its target goal.

4. Establish the means of assessment: This activity involves two aspects—data collection and data analysis. Based on the project characteristics such as size, complexity, level of control, etc., a decision should be made in terms of whether a manual or an automated data collection process should be used. If a nonautomated process is applied, then the availability of the collection medium at the right time should be emphasized. The following two types of data analyses should be considered:

   - Project analysis—This type of analysis, consisting of checkpoint analysis and continuous analysis (trend analysis), is concerned with verifying whether the intermediate targets are being met, to ensure that the project is on the right track.
   - Component analysis—This type of analysis concentrates on the finer level of detail of the end product, and is concerned with identifying those components in the product that may require special attention and action. The complete process includes deciding on the set of measures to be analyzed, identifying the components detected as anomalous using measured data, finding out the root cause of the anomalies, and taking corrective actions.

Process Improvement

Modifying a system or process to enhance productivity or obtain competitive advantage is referred to as process improvement. Instituting a program that continually searches for ways to improve processes is referred to as continuous improvement.

Once a company decides that continuous improvement is indeed key to competitive advantage, it must create and then manage a continuous improvement plan. The next question that needs to be asked is whether the company is able to articulate a continuous improvement plan for its operations. In Chapter 1, we briefly discussed the balanced scorecard. The goals of an information technology (IT) balanced scorecard are simplistic in scope but complex to execute:

1. Align IT plans with business goals and needs.
2. Establish appropriate measures for evaluating the effectiveness of IT.
3. Align employees' efforts toward achieving IT objectives.
4. Stimulate and improve IT performance.
5. Achieve balanced results across stakeholder groups.

The keyword here is *balanced*. It reflects the balance between the five goals, the four balanced scorecard perspectives (customer, business processes, learning and innovation, and financial), long- and short-term objectives, as well as between qualitative and quantitative performance measures.

Progressive scorecard practitioners track metrics in five key categories:

1. Financial performance: IT spending in the context of service levels, project progress, etc. Sample metrics include cost of data communications per seat and relative spending per portfolio category.
2. Project performance: Sample metrics include percentage of new development investment resulting in new revenue streams and percentage of IT R&D investment leading to IT service improvements.
3. Operational performance: Instead of concentrating measurement efforts on day-to-day measures, best-in-class practitioners seek to provide an aggregate, customer-focused view of IT operations. Sample metrics include peak time availability, critical process uptime.
4. Talent management: This category of metrics seeks to manage IT human capital. Measures include staff satisfaction and retention, as well as attracting external job seekers to the IT department. Metrics include retention of high-potential staff and external citations of IT achievement.
5. User satisfaction: Sample metrics include focused executive feedbacks and user perspective.

Bowne & Co. (www.bowne.com), a New York City–based documents management company initiated the IT balanced scorecard in 1997. Their process consisted of the following seven steps:

1. Provision of kick-off training for IT staff.
2. Ongoing strategy mapping: The annual IT strategy, as in most companies, is derived from the corporate strategy.
3. Metrics selection: A team, including the chief technology officer (CTO), created a list of metrics. The list was refined using analysis of each potential metric's strengths and weaknesses. The final list was approved by the chief information officer (CIO).
4. Metrics definition: A set of standard definitions is created for each metric such that the measurement technique as well as data collection process are defined. Initiatives that must be completed to allow tracking of the metrics are also outlined.
5. Assignment of metric ownership: Owners are assigned to each metric. They are responsible for scorecard completion. Their bonuses are related to their scorecard-related duties.
6. Data collection and quality assurance: Data frequency varies by metric on the basis of cost of collection, the corporate financial reporting cycle, and volatility of the business climate.
7. Metric review: CIO, CTO, and corporate officers review the scorecard every six months. Metrics are revisited annually.

A sample balanced scorecard is shown in Table 4.2.

Table 4.2 Typical Balanced Scorecard Measures, Targets, and Initiatives

Objectives	Measures	Target	Initiative
Financial			
Reduce administrative costs	Cost-to-spend ratio	Reduce administrative costs by 10 percent	Implement plan to improve efficiencies
Increase profits	Net earnings	Increase revenue	Improve volume and collection efforts
Internal Business Processes			
Decrease the number of fraudulent transactions	The number of fraud instances reported	Reduce the number by 10 percent	Implement stronger policies to penalize dishonest sellers
Reduce system downtime	Downtime, in minutes per month	Achieve 99 percent online per month	Schedule system maintenance during low customer use times
Learning and Growth			
Improve Internet marketing	Number of hits and site visits from Internet ads	Increase by 15 percent	Assess target market for effectiveness of current ad placements
Increase number of buyers and sellers by regions	Number of auctions and bids per auction	Increase by 5 percent per region	Form region-specific auctions
Increase participants in business-to-customer (B2C) auctions	Number of businesses selling surplus via auctions	Increase by 10 percent	Market push to businesses
Customer Relations			
Improve response time to respond to questions	Time from receipt of question to response	Decrease to 4 hours for 99 percent of responses	Empower first level CSRs to respond to questions
Decrease the number of disputes	Number of resolved and unresolved disputes	Decrease unresolved disputes by 5 percent	Implement plan to intervene earlier and faster in disputes

Example

Quality and productivity have always been an explicit part of Cupertino, California-based Hewlett-Packard's (HP) corporate objectives. To help develop and utilize metrics companywide, HP created the Software Metrics Council. Today, 80 productivity and quality managers within HP perform a variety of functions, from training to communicating the best software engineering and business practices, to establishing productivity and quality metrics.

HP has adopted a methodology called Total Quality Control (TQC). A fundamental principle of TQC is that all company activities can be scrutinized in terms of the processes involved; metrics can be assigned to each process to evaluate effectiveness. HP established the Systems Software

Certification program to ensure measurable, consistent, high-quality software through defining metrics, setting goals, collecting and analyzing data, and certifying products for release.

HP's results were impressive. Defects were caught and corrected early, when costs to find and fix are lower. Less time was spent in the costly system test and integration phases, and on maintenance. This resulted in lower overall support costs and higher productivity. It also increased quality for HP's customers.

HP's success demonstrates what a corporatewide commitment to continuous improvement can achieve. The commitment to these gains was so strong that HP invested in full-time productivity and quality managers, which is indeed unique.

Techniques to introduce quality programs vary from company to company, but there are some common features:

1. Perform a customer satisfaction survey.
2. Get management sponsorship to fix what you found wrong in #1.
3. Top management needs to make a visible and personal commitment to any quality program.
4. Customers as well as suppliers need to be involved.
5. Define the processes.
6. Come up with ways to improve the process.
7. Determine metrics to measure the improvement of the process.

Quality Control Techniques

Several techniques are commonly used by businesses to control the quality of products. A check sheet is one of the easiest ways to collect data that can be used in later analysis when determining quality issues. Graphs and histograms are graphical techniques that can be used to organize, summarize, and display data over time.

The old adage that 80 percent of the problems are caused by 20 percent of the causes is the reason for the popularity of Pareto analysis. This technique visually represents which factor or factors are causing the problem, as shown in Figure 4.4. In this example, "bad data" seems to be the culprit.

Creation of a Pareto diagram involves the following:

1. Select the problem you want to analyze.
2. Determine the categories of the problem, and collect the data you want to display.
3. Note the categories on the horizontal axis in descending order of value.
4. Determine measurement scale (cost, frequency, etc.), and note it on the left vertical axis.
5. Optionally, draw a cumulative line from left to right that shows the cumulative percentage of the categories.

The Ishikawa diagram (also called fishbone diagram or cause-and-effect diagram) is a diagram that shows the causes of a certain event. It was first used in the 1960s, and is considered one of the seven basic tools of quality management, along with the histogram, Pareto chart, check sheet, control chart, flowchart, and scatter diagram.

Figure 4.5 shows a first pass in creating a fishbone diagram for the problem of late projects. To create a fishbone diagram, the following steps must be performed:

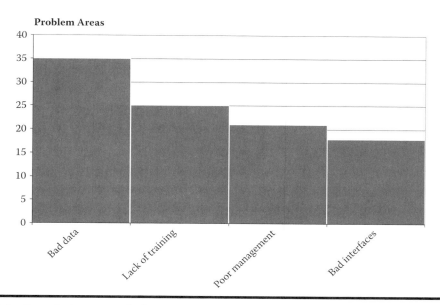

Figure 4.4   Sample Pareto analysis.

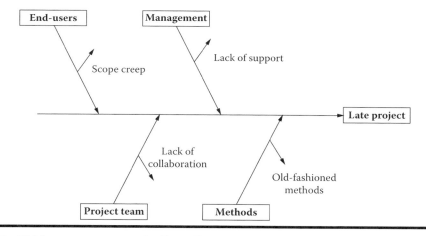

Figure 4.5   Fishbone, or cause-and-effect, diagram.

1. Define the problem clearly and objectively.
2. Write the problem statement in a box at the right of the diagram.
3. Define major categories of possible causes (use generic branches). Factors to consider include: data and information systems, dollars, environment, hardware, materials, measurements, methods, people, training, and equipment.
4. Construct the diagram by inserting the major categories at the ends of lines.
5. Brainstorm possible and specific causes, and list them under the appropriate category.
6. Vote to identify the probable root causes.

Performance Management and Management Systems

There are certain attributes that set apart successful performance measurement and management systems, including (*Guide to a Balanced Scorecard Performance Management Methodology*, 1999) the following:

1. *A conceptual framework is needed for the performance measurement and management system.* Every organization, regardless of type, needs a clear and cohesive performance measurement framework that is understood by all levels of the organization, and that supports objectives and the collection of results.
2. *Effective internal and external communications are the keys to successful performance measurement.* Effective communication with employees, process owners, customers, and stakeholders is vital to the successful development and deployment of performance measurement and management systems.
3. *Accountability for results must be clearly assigned and well understood.* High-performance organizations clearly identify what it takes to determine success, and make sure that all managers and employees understand what they are responsible for in achieving organizational goals.
4. *Performance measurement systems must provide intelligence for decision makers; they must not just compile data.* Performance measures should be limited to those that relate to strategic organizational goals and objectives, and that provide timely, relevant, and concise information for decision makers at all levels to assess progress toward achieving predetermined goals. These measures should yield information on the efficiency with which resources are transformed into goods and services, on how well results compare to a program's intended purpose, and on the effectiveness of organizational activities and operations in terms of their specific contribution to program objectives.
5. *Compensation, rewards, and recognition should be linked to performance measurements.* Performance evaluations and rewards need to be tied to specific measures of success by linking financial and nonfinancial incentives directly to performance. Such a linkage sends a clear and unambiguous message throughout the organization as to what's important.
6. *Performance measurement systems should be positive, not punitive.* The most successful performance measurement systems are not "gotcha" systems, but "learning" systems that help the organization identify what works and what does not, so as to continue with and improve on what is working and repair or replace what is not.
7. *Results and progress toward program commitments should be openly shared with employees, customers, and stakeholders.* Performance measurement system information should be openly and widely shared with an organization's employees, customers, stakeholders, vendors, and suppliers.

Conclusion

Over half of IT projects overrun their schedules and budgets, 31 percent are cancelled, and only 16 percent are completed on time according to the Standish Group (www.standishgroup.com). Unfortunately, these are not shocking statistics to those who manage IT departments. Although there are many reasons why systems go over budget or over schedule (e.g., changing requirements, departing employees, reallocated functionality, etc.), the biggest contributing factor to the problem is simply poor project management. Effective project management includes the processes of project tracking, promoting quality assurance, process improvement, performance measurement and management, and strict budget management.

Links

http://www.asq.org American Society for Quality.
http://deming.eng.clemson.edu/pub/tutorials/qctools/homepg.htm Quality control tools tutorials.
 http://www.juran.com/ Information about quality and Juran.
http://measurement.fetcke.de/ Software metrics meta-site.
http://www.sei.cmu.edu/sema/welcome.html SEI's SEMA (Software Engineering Measurement and Analysis) site.
http://www.rspa.com/spi/SQA.html Quality management meta-site.
http://www.rspa.com/spi/SCM.html Software Configuration Management meta-site.
http://www.rspa.com/spi/project-mgmt.html Software project management resources.
http://www.microsoft.com/technet/prodtechnol/visio/visio2000/maintain/picture.mspx Microsoft diagramming with Visio.

References

Guide to a Balanced Scorecard Performance Management Methodology (1999). U.S. Department of Commerce.
Linkman, S. G. and Walker, J. G. (1991). Controlling programs through measurement. *Information and Software Technology,* 33(1).

Chapter 5

Project Critical Success Factors

In this chapter, we will examine project critical success factors. Topics highlighted include managing people, dealing with politics, and managing for disaster.

Just What's Critical to Project Success

Quite a few things can go wrong with software development. McConnell (1996) neatly categorized these, as shown in Table 5.1.

Hyvari (2006) provides a different spin on this, as shown in Table 5.2.

A wide variety of management considerations (e.g., project scope, scheduling, risk, tracking, estimation, etc.) can "make or break" a project. We usually call these considerations *critical success factors*. There is a diversity of opinions on what drives project success. The Standish Group's "top ten" reasons include the following:

1. User involvement
2. Executive management support
3. Clear business objectives
4. Optimizing scope
5. Agile process
6. Project manager expertise
7. Financial management
8. Skilled resources
9. Formal methodology
10. Standard tool and infrastructure

In the discussion that follows, all of these critical success factors—except the last two—are from the Standish Group's study of successful and unsuccessful projects. The last two factors, "Contract negotiation and management" and "Implementation" are lessons learned from various

Table 5.1   Classic Project Mistakes

People-Related Mistakes	Process-Related Mistakes	Product-Related Mistakes	Technology-Related Mistakes
Undermined motivation	Overly optimistic schedules	Requirements gold-plating—i.e., too many product features	Silver-bullet syndrome—i.e., latching onto a new technology or methodology that is unproven for the particular project
Weak personnel	Insufficient risk management	Feature creep	Overestimated savings from tools or methods
Recalcitrant problem employees	Contractor failure	Developer gold-plating—i.e., developers using technology just for the sake of using technology	Switching tools in the middle of a project
Heroics	Insufficient planning	Push me, pull me negotiation—i.e., constantly changing schedule	Lack of automated source code control
Adding people to a late project	Abandonment of planning under pressure	Research-oriented development—i.e., stretching the limits of technology	
Noisy crowded offices	Wasted time before project actually starts—i.e., the approval and budgeting process		
Friction between developers and customers	Shortchanged upstream activities—e.g., requirements analysis, etc.		
Unrealistic expectations	Inadequate design		
Lack of effective project sponsorship	Shortchanged quality assurance		
Lack of stakeholder buy-in	Insufficient management controls		

Table 5.1 Classic Project Mistakes (Continued)

People-Related Mistakes	Process-Related Mistakes	Product-Related Mistakes	Technology-Related Mistakes
Lack of user input	Premature or too frequent convergence—i.e., release the product too early		
Politics over substance	Omitting necessary tasks from estimates		
Wishful thinking	Planning to catch up later		
	Code-like-hell programming		

governmental IT projects (a method for assigning a green, yellow, or red indicator to this category on the basis of these success factors is shown in Tables 5.3, 5.4, and 5.5):

- Executive support: The executive sponsor must have a global view of the project, set the agenda, arrange the funding, articulate the project's overall objectives, be an ardent supporter, be responsive, and finally, be accountable for the project's success.
- User involvement: Primary users must have good communication skills allowing them to clearly explain business processes in detail to the IT personnel. Primary users should also be trained to follow project management protocols. Finally, users must be realists; they should be aware of the limitations of the project.
- Experienced project manager: Project managers must possess technology and business knowledge, judgment, negotiation, good communication and organization. The focus is on softer skills such as diplomacy and time management.
- Clear business objectives: The project objectives must be clearly defined and understood throughout the organization. Projects must be measured against these objectives regularly to provide an opportunity for early recognition and correction of problems, justification for resources and funding, and preventive planning on future projects.
- Minimized scope: Scope must be realistic; it must be possible to complete the project within the specified duration. Scope must be measured regularly to eliminate scope creep.
- Agile business requirements process: Requirements management is the process of identifying, documenting, communicating, tracking, and managing project requirements, as well as changes to those requirements. An agile requirements process enables one to manage requirements quickly without generating major conflicts. This is an ongoing process and must stay in lockstep with the development process.
- Standard infrastructure: Establish a standard technology infrastructure that includes operational and organizational protocols. This infrastructure must be commonly understood and regularly assessed.
- Formal methodology: Following a formal methodology provides a realistic picture of the project and the resource commitment. Certain steps and procedures are reproducible and reusable, maximizing projectwide consistency.
- Reliable estimates: Be realistic.

Table 5.2　Success/Failure Factors

Factors Related to Project	Size and Value
	Having a clear boundary
	Urgency
	Uniqueness of project activities
	Density of the project network (in dependencies between activities)
	Project life cycle
	End-user commitment
	Adequate funds/resources
	Realistic schedule
	Clear goals/objectives
Factors Related to the Project Manager/Leadership	**Ability to Delegate Authority**
	Ability to trade off
	Ability to coordinate
	Perception of role and responsibilities
	Effective leadership
	Effective conflict resolution
	Having relevant past experience
	Management of changes
	Contract management
	Situational management
	Competence
	Commitment
	Trust
	Other communication
Factors Related to Project Team Members	**Technical Background**
	Communication
	Troubleshooting
	Effective monitoring and feedback
	Commitment
Factors Related to the Organization	**Steering Committee**
	Clear organization/job descriptions
	Top management support
	Project organization structure
	Functional manager's support
	Project champion

Table 5.2   Success/Failure Factors (Continued)

Factors Related to Project	*Size and Value*
Factors Related to the Environment	**Competitors**
	Political environment
	Economic environment
	Social environment
	Technological environment
	Nature
	Client
	Subcontractors

Table 5.3   Success Factors—Sample Assessment

Success Factor	*Standish Rank*	*Standish Weight*	*Assessment[a]*	*Score*
Executive support	1	18	3	54
User involvement	2	16	3	48
Experienced project manager	3	14	3	42
Clear business objectives	4	12	2	24
Minimized scope	5	10	2	20
Agile requirements process	6	8	2	16
Standard infrastructure	7	6	3	18
Formal methodology	8	6	2	12
Reliable estimates	9	5	2	10
Skilled staff	10	5	3	15
Contract negotiations and management	—	10	3	30
Implementation	—	8	2	16
TOTAL SCORE				301
WEIGHTED SCORE				86.5%

[a] In this example, the assessment is 3, 2, or 1 for High, Medium, or Low, respectively.

■ Skilled staff: Correctly identify the required competencies, the required level of experience and expertise for each identified skill, the quantum of resources needed within the given skill, and when these will be needed. When identifying competencies, remember that soft skills are as important as technical skills.

■ Contract negotiation and management: The Standish Group did not identify this as a success factor; however, on the basis of lessons learned from governmental projects, one can conclude that contract negotiation and management plays a major role in project outcomes.

■ Implementation: The Standish Group did not identify this as a success factor; however, on the basis of lessons learned from governmental projects, one can conclude that implementation plays a major role in project outcomes.

Table 5.4 Project Outlook Stoplight Criteria

Dashboard Area	Green	Yellow	Red
Scope	• Total cost of all change requests is 50 percent or less of change request budget, and • All major system components will be implemented as planned	• Total cost of all change requests is 75 percent or less of change request budget, or • Major system component will be deferred to later phase to meet the current phase's schedule or budget	• Total cost of all change requests is at least 75 percent of the change request budget, or • Major system component will not be implemented
Schedule	• Schedule variance does not impact completion date for current phase, and • Work plan is updated at least once every two weeks	• Schedule variance delays completion date for current phase but does not impact completion date for later phases or critical path, or • Major deliverable will be late by two weeks or less, or • Work plan has not been updated within last 30 days	• Schedule variance affects critical path, or • Major deliverable will be at least two weeks late, or • Work plan has not been updated for more than 30 days
Budget	• Budget variance is less than 5 percent of total budget, and there is project funding flexibility within the agency's control	• Budget variance is less than 10 percent of total budget, and there is project funding flexibility within the agency's control	• There is budget variance and there is no remaining project funding flexibility, or • Budget variance is at least 10 percent
Success Factors	• Weighted score is at least 90 percent	• Weighted score is at least 80 percent	• Weighted score is less than 80 percent

Some Critical Success Factors: A Closer Look

The Right People

Having the right people on a project team is certainly key to the success of a project. In a large pharmaceutical company, the lead designer walked off a very important project. Obviously, that set the team back quite a bit as no one else had enough experience to do what he did. Even if the IT staff stays put, there is still the possibility that a "people" issue will negatively affect the project. For example, a change in senior management might mean that the project you are working on gets canned or moved to a lower priority. A project manager working for America Online Time Warner had just started an important new project when a new president was installed. He did what all new presidents do—he engaged in a little housecleaning. Projects got swept away, and so did some people. When the dust settled, the project manager personally had a whole new set of priorities, as well as a bunch of new end users to work with. Although the project manager's most important project stayed high on the priority list, unfortunately, some of the end users didn't. The departure

Table 5.5 Project Outcome Stoplight Criteria

Dashboard Area	Green	Yellow	Red
Scope	• Project satisfies at least 95 percent of all business objectives, and • All major system components are implemented as planned	• Project satisfied at least 90 percent of all business objectives, and • No more than one major system component is deferred to later phase	• Project satisfies less than 90 percent of all business objectives, or • At least one major system component is not implemented
Schedule	• Project completion no later than 10 percent of original schedule duration	• Project completion no later than 20 percent of original schedule duration	• Project completion later than 20 percent of original duration
Budget	• Budget variance is less than 5 percent of total budget	• Budget variance is less than 10 percent of total budget	• Budget variance is at least 10 percent of total budget
Success Factors	• Weighted score is at least 90 percent	• Weighted score is at least 80 percent	• Weighted score is less than 80 percent

of a subject matter expert (SME) can have disastrous consequences. Lucky for our intrepid project manager, she was able to replace her "domain expert" with someone equally knowledgeable.

Today's dynamically changing business landscape can also play havoc with projects. Mergers and acquisitions can have the effect of changing the key players or adding whole new sets of stakeholders and stakeholder requirements. Going global adds an entirely new dimension to the importance of being able to speak the end user's language.

Personnel changes, mergers, and acquisitions pale beside the one thing that has the most dramatic effect on the success or failure of our projects—corporate politics. Politics is something that we are all familiar with and are definitely affected by. We can't change it, so we have to live with it. "Being political" is something we might look down upon. Nonetheless, it's something that we all have to learn to do if we are to shepherd our projects through to successful project completion.

Having the right people on your team and being on a team favored by current management are just two critical success factors. A wide variety of other factors will determine the success or failure of your project.

Technological Issues

I once worked on a project where the technical lead selected software based on the technology he wanted to put on his résumé, rather than what the project required. The software was implemented, but had to be replaced within a few years owing to frequent system failure. An important critical success factor, as you can surmise, is making sure the technology fits the project.

The team must have the wherewithal to develop the software using the tools and technologies selected. The system itself must be fully specified, with all dependencies listed, so that all developers can readily understand what they need to do and how their piece of the pie relates to what everyone else is doing.

Lest the system fail repeatedly, as ours did, it's a good idea to strive for "simple is better." In other words, the architecture should be simple and straightforward, where possible.

Companies should use formal software engineering methodologies, with validation at each major milestone: systems analysis, design, etc. This ensures that what was designed actually makes its way into production. Along this line, it's best to opt for incremental development, where possible. Massively large systems, with hundreds of processes and programmers, are just too large to effectively manage for a single implementation. It's best to divide this massive project up into smaller, more manageable projects instead.

Effective Communication

In Chapter 2 we discussed the skill sets that a project manager must have to be successful. This included the ability to manage expectations, resolve conflict, overcome fears, facilitate meetings, and motivate team members.

One of the most important abilities a project manager can have is interpersonal skills. He or she must be able to effectively communicate with a wide variety of people across the entire organization. The project manager must be equally at ease when working with the chief executive officer (CEO) as he or she is when working with data entry clerical staff.

The project manager must be able to do the following:

1. Make the person being spoken to feel at ease.
2. Understand the language of the end user.
3. Understand the business of the end user.
4. Interpret what the end user is saying correctly and completely.
5. Write effectively, using the proper style.
6. Be able to make meaningful presentations.
7. Be articulate.
8. Be able to mediate disputes.
9. Understand the politics of the organization.

The Proper Utilization of Standards

There are many methodologies a project manager might employ when doing his or her job. The Software Engineering Institute's Capability Maturity Model (CMM) defines five levels of software process maturity. The lowest level, Initial, is typified by little formalization. The highest level, Optimized, is defined by the use of quality standards such as formal use of a methodology and process measurement. The project manager should strive to utilize the very highest levels of standards of practice such that the highest level of CMM can be achieved.

Software engineering (i.e., development) consists of many components: definitions, documentation, testing, quality assurance, metrics, etc. Standards bodies (i.e., ANSI, ISO, IEEE) have crafted standards for many of these.

Standards enable software developers to develop quality-oriented, cost-effective, and maintainable software in an efficient, cost-productive manner. The goal of each standard is to provide the software developer with a set of benchmarks, enabling him or her to complete the task and be assured that it meets at least a minimum level of quality. Indeed, the dictionary definition of standard is, "an acknowledged measure of comparison for quantitative or qualitative value; a criterion." Thus, standards provide the developer with the criteria necessary to build a system. It is the role of the project manager to ensure that the proper standards are being adhered to.

Ethics

One of the very highest standards a project manager can aspire to is a heightened sense of ethics. The newspapers have been filled with stories of the results of a lapse of ethics (e.g., Parmalat, Enron, Arthur Andersen). When dealing with individuals, the organization as a whole, or society at large, the project manager must follow these guidelines:

1. Be fair.
2. Be impartial.
3. Be honest.
4. Be forthright.

Political Aspects

A project must be developed from a position of strength. Because the project manager is the one in charge of the project, the PM must be powerful, know how to get power, or align himself or herself with a powerful sponsor.

What do you do if political gamesmanship is getting in the way of your project's success? Shtub (1994) recommends a series of steps that serve to neutralize opposition or attacks on a project:

1. Identify persons who are opposed to the project.
2. Determine why they feel the project isn't to their advantage.
3. Meet with anyone who directly attacks you or the project, and ask that person what is troubling him or her. Show this person how his or her actions will affect the project and the organization, and then ask for suggestions to get him or her to support the project.
4. Place all agreements and progress reports in writing. This provides an audit trail.
5. Speak directly and truthfully; never hedge your comments.
6. Distribute a memo to stakeholders, including the opposition, to clarify all rumors. Project opponents frequently use the office rumor mill to distribute misinformation about the project.
7. Be prepared to defend all actions that you take. Make sure you have a solid rationale for your decisions.

Legal Aspects

Legal and regulatory issues will also influence whether or not the system will ultimately be successful. Examples of regulatory or legal changes precluding the successful completion of a project include the following:

1. Internet gambling systems built by U.S.-based organizations. Offshore companies currently host Internet gambling systems as it is illegal to do so in the United States.
2. P2P (peer-to-peer) systems that enable Web surfers to "pirate" music have been deemed illegal.

Organizational Aspects

Computer systems can benefit organizations in many ways. However, some changes required by the introduction of a system might be considered disruptive and, thus, undesirable. For example, a system that requires the entire company to be reorganized, might be deemed infeasible.

Conclusion

My students studied the issues surrounding project failure and came up with their own list of critical success factors:

1. Successfully relating to end users.
2. Understanding and dealing with organizational politics.
3. Resolving conflicts.
4. Motivating internal stakeholders.
5. Being a visionary who can see the end product right from the start.
6. Being able to relate to tech gurus.
7. Successful team building.
8. Being an SME.
9. Understanding risk analysis.
10. Willingness to commit "intelligent disobedience" (McGannon, n.d.). This is the ability to disagree with stakeholders who might pose threats leading to the derailment of the project.

Links

http://zzyx.ucsc.edu/~boxjenk/C11/sld001.htm Strategy and leadership PowerPoint presentation.
http://www.bredemeyer.com/CSFs_pitfalls.htm Software Architecting Success Factors and Pitfalls.
http://www.tarrani.net/mike/docs/CSF4SPI.pdf 15 Success Factors for Software Process Improvement.
http://www.teamworkdynamics.com/id20.html Success Factors for Teamwork.
http://builder.com.com/5100-6404-1049484.html Personal Success Factors.
http://www.sei.cmu.edu/cmm Capability Maturity Model.
http://www.projectmagazine.com Project Magazine.

References

Hyvari, I. (September 2006). Success of projects in different organizational conditions. *Project Management Journal, 37*(4).

McConnell, S. (1996). *Rapid Development: Taming Wild Software Schedules*. Redmond, WA: Microsoft Press.

McGannon, R. (n.d.). *Intelligent Disobedience: The Difference Between Good and Great Project Managers*. Retrieved from http://www.projectsmart.co.uk/difference-between-good-and-great-project-managers.html.

Shtub, A. (1994). *Project Management: Engineering, Technology and Implementation*. New York: Prentice Hall.

BASICS OF PROJECT MANAGEMENT

III

BASICS OF PROJECT MANAGEMENT

Chapter 6

Project Scope Management and System Requirements

In this chapter, we will examine project scope management. Definition of goals and objectives, scope, general requirements, system context, use of external resources, and major constraints will be analyzed. The work breakdown structure (WBS) will be introduced and the concept of the project plan document emphasized.

Managing Ideas

Ideas for new computer systems can originate from anyone or any place. Your marketing department might want a brand-new way of tracking customers. Your finance department might require some changes because of a modification of the tax code. Even your customers might be the source of a great idea. If there's one constant in business, it's change.

Change needs to be managed, however. Projects have a tendency to grow from the manageable to the not so manageable fairly quickly. This is usually referred to as *scope creep*, and it's something good project management must overcome.

Once an idea has been formalized, deemed feasible, and approved by the managers of the organization, a project plan is created. The plan will detail the scope, resources, cost estimates, and schedule for development of the software. If development is to be outsourced to an external organization such as a consulting company, a request for proposal (RFP) must be carefully crafted.

An RFP has many of the attributes of a project plan. It defines the project scope, business goals, constraints, technical requirements, and administrative information, and also provides some preliminary information on scheduling and task allocation. Those responding to the proposal will flesh it out to ultimately provide a completed project plan and, if selected, will complete the project itself.

Defining Business Goals

Organizational goals are usually quite dynamic. Last month's goals are not necessarily this month's goals. So, it's important to make sure that the goals listed are consistent with the true goals of the organization.

Most companies review their mission and goals annually. In fact, this is usually a corporatewide activity, with each department determining its own mission and goals as they relate to the corporatewide statement. Goals are usually determined after an intensive SWOT analysis (i.e., strengths, weaknesses, opportunities, and threats), in which a company rigorously compares itself to its competitors.

There are actually two sets of goals, short term and long term. Short-term goals usually have a window of three to five years. However, the increasingly competitive and very global nature of business has collapsed the short-range planning cycle—in some cases—into months.

Both long-term as well as short-term goals can be articulated in terms of corporate scope, products and services the company currently offers and desires to offer, market share, company size, and profitability.

Examples of business goals are as follows:

1. Increase earnings per share by ten percent within two years.
2. Introduce one new product per quarter within one year.
3. Introduce one new service per year within the next two years.

Note that business goals are associated with a quantifiable metric. For example, goal number one indicates that to be successful the company is required to increase earnings per share by a certain percentage.

Defining Project Goals

Project goals are always subsets of business goals. In a project plan, one or more project goals are described and tied back to the business goals of the organization.

For example, a company might decide to develop a Web-based system that matches pets with potential pet owners. The goal of this project might be defined as follows:

> The goal of the dog e-adoption system (DEAS) is to bring together potential pet adopters and animal shelters across the country.

We can then tie this project goal to one or more of the company's stated business goals, thus:

> The goal of the dog e-adoption system (DEAS) is to bring together potential pet adopters and animal shelters across the country. DEAS is aligned to the corporate business goal of introducing one new service or product per year.

Defining Project Scope

The project scope is a short description of the project, which includes the following:

1. Justification for the project

2. What the system will do
3. How the system will generate revenue, if applicable

The project scope will flesh out the list of project goals. An example of a scope statement follows:

> The problem of pet overpopulation is severe in the United States. Animal shelters have limited capacity and every year millions of healthy animals are killed due to the shortage of potential pet adopters. The problem is economic as well as moral. Disposal of these animals is an expensive procedure, and the moral implication of animal destruction is obvious.
>
> One way to address the problem is through an Internet adoption service. The potential of the Internet is not utilized in this area. There are few, if any, search engines with the ability to search a network of shelters for a pet or for the range of additional services and information provided by shelters.
>
> The aim of the dog e-adoption system (DEAS) is to bring together potential pet adopters and animal shelters across the country. Shelters will have a fast and convenient option to upload a range of information about their pets to prospective pet adopters. Prospective pet adopters receive an equally fast and convenient way to look for a pet through the service. They will also gain access to a broad spectrum of information on various aspects of pet adoption and ownership—from applicable government regulations to pet care.
>
> The system will have the functionality to work with any pets present in the shelters, but the design focus will be on dogs. Dog adoption holds the possibility of being the best source of pet adoptions, thus driving the economic success of the system. The system will generate revenue through shelter or adopter fees, advertising, and donations.

Like anything else, scope has to be managed. There are five components to scope management, as shown in Figure 6.1. They are as follows:

Scope planning—During this phase, the project team and key stakeholders plan how they will define the scope, create the WBS, and then verify and control the scope.
Scope definition—As the project evolves, and goals and methods become clearer, the scope definition will change to include these requirements.
Project Initiation—This includes all deliverables within the project as a time-constrained projection—it basically lays out what will be done and when. Once specified within the WBS, the work is tied to timeframes and costs. The project is then initiated.
Scope verification—This involves formal acceptance of the completed project scope by the key stakeholders.
Scope control—This is the set of policies and procedures for controlled scope change.

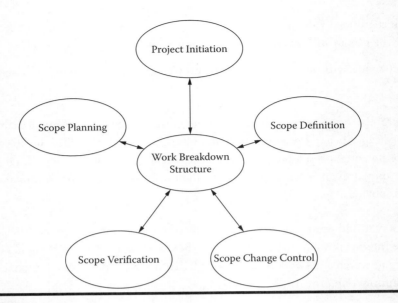

Figure 6.1 Scope management.

Constraints

The project plan will usually determine the cost, resources, and time requirements for the proposed project. However, regulatory, legal, and competitive pressures might impose a specific deadline. This is referred to as *timeboxing*. It is interesting to note that many governmental contracts impose a financial penalty on a contracting company that delivers the project late.

If the project is to be constrained by a set dollar amount, then this too is required to be clearly articulated. Many companies create a yearly business plan that allocates financial resources to each department. Project plans, therefore, will have to live within the constraints of this preallocated budget. Savvy companies will always add a contractual stipulation that mandates the absorption of all overages by the consulting company, unless extenuating circumstances can be proved (e.g., act of war, etc.).

Additional RFP Information

The point of an RFP is to supply a sufficient amount of detail so that the bidders to the project can develop a complete and accurate proposal.

In this section, any information not supplied elsewhere in the RFP should be provided. This information might include, but is not limited to, the following:

1. Information about the company
2. Information about the competitors
3. Information excerpted from the annual report
4. Marketing literature
5. Hyperlinks to articles and Web sites relevant to the project
6. Copies of relevant feasibility studies or cost–benefit analyses

General Requirements

The requirements section is the heart of the project plan. Requirements usually take the form of a list of features that the system must have. For example:

The following general requirements were specified for the Online Resource Scheduling System (ORSS) project:

- A Web-based application allowing users easy access and use
- The ability to originate or update resource reservations
- The ability to link to the Faculty database to verify "Authorized Users"
- A method to maintain and update a resource database
- The ability to limit simultaneous reservations (of classrooms) against total resources available
- A way to search for resources available
- A method to disallow duplication of "special" classrooms
- The ability to disallow duplicate orders from the same user
- A method to print a confirmation from the Web site
- The ability to send e-mail confirmations to the user
- The ability to print a daily list

This feature set was most likely collated during the feasibility phase of the systems development life cycle (SDLC). Many of the desired features might have been selected as a result of competitor analysis. Web sites such as Hoovers.com or governmental regulatory agencies such as the Securities and Exchange Commission provide a wealth of detail about a company's competitors. The competitor's Web site also provides much detail, including marketing brochures, and even downloadable trial software.

As can be seen in Figure 6.2, the feasibility study is the very first phase of the systems development effort. This is the phase where ideas are discussed, evaluated, and then deemed either feasible or not feasible. If the ideas are deemed feasible, the next phase, the project plan, can then be initiated.

In some organizations, feasibility studies are not performed. The project plan is created as the requirements are being determined within the analysis phase of the SDLC.

In all cases, the functionality of a system must be ascertained, because scheduling and cost estimation is dependent on knowing what the system is going to do.

Technical Requirements

Most projects are built under a series of constraints. For example, a particular system must be built using the Oracle database. These constraints must be addressed in the project plan. This includes, but is not limited to, the following: standards, existing systems, hardware, software, operating systems, networking, application software utilized, security, disaster recovery, availability, scalability, and reliability.

Figure 6.2   The typical systems development life cycle (SDLC).

Standards

Software engineering (i.e., development) consists of many components: definitions, documentation, testing, quality assurance, metrics, etc. Standards enable software developers to develop quality-oriented, cost-effective, and maintainable software in an efficient, cost-productive manner. The goal of each standard is to provide the software developer with a set of benchmarks, enabling him or her to complete the task and be assured that it meets at least a minimum level of quality.

An organization might adhere to one or more standards. In particular, ISO 9000 is frequently cited as a requirement for many companies. ISO 9000 is the most recognizable of ISO standards. It defines the criteria for quality in the manufacturing and service industries. It was first popularized in Europe, but its popularity has spread worldwide as more and more companies deem "ISO certification" to be a competitive advantage.

ISO 9000 is actually a "family" of standards:

1. ISO 9000 is the actual standard. ISO 9001, ISO 9002, and ISO 9003 are the three quality assurance (QA) models against which organizations can be certified.
2. ISO 9001 is the standard of interest for companies that perform the entire range of activities, from design and development to testing. ISO 9001 is of most interest to the software developer. It is this standard that provides the all-important checklist of quality initiatives such as:
   a. Develop your quality management system.
   b. Implement your quality management system.
   c. Improve your quality management system.
3. ISO 9002 is the standard for companies that do not engage in design and development. This standard focuses on production, installation, and service.
4. ISO 9003 is the appropriate standard for companies whose business processes do not include design control, process control, purchasing, or servicing. This standard focuses on testing and inspection.

Existing Systems

Not all projects involve the development of new systems. In many cases, existing systems will need to be modified. This is referred to as *maintenance*. If a system does indeed exist, then the following information (or links to this information, if digital) should be included in the appendices of the Project Plan:

1. Feasibility study for the existing system.
2. Requirements document, including all diagrammatic models such as data flow diagrams (DFDs), class diagrams, entity relationship diagrams (ERDs), state transition diagrams (STDs), etc., that were created for the existing system. The Software Engineering module provides a great source of information on these documents and diagrams. Other sources of information can be found in the Links section at the end of this chapter.
3. Design specification, including all diagrammatic models for the existing system.
4. Data dictionary or repository for the existing system.

This section should also include information on existing systems that the system is required to be interfaced to.

Hardware

This section describes the following:

1. Existing hardware that is required to be used
2. Proposed hardware that is desired to be used

The information might take the following form:
Minimal Hardware Requirements

Development
Three IBM PCs or compatibles, with the following configuration:
- Pentium* 4 processor with HT technology
- 3.2 GHz w/800 MHz FSB
- 4 GB of dual channel DDR 400 MHz SDRAM
- 60 GB hard disk space
- Internet connection

User Server-Side
IBM PC or compatible, with the following configuration:
- Pentium* 4 processor with HT technology
- 3.2 GHz w/800 MHz FSB
- 4 GB of dual channel DDR 400 MHz SDRAM
- 60 GB hard disk space
- Internet connection

User Client-Side
IBM PC or compatible, with the following configuration:
- Intel* Pentium* 4 processor up to 2.8 GHz with 533 FSB or Intel* Celeron* processor
- 2.7 GHz with 400 MHz FSB
- 1 GB of shared² single channel DDR 333 MHz
- 1 GB hard disk space
- Internet connection

Operating Systems

If there is a requirement for one or more operating systems, it should be specified in this section. The usual format is as follows:

User Server-Side
- Windows 2003 Server version with Internet Information Server (IIS)

User Client-Side
- Windows XP or higher operating system

Networking

Computer systems may be designed using a variety of physical architectures. A system may utilize a one-tier (e.g., PC only, mainframe only), two-tier (e.g., PC and mainframe, PC and server), or three-tier (e.g., PC, server, mainframe) architecture. Computer systems might use one server, two

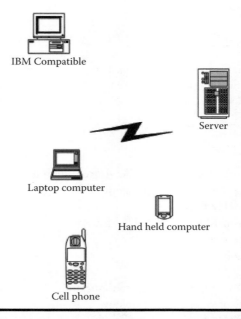

Figure 6.3   A network model. This sample network supports multiple PCs, wireless laptops, cell phones, and PDAs.

servers, or many servers. The system might comprise one PC or 10,000 PCs (usually called *clients*). The system might be Internet based, intranet based, or conventionally based (i.e., not connected to the Internet). The system might comprise support wireless devices, PDAs, and even cell phones. If the new system is required to work within the constraints of a particular network, a network diagram should be included in the project plan, as shown in Figure 6.3.

Application Software

This section of the project plan specifies the software required to be used. The usual format is as follows:

Development
  – Windows XP Professional version
  – FrontPage 2003 or Dreamweaver MX 2004
  – SQL Server 2000
User Server-Side
  – Windows 2003 Server version with IIS
  – SQL Server 2000
User Client-Side
  – Windows XP or higher operating system
  – Internet Explorer Browser 5.0 or above, Netscape Navigator 5.0 or above

Security

Most organizations have security requirements that must be adhered to by all systems. This should be included in the project plan. A security statement might contain the following information:

> The system will provide a number of different security features. First, all members must log into the system at member PCs and must provide a username and password before gaining access to the system. Similarly, the librarian and administrator access the system via their respective PCs and are authenticated by username and password. Second, remote users access the system via a gateway that provides a firewall. The firewall allows access to services designated as remote access services, but blocks access to all other services, such as administrator services. Cookies will also be used to aid in identifying remote users.

> The database management system (DBMS) provides a high level of security. Security profiles for the different user types will be created so that only specific users have the permissions (create, update, delete) on selected data objects. For example, only the administrator will have create and delete permissions in the asset database. Stored procedures will be used to maintain referential integrity in the databases.

Scalability

Scalability refers to how much a system can be expanded. A scalability statement might specify the following:

> The system will be able to expand to 200 users without breaking down or requiring major changes in procedure.

Availability

Availability refers to the percentage of time that a system is available for use. It is also referred to as *uptime*—i.e., "the amount of time the system is up." Availability is an important component of information systems. An availability statement might specify the following:

> System uptime will not be lower than 99 percent. Providing reliable and continuous service to users is one of the key requirements of the system. When a failure occurs, system downtime will be kept to a minimum. The target is to have the system operational within two hours following a serious failure.

Reliability

Reliability refers to the accuracy, correctness, and quality of the system. Several IEEE standards were written with the objective of providing the software community with defined measures that can be used as indicators of reliability. By emphasizing early reliability assessment, this standard supports methods through measurement to improve product reliability. Some common measures are as follows:

1. Fault density—This measure can be used to predict whether faults remain, by comparison with expected fault density; determine if sufficient testing has been performed; and establish standard fault densities for comparison and prediction.

$$FD = F/KSLOC$$

where
   F = total number of unique faults found in a given interval, resulting in failures of a specified severity level
   KSLOC = number of source lines of executable code and nonexecutable data declarations in thousands

2. Defect density—This measure can be used after design and code inspections of new development or large block modifications. If the defect density falls outside the norm after several inspections, it indicates a problem.

$$DD = \sum_{i=1}^{I} (Di/KSLOD)$$

where
   Di = total number of unique defects detected during the ith design or code inspection process
   I = total number of inspections
   KSLOD = in the design phase, this is the number of source lines of executable code and nonexecutable data declarations in thousands

3. Cumulative failure profile—This is a graphical method used to predict reliability, estimate additional testing time to reach an acceptable reliable system, and identify modules and subsystems that require additional testing. A plot is drawn of cumulative failures versus a suitable time base.

4. Fault-days number—This measure represents the number of days that faults exist in the system, from their creation to their removal. For each fault detected and removed, during any phase, the number of days from its creation to its removal is determined (fault-days). The fault-days are then summed for all faults detected and removed, to get the fault-days number at the system level, including all faults detected and removed up to the delivery date. In those cases where the creation date of the fault is not known, the fault is assumed to have been created at the middle of the phase in which it was introduced.

Maintenance

The maintenance statement should discuss policies and procedures that the company has put in place to handle the various types of maintenance. This should address any configuration management or change control policies the company already has in place. Alternatively, the maintenance statement might specify a requirement that those bidding on the RFP create a set of policies and procedures to deal with maintenance issues.

Disaster Recovery

Disaster recovery is associated with risk analysis and mitigation planning. Before a disaster recovery (contingency) plan can be created, risks associated with the project should be identified. A sample risk plan can be seen in the following table. Each "risk" should have an associated contingency plan.

Risks	Category	Probability (percent)	Impact
Customer will change or modify requirements	PS	70	2
End users will lack sophistication	CU	60	3
Users will not attend training	CU	50	2
Delivery deadline will be tightened	BU	50	2
End users will resist system	BU	40	3
Server may not be able to handle larger number of users simultaneously	PS	30	1
Technology will not meet expectations	TE	30	1
Number of users will be greater than the planned number	PS	30	3
End users will lack training	CU	30	3
Project team will be inexperienced	ST	20	2
System (security and firewall) will be hacked	BU	15	2

Note: Impact values: 1 = catastrophic, 2 = critical, 3 = marginal, 4 = negligible; category abbreviations: BU = business impact risk, CU = customer characteristics risk, PS = process definition risk, ST = staff size and experience risk, TE = technology risk.

The preceding table was sorted first by probability and then by impact value. Risks will be discussed more in detail in Chapter 9. For the purpose of the goals and objectives statement, all that is required is a brief statement such as the following:

> The DBMS software will provide a backup capability to ensure protection of the data in the database. In addition, the DBMS software will provide a transaction-recording feature that can be used to keep track of all transactions during normal daytime operation. If a failure occurs, the transaction record can be used to rollback to the last successful transaction so that a minimum amount of information is lost.

Other

Any additional technical requirements not already included in any other section should be included here. This might include information about required interfaces, competitive information, etc.

Training and Documentation

All documents created as a result of systems development should be assigned a tracking number and stored in a repository for future use. This is one of the basic tenets of configuration management.

While a system is under development, a wealth of documentation is created. This documentation includes the following:

1. The Feasibility Report discusses the economic, organizational, and technological feasibility of creating the system.
2. The Project Plan (i.e., the statement of work, or SOW) defines the mission and scope of the system, and lists the resources—both human and economic—for systems development.
3. The System Requirements Specification (i.e., the SRS) defines the system requirements. It is a lengthy document that includes diagrams (e.g., class diagrams, data flow diagrams, entity relationship diagrams, etc.), a list of required data, as well as a detailed discussion of the processes that the system should perform.
4. The System Design Specification (i.e., the SDS) provides the actual detailed blueprint for building the system. This document provides specific instructions for writing each program and how each program relates to other programs as well as to external systems and data.
5. The Test Plan provides a schedule as well as test cases (e.g., inputs, outputs, and steps) for testing each component of the system.
6. System Operator's Policies and Procedures provides a set of instructions for the proper running and handling of the system by the systems administrator or network administrator. Computer systems are made up of many components and could include a variety of resources, such as a network, electronic document interchange (EDI), tape drives, etc. Many of these components are invisible to the actual end user but do require some manual intervention if the system is to run properly. This is the job of the computer operator. Depending on the way the organization is configured, some responsibility for these functions might be allocated to a systems administrator (i.e., changing the settings on the user profiles) or a network administrator (e.g., adding a node to the network).

The plan should also specify the types and requirements of all user-facing documentation. User documentation includes user manuals and online help (including contextual help).

User manuals have the following features:

1. They may be paper based, but are increasingly available solely on CD-ROM or hard disk and product sites on the Internet.
2. They contain a detailed table of contents and an index so that the end user may easily locate the answer to a question.
3. They provide detailed instructions for use of the system.
4. They provide numerous screen shots of the system that "walk the user" through the steps of performing a function.

Organizations have a wide variety of training options. Most do not settle for just one mode of training, particularly because training is an ongoing process. The project plan should specify which training options should be utilized.

Training options include the following:

1. Tutorials
2. Courses and seminars
3. Computer-aided instruction

Installation Issues

The project plan should specify what, if any, requirements are to be imposed on the installation of the developed system. These may include the following:

1. Timing constraints—There might be certain periods of time when installation processes are prohibited, e.g., end-of-month reconciliation, start of day, etc.
2. Resource constraints—Installation might require the participation of a wide variety of people, e.g., database administrator, various end users, etc. One or more of these people might have limited availability.
3. Redundancy requirements—The RFP should specify whether or not redundant systems are to be maintained after installation of the proposed system.

In addition to the constraints imposed on the installation process, the RFP should specify that a detailed log of all installation issues be maintained. Issues might be categorized as follows:

- 0—only severe errors logged
- 1—errors
- 2—warnings
- 3—information
- 4—detailed information useful for debugging

The Work Breakdown Structure (WBS)

Configuration management, or CM as it is often referred to, is a standards-based engineering methodology that provides a superstructure around software engineering activities. Endorsed by the government, and adhered to by organizations interested in quality control (QC), one of the fundamental components of CM is the breakdown of a project into its subordinate tasks, resulting in what is called a work breakdown structure or WBS.

A project is composed of one or more tasks. Each of these tasks has interdependencies, usually based on their sequence. Most projects have more than one person involved in the engineering process, so it is likely that some tasks will be done in parallel; e.g., Task A and Task B are developed concurrently. It is very important that these tasks be carefully coordinated so that Task B has available to it on time the work product outputted by Task A.

Figure 6.4 shows a WBS, also referred to as a task network, for a software engineering project that is developed using an incremental methodology. Note that there are three 1.4 and three 1.5 tasks. This reflects the fact that design, coding, and testing are split in this system into three increments. Each increment may be done in parallel, as shown in this diagram, or completed on a staggered schedule.

The WBS, which we discuss in greater depth in chapters 7 and 8, provides the basis for planning and managing project schedules, costs, resources, and changes.

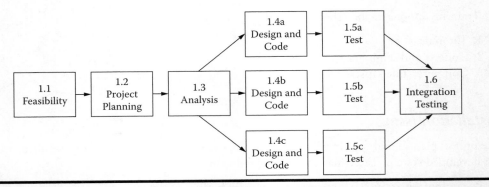

Figure 6.4 A work breakdown structure (WBS) for an incremental software development project.

Conclusion

The project plan must be carefully constructed, because it is the controlling document for the creation of a system and the expenditure of resources. Project managers must work with the various project stakeholders (i.e., managers, end users, clients, customers, etc.) to determine all internal and external constraints on the development effort as well as the scope and general requirements of the system itself.

Links

http://www.praxiom.com/ ISO 9000 translated into plain English.

http://en.wikipedia.org/wiki/Work_breakdown_structure How to build a WBS.

http://www.e-programme.com/articles/progscoping.htm Scope Creep.

http://www.smartdraw.com/resources/examples/software/index.htm Samples of a variety of diagrams (e.g., ERD, DFD).

http://www.rspa.com/docs/ Software Engineering document templates. Includes templates for project plans, requirements specifications, design specifications.

http://www.techweb.com/encyclopedia/ TechWeb's encyclopedia engine for the definition of software engineering and other technical terms.

Chapter 7

Project Scheduling

In this chapter, we will examine the concept of scheduling. Students will examine the utility of the work breakdown structure (WBS) as a basis for scheduling, network diagrams, PERT (Program Evaluation and Review Technique) and Gantt charts, as well as critical path.

The Task Network

A project is composed of one or more tasks. These tasks have interdependencies, usually based on their sequence. Most projects have more than one person involved in the engineering process, so it is likely that some tasks will be done in parallel (e.g., task A and task B are developed concurrently). It is very important that tasks be carefully coordinated so that, for example, if task C depends on task D then task D has available to it on time the work product outputted by task C.

Figure 7.1 shows the WBS we introduced in Chapter 6. A WBS is sometimes referred to as a task network for a software engineering project that is developed using an incremental methodology. Note that there are three 1.4 and three 1.5 tasks. This means that design, coding, and testing

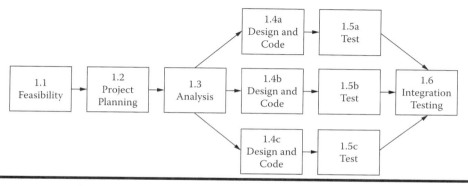

Figure 7.1   A WBS for an incremental software development project.

are split into three increments in this system. Each increment may be implemented in parallel, as shown in this Figure 7.1, or completed on a staggered schedule.

Creation of a WBS will require much information about the project to be tasked. In general, the steps required to create a WBS include the following:

1. Start with the project statement of work (SOW). Place a task at the top of the list.
2. Define the inputs, outputs, resources, and milestones for the task.
3. If task as defined can be achieved as a stand-alone task, then go to #5, otherwise go to #4.
4. Create subtasks for the task, and repeat #2 and #3 for each subtask.
5. Return to #2 to work on the next task until all tasks are accounted for.

Task Identification and Descriptions

Generating a WBS will require much task information to be collected and understood. At minimum, the following information should be available for each task—the purpose or objective of the task and the deliverables for each task.

The task description should consist of the following:

1. Number (the first column in Table 7.1): Numbering was done according to task numbering as explained in a later section.
2. Task title (the second column in Table 7.1): The title should be descriptive. A combination of a noun and a verb is recommended such that the task is described actively rather than passively. For example, the task title for the first task in Table 7.1 is "hold meetings," where "hold" is the verb and "meetings" is the noun.
3. Deliverables (the third column in Table 7.1): Each task will have one or more deliverables associated with it, e.g., training manual, meeting notes, and specification.
4. Subtasks: Some systems developers equate deliverable with subtask. In Table 7.1, deliverables are denoted as subtasks because the act of creating the deliverable is actually a task.

We will explain the rest of the columns in the following sections.

Readers may wonder just how the scheduler arrived at the dates, seemingly out of thin air, in Table 7.1. As will be discussed in Chapter 8, both art and science are involved in the process of project management. Just as one might use "guesstimation" techniques to arrive at a cost estimate, a scheduler might use a best estimate to arrive at the first cut of a schedule. The key here is that this is a first cut. Project management is a discipline within the field of software engineering. As with all components of software engineering (i.e., requirements document, design specification, test plan), a project plan is continually revised when more is understood and known about the project. In other words, the development of a project plan is an iterative process.

An alternative way to tackle the first cut of a schedule appears in the following text. This project plan was developed by a project manager (PM) who used a different method of date handling.

Timeline Details

The following outline of activities is based on dates relative to the project start date, and reflects weekly increments. Any slippage of the start date will result in a corresponding offset of all other dates and milestones. Major activities and project **milestones** (indicated by bold font) are indicated

Table 7.1   A Typical Systems Development Task List

Number	Tasks	Deliverable	Dates/ Days	Precedence	Milestone
A0000	Start of project	Agreement / contract	02/04/07		
A9999	Project ends	Delivery			10/05/07
A0010	Hold meetings	Weekly meetings	02/04/07		07/05/07
A0101	Develop requirements	Assess functional requirements	4	A0102, A0103, A0104	01/03/07
A0102		Demonstrate system	8		
A0103		Evaluation of testing needs	2		
A0104		Assess nonfunctional requirements	9		
A0105		Final requirements specification	4		
A0201	Develop documentation	Quality assurance plan	2		03/05/07
A0202		Project plan	8		
A0203		Requirements document	13		
A0204		Design document	11		
A0205		User guide	5		
A0206		Final project notebook	4		
A0207		Maintenance plan	4		
A0301	Produce programmer training	Web design training	6	A0202, A0204	03/12/07
A0302		Database design training	4		
A0401	Create preliminary design	Brainstorming	1	A0203, A0204	03/20/07
A0402		Architectural layout	5	A0204, A0401	
A0501	Create detailed design	Design user interface	10		04/01/07
A0502		Database design	10		
A0602	Perform coding	Build database	0		04/19/07
A0603		User interface of campus version	14		
A0604		User interface of in-house version	14		
A0701	Perform integration testing	In-house testing	4	A0104	04/26/07
A0702		Necessary modifications	3		
A0801	Perform post-test	On-campus testing	4	A0701, A0702	05/03/07
A0802		Necessary modifications	4		
A0901	Develop modification	Clean up and finalize for delivery	1		05/07/07
A0902		Additional perks			
A1001	Produce faculty training	In-house training	0	A0901, A0205	05/10/07
A1002		Campus training	1		

separately, though they will often occur simultaneously. Upon receipt of formal start date, the schedule will be entered into, and managed using Microsoft Project software.

Project Start (PS) (start planning)

 PS + 1 wk Complete Project Plan (start Software Requirements Specification [SRS])

 PS + 2 wk Complete SRS (start design)

   PS + 4 wk   Complete Architectural Design

   PS + 4 wk   **Conduct Preliminary Design Review (PDR)**

   PS + 5 wk   Complete Test Plan

   PS + 6 wk   Complete Detailed Design (start code)

   PS + 6 wk   **Conduct Detailed Design Review (DDR)**

   PS + 6 wk   Begin Code Development

   PS + 8 wk   Complete GUI Development

   PS + 8 wk   Complete Server Framework

   PS + 8 wk   Complete 75 percent Database Implementation

   PS + 8 wk   **Conduct Code Review**

   PS + 9 wk   Complete Code Development (start testing)

   PS + 9 wk   Complete Test Cases

   PS + 11 wk   **Conduct Integration Testing**

   PS + 13 wk   **Conduct System Testing**

   PS + 14 wk   **Conduct Acceptance Testing**

   PS + 15 wk   Deliver system, Install, and Train Customer

 Project End (PS + 16 wk)

Once a preliminary schedule is articulated, it can be fine-tuned as the PM gains a better understanding of tasks, dependencies, and specific milestone and due date requirements (see Table 7.1). At this point, the PM will usually start using the functionality of Microsoft Project for schedule revision.

Many systems developers use a top-down approach to task identification. Using this methodology, a complex project is decomposed (i.e., divided up) into less complex subprojects or tasks. Top-down design is a tenet of good software engineering, so it follows that the top-down approach to task identification would offer similar quality attributes. Top-down methodologies promote usability, efficiency, reliability, maintainability, and reusability.

When using a top-down approach, we conceptualize the highest-order tasks and then break these down into subtasks. For example, two high-order tasks might be the following:

Develop modifications to system
Produce faculty training

Next, we proceed to identify the subtasks for each of the higher-order tasks that we have already identified:

Develop modifications to system
 Clean up and finalize for delivery
 Develop additional perks
Produce faculty training
 Create in-house training
 Create campus training

An alternative to the top-down methodology is the bottom-up ("grass roots") methodology. In a bottom-up approach, you start by defining the low-level tasks, such as "develop additional perks," and then figure out how these will be put together to create successively higher-level tasks (i.e., develop modifications to system), and ultimately, the entire system.

There are many advantages to using a bottom-up methodology. The most important advantage is that we are assured of conformance with requirements as each requirement is tasked at a low level, thus satisfying our end users. Therefore, it can be said that bottom-up estimating is the most precise of all methodologies.

The system developer creating Table 7.1 could have created this task list using a bottom-up approach. He or she would have done this by listing the deliverables (column 3), grouping them (i.e., subtasks), and finally, creating the major tasks (column 2). Creation of a bottom-up task list requires the developer to have detailed information, and therefore, it can be quite a time consuming process.

Accurate task identification is critical to the successful development and implementation of a project. Guidelines should be developed and published such that the methodology deployed to create the WBS is a repeatable process within the organization.

Configuration management (CM) is the recommended repeatable process by which task identification is managed.

Task Numbering

Although the figures in the prior sections do not adhere to a numbering sequence, good CM technique dictates that each task be identified not only through the use of a title but also with a sequence number.

Consider the following tasks:
    Develop modifications to system
        Clean up and finalize for delivery
        Develop additional perks
    Produce faculty training
        Create in-house training
        Create campus training
The foregoing tasks could be numbered as follows:
    A2000 Develop modifications to system
        A2010 Clean up and finalize for delivery
        A2020 Develop additional perks
    A3000 Produce faculty training
        A3010 Create in-house training
        A3020 Create campus training

The numbering system chosen, referred to as configuration identification in CM parlance, clearly shows the relationship between main task (e.g., A2000) and subtask (A2010 and A2020).

Task Sequence

Tasks will be performed in a particular sequence. The WBS diagram does a good job of helping one visualize task sequence. In Figure 7.1 we see that task 1.1 is done first, followed by tasks 1.2 and 1.3. We then see that tasks 1.4a through 1.4c are performed in parallel followed by tasks 1.5a through 1.5c, which are also executed in parallel. Finally, at the completion of tasks 1.1 through 1.5, task 1.6 is initiated.

A Gantt chart, shown in Figure 7.2, is another task-modeling technique that is frequently used to show task relationships as well as scheduling and resource requirements. We will discuss Gantt charts later in this chapter.

Task Precedence

Precedence is an indicator of task interdependency. In other words, it tells us when each task can start. Although the following list clearly indicates tasks and their subtasks, it does not really tell us whether it is necessary for A2000 to begin and end before A3000 or whether A2000 and A3000 can be performed concurrently:

A2000 Develop modifications to system
    A2010 Clean up and finalize for delivery
    A2020 Develop additional perks
A3000 Produce faculty training
    A3010 Create in-house training
    A3020 Create campus training

Task precedence, therefore, is an indicator of the interrelationship between task start and stop times. Time intervals can be evaluated using several methodologies:

1. Start to finish time of each task: This is the most common of precedence relationships between tasks. It requires that a task can start only after its predecessor has been completed.
2. Start to start time of two tasks: In this relationship, an activity can start only after a specified activity has already begun.
3. Finish to finish time of two tasks: In this relationship, a task cannot end until a specified task has been completed.
4. Overlap between tasks: In this relationship start and end times of tasks are permitted to overlap.
5. The gap between tasks: In any of these relationships a time delay or gap may be added. This is usually done to allow for uncertainty.

A task precedence graph is a form of PERT chart. It is a network of nodes and arrows, which can be evaluated to figure out task precedence as well as the critical path (i.e., the longest path) through the network.

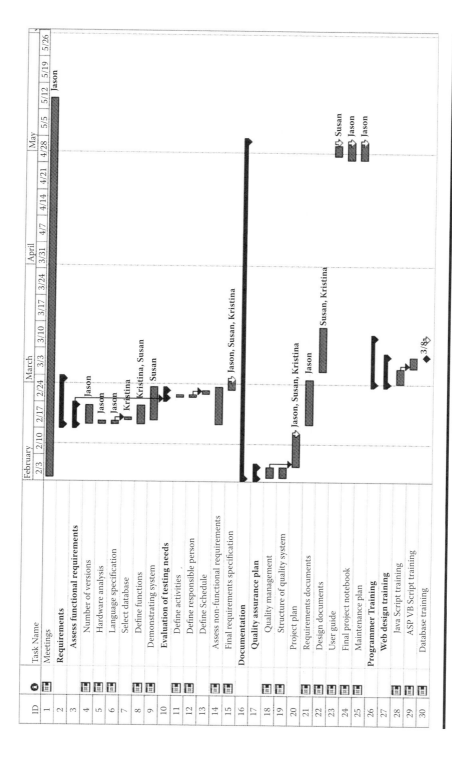

Figure 7.2 A Gantt chart.

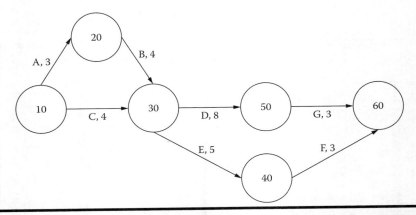

Figure 7.3   A task precedence graph. This is sometimes called a project network diagram.

Figure 7.3 shows a task precedence network of seven tasks (A through G) and six nodes (labeled 10 through 60). The tasks can be identified as follows:

Task	Precedence	Duration
A Interview staff	None	3
B Distribute questionnaires	A	4
C Analyze competitive data	None	4
D Elicit requirements	B, C	8
E Create prototype	B, C	5
F Observe reactions	E	3
G Write specification	D	3

In this example, we used the "start to finish" cycle time of each task.

The Task List

Generating a WBS requires much information about each task to be collected and understood. At minimum, the following information should be available for each task:

1. The purpose or objective of the task: An example of this would be "training end users to use the new system."
2. Deliverables for each task: In the case of our end-user training objective, several deliverables might be required, e.g., development of training materials, development of online training module, etc.
3. Scheduled start and completion time for each task.
4. Budget.
5. Responsibility: Each task should have an owner, i.e., the person responsible for getting the task done.
6. Metrics: Whether or not a task has been successfully completed should be made quantifiable. Metrics can be of the following form: days overdue, cost overrun amount, user acceptance ratio, etc.

Before one can identify the criteria for each task, the task itself has to be identified. Figure 7.1 shows a typical task list, containing six columns.

Column 1: The numbering of the activities.

Column 2: Name of the task.

Column 3: Deliverables associated with each task.

Column 4: The date the project is initiated, and the duration of each activity.

Column 5: The dependencies of the completion of previous activities.

Column 6: The milestone date usually coincides with the last completion date for the task. It is the date on which the work product is delivered. A task will have at least one milestone, although it might have more. A milestone is a deliverable that is due on a certain date. In Figure 7.2, a "final requirements specification" is due on 2/24. The delivery of that document on the specified date is a milestone.

It should be noted that for many systems developers Table 1 represents the WBS itself.

Project Scheduling

People who perform project scheduling are often referred to as estimators. These employees are usually senior members of the staff who have years of experience working on a wide variety of projects, and in-depth knowledge of the organization and its systems.

After a WBS has been developed, each of the tasks must be scheduled.

Just how long will it take to perform a particular task? There are several estimation approaches to choose from:

1. Stochastic approach: It is unlikely that one can ever calculate the duration of a task with certainty. The stochastic approach takes this uncertainty into consideration by estimating task duration along with a variance.
2. Deterministic approach: Most project schedulers do not want to deal with uncertainty, so the deterministic approach is the preferred method. A deterministic estimate is based on past experiences, where the average time it took to perform the task in the past is used.
3. Modular approach: A task is first decomposed into its subtasks. Each subtask is then estimated. The sum of the estimates is rolled up to provide an estimate for the major task. For example, consider the following tasks:
   A2000 Develop modifications to system
       A2010 Clean up and finalize for delivery
       A2020 Develop additional perks
   A2000 has two subtasks. If we estimate A2010 to take 20 days and A2020 to take 30 days, then the duration for task A2000 is calculated to be 50 days.
4. Benchmark job technique: This technique is best used for repetitive tasks in which, task duration has proved to be consistent over time (i.e., a benchmark). For example, let's say it takes 20 minutes to install antivirus software on a PC. The company has 100 PCs. Given that every PC is similar and the process of installing the antivirus software is the same for every PC, we can estimate the duration for the complete installation task to be (20 minutes × 100 PCs) 33.33 hours.

5. Experience is best: The very best estimators are those with years of analogous estimate experience in the organization, and with in-depth knowledge of the systems, policies, and procedures used by the organization. The experienced estimator can use the actual cost of previous projects to extrapolate the cost of the current project.

The most prevalent unit of measure for a schedule is days. In a time-critical system (i.e., human-rated, where life and death is often at stake), it is quite possible that hours and even minutes might need to be used as units. When summarizing the project schedule, it is customary to roll up the schedule to provide an overview. In this case, time spans longer than days are permissible.

Project Management Charts

There are a variety of project management charting techniques that can be used to assist the resource allocation activity:

1. Gantt charts assist the PM to schedule tasks.
2. PERT utilizes a systematic network of nodes and arrows to allocate the various project tasks or activities. These nodes are then analyzed to determine the critical path (i.e., the longest path) through the tasks.

PERT charts show task interdependencies (i.e., which tasks are dependent upon which other tasks for their successful completion), but do not clearly show how these tasks might overlap. Gantt charts, on the other hand, do show task overlap as well as interdependencies.

Most PMs prefer Gantt over PERT as Gantt is far easier to use and easier to understand. However, both Gantt and PERT can be used simultaneously.

A good resource for charting examples is the smartdraw.com site (http://www.smartdraw.com/resources/examples/business/gantt.htm). SmartDraw and Microsoft Visio are the two premier business charting software tools available. (Please note that these are commercial software packages.)

Gantt Chart

The Gantt chart is the most commonly used of all business charting tools. It is widely used outside of the information technology department as all business processes are task based.

Figure 7.4 is an example of a typical Gantt chart as created by Microsoft Project. Note that it is a chart with two dimensions: tasks and time.

Gantt charts are easy to understand:

1. Tasks are listed on the vertical dimension.
2. Time is shown on the horizontal dimension using a bar whose length signifies the time it will take to complete the task. In our example, the name of the person assigned to the task is located at the end of the bar.

Aside from Microsoft Project, there are a variety of other diagramming tools that enable the PM to create a Gantt chart. One of these is Microsoft Visio.

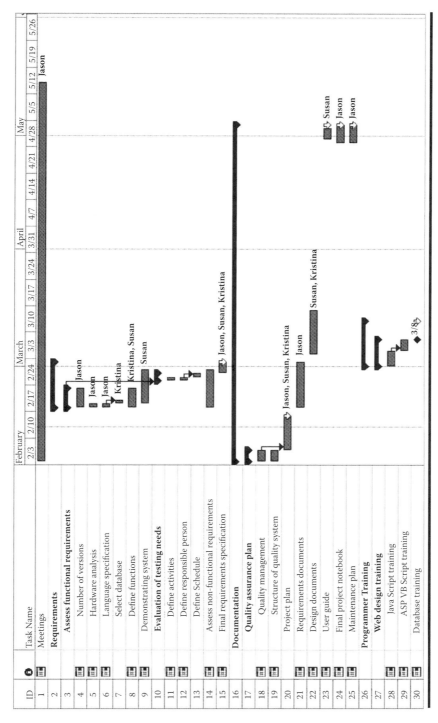

Figure 7.4 Gantt chart as created by Microsoft Project.

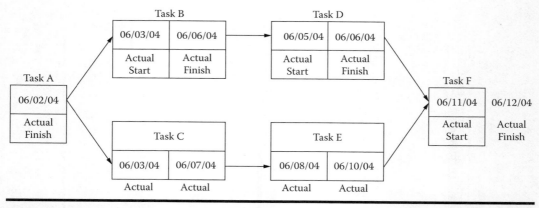

Figure 7.5   A sample PERT chart with six tasks.

Program Evaluation and Review Technique (PERT)

PERT was developed by the U.S. military for use on the U.S. Navy's Polaris nuclear submarine project. It is said that PERT saved the U.S. government two years' worth of development time.

PERT charts—also known as network diagrams or precedence diagrams—show tasks and the dependencies between tasks. Figure 7.5 shows a network of six tasks (i.e., task A through task F). Each task contains a task description as well as a scheduled start and finish date (the two dates we see in each task box), and an actual start and finish date. We can clearly see, for example, that task A must be completed before tasks B and C are initiated. We can also see that tasks A through E must be completed before task F is begun. In other words, the PERT chart enables us to visualize the order of the tasks as well as the dependencies between them.

The PM can also use the Microsoft Visio software tool to create a PERT chart. There are variations on this format. One might also choose to include slack (i.e., free time) and duration in the diagram.

Critical Path

The critical path is the sequence, or chain, of tasks that determines the duration of the project. It is calculated by figuring out the longest path through the tasks, thus giving us the "outside date" the project will be completed.

A variation on the PERT chart is the task activity network or network diagram, shown in Figure 7.6. Circles are called events and are arbitrarily identified in this figure as events 10 (the initiating task) through 50 (the final task). In Figure 7.6, the arrows represent the activities and duration of each activity. "A, 5," for example, refers to an activity named "A" that takes five days to complete.

As you can see, the duration (critical path) for the project can be easily calculated. To determine the length of the project, all we need to do is add up the total number of days along each path and select the one with the longest duration.

Path 10-20-40-50 has a length of (5 + 20 + 3) 28 days.
Path 10-30-40-50 has a length of (10 + 20 + 3) 33 days

The critical path is 33 days as it is the longest of the two paths calculated.

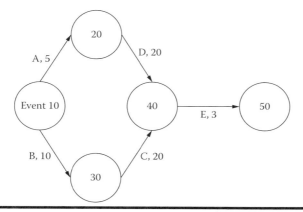

Figure 7.6   Using a task activity network to calculate critical path.

Leveling and Resource Allocation

In a typical work environment, there will always be staff members who are overutilized and others who are underutilized. This is especially true for key human resources assigned to a project. Leveling refers to the optimization technique of efficiently allocating human resources to a project by essentially evening out the workload through the reallocation of tasks. The manager first looks at how each human resource is utilized. Next, slack time (i.e., free time) for each resource is examined. Finally, tasks are reallocated based on an analysis of resource utilization and available slack time. On occasion, reallocation will be done regardless of the amount of slack time available.

There are several methods that can be used to level human resource utilization, including the following:

1. Split a task into subtasks so that work can be suspended and then restarted when a resource is available.
2. Allocate additional human resources to a particular task.
3. Replace the human resource assigned to the task.
4. Delay lower-priority tasks until higher-priority tasks are completed.

Leveling can be a complicated statistical process, particularly when precedence of tasks must be considered. This is why tools such as Microsoft Project are so useful. When leveling is used, Microsoft Project checks each of the selected resources. If a resource is overallocated, the tool searches for the tasks that are causing the overallocation and identifies which of those tasks can be delayed. Microsoft Project does not delay tasks that have the following features:

- Have a constraint of Must Start On, Must Finish On, or As Late As Possible.
- Have a "Do Not Level" priority.
- Have an actual start date.

After determining which tasks can be delayed, Microsoft Project picks the task to delay based on its task relationships, start date, priority, and constraints. Note that Microsoft Project cannot resolve overallocations in projects that are scheduled from the finish date.

Questions to ask prior to resource optimization include the following:

1. Which human resources can be allocated to which tasks (e.g., skill sets required for each task)?
2. Can the project finish date be deferred?
3. Can a task be subdivided?
4. What are the task's dependencies?
5. Can a task be shared?

Slack Management

In terms of project management, slack is the timing difference between an activity's earliest start date and its latest possible (critical) start date. If the slack of an activity is zero, then that activity can be considered to be on the critical path. The critical path is the succession of tasks such that if any one of them is completed X days late, the project itself will be X days late.

Slack management is the process by which a PM fine-tunes a schedule to correspond to the project's budget dollars availability. At times the cash flow of a budget (i.e., the budget dollars available during a certain period) precludes one or more tasks from being completed as per the schedule. Slack management is the art and science of redistributing the tasks so that the project stays within budget and on schedule and, at the same time, allowing a buffer for emergencies. For example, if critical task A is redistributed to the tail end of the schedule because of budgeting problems, and an unforeseen emergency precludes task A from being completed on schedule, the entire project might be delivered late.

Slack time management is also used heavily in manufacturing. Jobs are prioritized in accordance with their slack time, the slack time being divided by the number of operations remaining. Each operation could introduce a delay. The lower the slack time per operation, the higher the job's priority.

Crashing the Activities

What do you do if the project is behind schedule and is in danger of being late? *Crashing* is the practice of performing one or more activities in a shorter-than-normal period of time. This can be accomplished by the following steps:

1. Using different technologies to speed up the process
2. Adding or deleting resources

Questions that should be answered prior to crashing:

1. How much does it cost to crash activities?
2. Do the benefits of completing the project in a shorter-than-normal time outweigh the extra cost of crashing the activities?

When the Resources Are Human

PMs should be reminded that each task on a Gantt chart, PERT chart, or Critical Path represents something done by a human being (i.e., resource). When creating a schedule, estimators need to take into account the following facts:

1. The experience of the resource
2. The educational level of the resource
3. The amount of work the resource has already been allocated
4. How long it typically takes a particular resource to complete a specific task
5. How well the resource works with team members

To ensure smooth sailing, the PM should take the following measures:

1. Make continuous training of human resources a priority.
2. Keep the staff motivated.
3. Utilize effective project control techniques.
4. Institute reward and recognition systems.
5. Develop an organizational culture that rewards group efforts.
6. Take up active efforts to disperse crucial application knowledge across project staff.
7. Improve communication and coordination across organizational layers.
8. Adopt egoless-programming techniques.

Large performance differences between individuals negate productivity increases. Boehm (1991) estimates that productivity ranges of 3:1 to 5:1 are typical, with some studies documenting differences as high as 26:1 among experienced programmers. Techniques to increase the effective level of productivity include the following:

1. Enhanced training
2. Investment in productivity tools (tools, methods)
3. Use of standard practices
4. Professional development opportunities
5. Recognition
6. Effective staffing
7. Using top talent
8. Matching the job to the employee's skill sets
9. Providing a career progression
10. Providing team balance

Conclusion

Creating the project schedule is one of the most difficult project management tasks. Many, if not most, projects wind up exceeding time estimates. Successful time estimation requires a great deal of experience, the use of tools (i.e., PERT, Gantt, etc.) with which to model the project's tasks, and an in-depth understanding of the human resources being scheduled.

Links

http://www.mindtools.com/critpath.html Critical path, Gantt, and PERT.
http://hadm.sph.sc.edu/COURSES/J716/CPM/CPM.html Critical path method tutorial.
http://www.rspa.com/spi/project-sched.html Scheduling resources.
http://www.smartdraw.com/resources/examples/business/gantt.htm SmartDraw charting examples.

References

Boehm, Barry W. (1991). *Software Engineering Economics*. New York: Prentice Hall.

Chapter 8

Project Estimation

In this chapter, we will explore the concept of project estimation on the basis of the work breakdown structure (WBS). Readers will examine a variety of estimation techniques such as process-based, bottom-up estimation, and the Cost Construction Model (COCOMO). Use of historical data and estimation of hardware, software, and external resources will be addressed. Various budgeting methodologies such as top-down, bottom-up, iterative, and overburden will be examined. Budget analysis techniques such as cost–benefit analysis, break-even analysis, return on investment (ROI), and net present value (NPV) will be analyzed.

The Importance of Project Estimation

Menlo Worldwide had been reworking its transportation and supply-chain management (SCM) system, known as EMCON, since 1996. Over time, the project size grew and the scope began to drift. Then, 9/11 happened and in its wake, the U.S. Transportation Security Administration (TSA) created the "known shipper" program to electronically match cargo to legitimate shipping companies.

This new requirement threw a wrench into EMCON's fragile works. Not only did the entire system need to be retrenched, but all the E-business processes associated with it as well.

The chief information officer (CIO) had a real problem on his hands. He was faced with a project that had been creeping along for years and a technology architecture that was over 30 years old. His decision was to overhaul this most critical application, but to do so in a carefully controlled, planned way.

The CIO put the project back into a business context and narrowed its scope, including a total redesign of some of the base architecture, to remove some of the complexity that was impeding progress. He also decided to delay some components, such as handheld devices for delivery drivers, until later in the project. The newly revised EMCON system is a combination of mainframe and client/server architectures as well as some off-the-shelf software, including a new transportation management application from Baan and a new SCM application from Viewlocity.

Achieving all of this was no easy feat. According to the CIO, the most difficult part of the project was understanding what had to be changed and then developing a viable project plan and accompanying estimate.

WBS—The Basis for Project Estimates

One of the first things EMCON's CIO did was create a WBS. This enabled him to understand and then effectively allocate and organize project tasks. To execute these tasks, EMCON's CIO had to also allocate sufficient resources, time, and budget dollars.

Project managers (PMs) develop project plans in these three dimensions, each being a constraint on what he or she can do. This is why they are often called triple constraint.

1. Resources—This answers the question, "What kinds of human and nonhuman resources, including hardware and software, are required?"
2. Time—This answers the question, "How much time needs to be allocated to the project in its entirety, and specifically to each individual task?"
3. Money—This answers the question, "How much will the project cost in its entirety, and specifically how much does each individual task cost?"

Figure 8.1 shows a partial WBS for a Web-based veterinarian service called Dog E-Doctor System (DEDs). Once a project is broken down into manageable tasks, it becomes possible to begin the estimation process.

The Process of Human Resource Estimation

PMs use a wide variety of techniques to perform the project cost estimation effort. It is customary, in fact, for the estimator to use at least two techniques and then triangulate the two (i.e., discuss the reasons why the two estimates have differences). Often, the best estimate is the average of the results of the various estimation methods used.

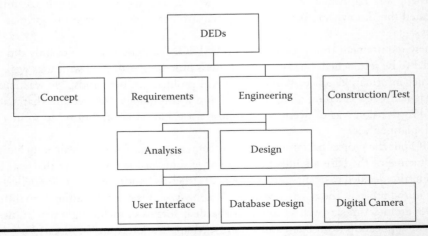

Figure 8.1   The work breakdown system (WBS) assists the project planner in identifying discrete project tasks. The WBS in this figure is a small subset of the complete WBS for this project.

A real-world example of this methodology follows. Notice that all three dimensions of the triple constraint are accounted for. Explanatory comments are italicized.

Project Estimates

This portion of the document provides cost, effort, and time estimates for the project using various estimation techniques.

Historical Data Used for Estimates

Local data was collected to determine the average salaries of IT professionals in Roanoke, Virginia. Table A summarizes this data.

Table A   Average Salaries

Profession	Average Salary ($)	40 Percent Average Adjustment ($)	Per Month ($)
Computer programmer 2	50,328	70,459	5,871
Computer programmer 3	44,949	62,928	5,244
Database administrator	53,923	75,492	6,291
Database analyst	48,406	67,768	5,647
Software design manager	77,619	108,666	9,055
Software design supervisor	58,325	81,655	6,804
Software engineer	58,395	81,753	6,812

The foregoing table shows the average salary of IT professionals. The average salary values do not include the administrative costs associated with the employee. These administrative costs are typically 40 percent of the employee's salary. Therefore, the real cost of the employee is 1.4 times the average salary. This adjusted salary value is shown in the second to last column of the table. The last column adjusts the salary to a per-month basis.

The programmers surveyed in this project were a well-rounded group with several years of experience in IT-related fields. Therefore, the adjusted average salary from Table A will be used for estimation purposes.

It is important that current real world data always be used. All too often, estimates are based on gut feelings about what the true cost of development is. Many IT Web sites provide comparative cost data. In addition, the Human Resources department presumably has accurate cost information as well.

Applied Estimation Techniques and Results

Two estimation techniques were used for planning purposes: process-based estimation and the COCOMO II Model. Two techniques were used so that the results could be compared and contrasted to ensure that the plan is as accurate as possible.

There are a wide variety of other estimation techniques. This PM selected these two techniques. Read on through this chapter for information on other estimation techniques.

Process-Based Estimation

Process-based estimation is accomplished by breaking (decomposing) the project down into a relatively small set of tasks. The time required to accomplish each task is then estimated. The major functions of this system are as follows:

- User interface/control engineering   (UICE)
- Search interface/algorithm engineering   (SIAE)
- Database design/management   (DDM)
- Automated notification algorithms   (ANA)
- Digital camera system   (DCS)
- Credit card transaction   (CCT)
- Automated backup recovery system   (ABRS)

This is where the WBS comes in handy. WBSs enable the estimator to successively decompose a system into multiple levels of subtasks. This makes it easier to provide an accurate cost estimate.

Estimation is part science and part "guesstimation." Table B represents a series of time estimates based on months for each task. For example, the project manager who created this estimate decided that it would take about a quarter of a month (0.25) to complete the analysis of the user interface (UICE).

The project team will be made up of three software engineers, one database analyst, and one software design manager. The software design manager will be shared between this project and four others. Therefore, one fifth of the cost of the software design manager will be applied to this project.

Table B shows that the project requires 9.15 person-months of work. However, this does not mean that four developers can complete the project in a quarter of the time. There are two reasons for this—the increase in lines of communication between developers and the time taken to complete the critical path.

The more developers on a project, the more lines of communication that must be maintained.

Communication problems can lower productivity. Most project problems arise because of poor communication between workers. If there are n workers on the team, then there are $n(n-1)/2$ interfaces across which there may be communication problems (Simmons, 1991). Maintaining these lines of communication takes project resources away from the actual development work. Also, the critical path may not be completed in a quarter of the time. Therefore, the actual amount of time required to complete the project is estimated to be 35 percent higher than the time shown in Table B. Then, the time required to complete the project is $(9.15 \times 1.35)/4 = 3.08$ months.

The PM might need to reduce or increase this figure depending on political, administrative, or other constraints.

The critical path is the longest path through a project. It determines the earliest date a project may be completed.

Table B Process-Based Human Resources Estimation Table

Activity	Customer Communication	Planning	Risk Analysis	Engineering		Construction Release		Customer Evaluation	Totals
				Analysis	Design	Code	Test		
UICE	0.38	0.08	0.03	0.25	0.38	0.38	0.38	0.15	2.03
SIAE	0.23	0.03	0.02	0.13	0.25	0.15	0.25	0.08	1.14
DDM	0.08	0.03	0.05	0.38	0.5	0.13	0.25	0.03	1.45
ANA	0.15	0.03	0.03	0.13	0.15	0.13	0.13	0.03	0.78
DCS	0.08	0.03	0.02	0.13	0.38	0.5	0.38	0.03	1.55
CCT	0.08	0.02	0.02	0.13	0.25	0.25	0.25	0.03	1.03
ABRS	0.08	0.03	0.02	0.13	0.25	0.25	0.38	0.03	1.17
Total	1.08	0.25	0.19	1.28	2.16	1.79	2.02	0.38	9.15
Effort (percent)	12	3	2	14	24	20	22	4	100

Note: The process-based estimation results show that the project will require 9.02 person-months of time to complete.

■ Software engineer 1—$20,708
(From Table A, a software engineer is costed at $6,812. Multiply this by 3.04 months, a reduction from the 3.08 months mentioned earlier and one gets $20,708). Therefore:
■ Software engineer 2—$20,708
■ Software engineer 3—$20,708
■ Database analyst—$17,166
■ Software design manager—$5,505

Then the cost of the project team is estimated at $84,795.

Function Point-Based Estimation

All project plans should be estimated using a minimum of two estimation techniques. To help ensure the accuracy of the estimation, the COCOMO II estimation model was used in conjunction with the process-based estimation technique discussed in Section 1.2.1.

COCOMO is an acronym for COst COnstruction MOdel. Developed by Barry Boehm and popularized by his book, Software Engineering Economics *(Prentice Hall, 1981), it is a formula that describes factors which affect the ultimate cost of computer software. The factors fall into four broad categories: product, computer, personnel, and project.*

The COCOMO II Model uses either lines of code (LOC) or Function Points (FPs) for the analysis. For this project, FPs were defined for the major software LOC functions:

■ User interface/control engineering (UICE)
■ Search interface/algorithm engineering (SIAE)
■ Database design/management (DDM)
■ Automated notification algorithms (ANA)
■ Digital camera system (DCS)
■ Credit card transaction (CCT)
■ Automated backup recovery system (ABRS)

The FPs for each major software function are shown as follows in Table C.

Table C   Function Points for the Major Software Functions

	Inputs	Outputs	Files	Interfaces	Queries
UICE	1	1	0	0	0
SIAE	0	0	0	0	1
DDM	0	0	0	1	0
ANA	0	1	0	0	1
DCS	0	0	0	1	0
CCT	0	0	0	1	0
ABRS	1	0	0	0	0

These FPs were plugged into the COCOMO II model. The screen shot in Figure 8.2 shows the results.

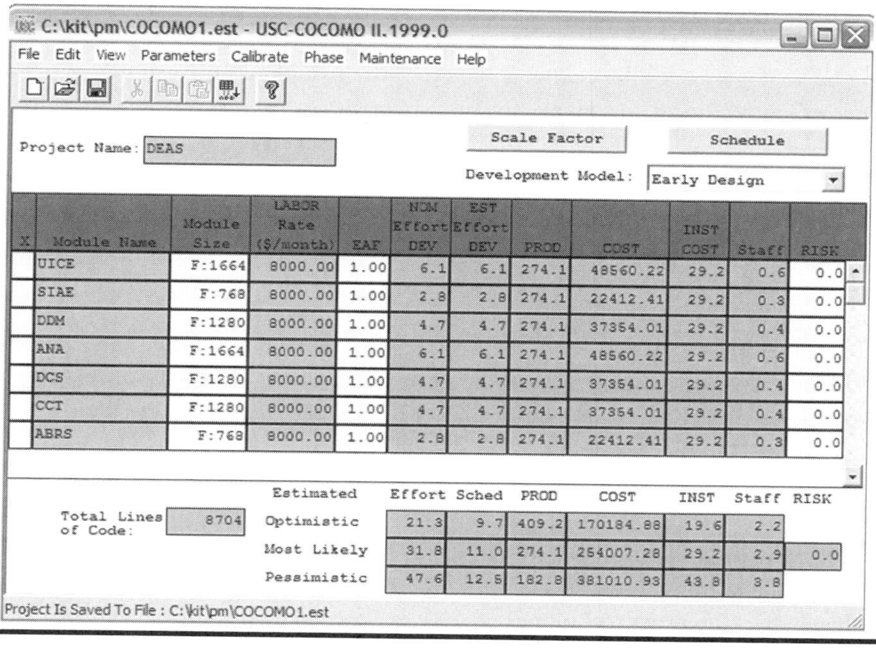

Figure 8.2   The COCOMO II project estimation.

Note that although FPs were used for the estimation, the COCOMO outputted its results in lines of code. The COCOMO II toolset will convert this automatically.

The COCOMO II estimation model results show that the project will require 31.8 person-months of time to complete, at a cost of $254,000. This is significantly different from the 9.15 person-months of time calculated using process-based estimation. Part of the reason for the wide difference in results is the fact that the project is still in the very early phases. This document, as well as the estimation models, will be updated throughout the project to ensure that accurate estimation data always exists and any issues with the project will be found as early as possible.

Note that a reason was given for the discrepancy between the two estimations. This is referred to as triangulation. At this point, the estimator will either select one of the two estimates or utilize the average of the two. The final determination, therefore, will become the cost estimation for the human resource component of the project plan.

Automated estimation tools are available. A COCOMO shareware tool, which was used above, can be downloaded from http://sunset.usc.edu/research/COCOMOII/.

Cost Xpert, which is available for a ten day free trial from http://www.costxpert.com/dynamic/trial-en.aspx, provides a great deal of functionality and is more intuitive in its end-user interface.

Other Estimation Techniques

The most important thing for you to understand about project estimation is that uncertainty is inherent in most estimation endeavors—so you need to plan for it! Using a variety of estimation techniques will ensure that your estimate is as accurate as possible.

Estimating by Analogy

Estimating by analogy relates the cost of a system to the cost of a known similar system through comparisons of key technical and management characteristics.

   Advantages
   - Provides estimates even when little data is available
   - Requires limited data collection
   - Based on "actual" costs (depending on adjustments)

   Disadvantages
   - Based on limited data
   - Subjective adjustments may be difficult to validate
   - Accuracy highly dependent on similarity between items
   - Does not identify cost drivers
   - Difficult to assess impact of design changes

   Uses
   - When little data is available
   - For a quick, rough order of magnitude
   - For a check on other techniques

Bottom-Up (Grassroots) Estimating

This technique builds up an estimate of a system, using detailed information (i.e., you start from the lowest-level tasks and build your system upward. It's analogous to bottom-up design versus top-down design when designing software systems).

   Advantages
   - Sensitive to changes in design
   - Visibility provided into cost drivers
   - The most precise cost-estimating methodology

   Disadvantages
   - Detailed design information required
   - Time consuming
   - Difficult to perform cost trade-offs
   - Accuracy depends on stability of design and skill of team

   Uses
   - In production estimating
   - To estimate development of firm designs

Parametric Estimation

This method relates the cost of a system to one or more parameters of the system, such as physical or performance characteristics, utilizing a mathematical model. Parametric cost-modeling techniques were first developed in the 1950s by the Rand Corporation.

Advantages
- – Sensitive to significant design changes
- – Quantifies effects of cost drivers
- – Based on real-world experience of many systems
- – Gives quick, reproducible results

Disadvantages
- – Subjective inputs
- – Results not as precise as bottom-up estimation
- – Requires skilled analyst to develop

Uses
- – For cost estimates and trade-offs for systems in early development
- – For quick reaction estimates
- – For an independent check on other estimates

Estimating Nonhuman Resources

In Chapter 6 we discussed how the scope of the project plan should detail the nonhuman resources required by the project. This includes all hardware, software, office supplies, training, and even travel-related expenses necessitated by the project. The cost of these resources must be estimated as well. These costs may be ascertained by researching the Internet or obtained directly from the various vendors. The total estimated project cost, therefore, is the sum of the human resource estimate and nonhuman resource estimate.

Managing Project Resources

A number of human resources may be assigned to a project. These people have a variety of titles and pay scales. The project plan's section on estimation will contain historical data for these various pay scales, which is then used to calculate the project's cost. The project plan will also contain much information that describes the people involved in the project as well as the equipment (i.e., nonhuman resources) needed for the project.

Human resources—An excerpt of a typical project plan that deals with this requirement follows:

> This project will require four developers. Three of them are software engineers and one is a database analyst. A software design manager will manage the project. The team is well rounded, and each team member has several years of experience in the IT field. Because the team members have a wide range of expertise, this project should require very little additional training.
>
> The part of the project that may require some (minimal) training is the digital camera system. One of the software engineers will be sent to a two day training course on the system that will be purchased. This will ensure that the risks involved with the most technically challenging aspect of the project will be limited. The cost of the training class and travel will be $2000.
>
> The project team will also be made up of a Society for the Prevention of Cruelty to Animals (SPCA) employees who will be the main point of contact for gathering

end-user feedback from the SPCA's perspective. This end user will not be paid for participation because he or she may then have a vested interest in ensuring the project's success.

There will also be a group of five end users who will be paid for testing the system. They will provide feedback from the users' perspective (individuals looking to adopt a dog). Their feedback will be solicited during regular dinner sessions. They will be served dinner while the latest changes to the system are discussed. After dinner, they will be allowed to test out the system for approximately one hour. They will each be paid $20 for each of testing sessions (five sessions).

Nonhuman resources—This includes costs for resources such as hardware (e.g., personal computers, servers, digital cameras, etc.), software (e.g., operating system, database management system, etc.), and even office supplies (e.g., desks). The project manager determines the nonhuman resources for each low-level task by asking, "What does the human resource require to perform this task?"

Budgeting

All projects have budgets. A budget is the total sum of all costs of a project. This includes the following:

1. Salaries.
2. Hardware.
3. Software.
4. Training, as applicable.
5. Other equipment such as telephones, stamps, paper, etc.

One talks about costs from two perspectives:

1. Fixed costs are costs that never vary. For example, let's say that a proposed system requires the company to purchase Microsoft Visual Basic (VB). The price of VB is fixed. Therefore, this can be identified as a fixed cost.
2. Overhead costs are costs not directly related to the project. For example, the project team's office space is considered an overhead. Most project estimations include overhead as a factor of salaries. This is referred to as an *administrative overhead* and is generally estimated to be 30–40 percent of the salary. For example, if $50 is the dollar amount we are using for a typical programmer's hourly cost, then the PM will craft a budget using an hourly rate of $65 (i.e., $50 + (30 percent of $50)).

There are several different methods of preparing a budget: top-down, bottom-up, and iterative. In all cases, the main goal of the budgetary process is to craft an accurate assessment of the costs of completing the project without overburdening the budget with extraneous costs.

Top-Down Budgeting

Budgeting within organizations is multitiered. The organization itself prepares a budget (strategic) as do the departments within the organization (tactical). The organization's master budget is the result of long-range planning, whereas each department prepares a budget based on short-range planning.

Top-down budgeting requires the project planner to be constrained by whatever dollar allocations are made available to the budget via the long-range plan. Problems with this methodology include the inevitable competition for scarce budget dollars and a lack of understanding on the part of senior management of the specifics of the project.

Bottom-Up Budgeting

Bottom-up is the preferred budgeting approach from the PM's perspective. In this scenario, each PM prepares a budget proposal for each project under his or her direction. The advantages of this approach are a granular level of detail for each project's budget, making the budgeting process far more accurate.

A disadvantage of this methodology is a loss of control by senior management. Once the many project budgets are aggregated, it is very likely that the gap between the resultant tactically created budget and the organization plan and budget is quite wide.

Iterative Budgeting

An iterative approach to budgeting tries to combine the advantages of both bottom-up and top-down budgeting while avoiding their respective disadvantages.

The iterative approach starts with management's crafting of a strategic budgetary framework that is passed down to the lower levels of the organization. PMs use guidance from the framework to develop their respective project budgets. These project budgets are aggregated at the departmental (i.e., functional) level, and then finally, into an organizational budget. Then senior management reviews this budget on the basis of organizational goals, schedule, available resources, and cost, makes its comments, and returns the budget to the functional areas for revision. Once revised, the project budgets are reaggregated at the functional level and resubmitted to senior management. This process is iterative and, at times, quite time consuming.

Financial Analysis

Before the inception of a project, its feasibility is analyzed. Aside from whether the project is technologically feasible, the costs and benefits of the system are also examined to determine economic feasibility.

Cost–Benefit Analysis

The cost-benefit analysis process compares the costs of the system to the benefits of having that system. We all do this on a daily basis. For example, if we go out to buy a new $1000 PC, we weigh the cost of spending that $1000 against the benefits of owning the PC. These benefits might be the following:

Table 8.1 Cost–Benefit Analysis

Costs (one-time)	Benefits/Year
$1000	Rental computer savings: $75 × 12 = $900
	Typing income: $300 × 12 = $3600
Totals $1000	$4500
Potential savings/earnings	$3500 (first year); $4500 (subsequent years)

1. No longer having to rent a computer, allowing cost savings of $75 per month.
2. Possibility of earning extra money by typing term papers for students, allowing potential earnings of $300 per month.

This is summarized in Table 8.1:

One-time capital costs such as computers are usually amortized over a certain period of time. For example, a computer costing $1000 can be amortized over five years, which means that instead of comparing a one-time cost of $1000 to the benefits of purchasing the PC, we can compare it to a monthly cost instead.

Not all cost-benefit analyses are so clear-cut, however. In our example, the benefits were both financial. Not all benefits are so easily quantifiable. Benefits that can't be quantified are called intangible benefits. Examples:

1. Reduced turnaround time
2. Improved customer satisfaction
3. Compliance with mandates
4. Enhanced interagency communication

Aside from having to deal with both tangible and intangible benefits, most cost–benefit analyses also need to deal with several alternatives. For example, let's say that a bank uses a loan–processing system that is old and often experiences problems. There might be several alternative solutions:

1. Rewrite the system from scratch.
2. Modify the existing system.
3. Outsource the system.

In each case, a spreadsheet should be created that details one-time as well as continuing costs. These should then be compared to the benefits of each alternative, both tangible as well as nontangible.

Break-Even Analysis

All projects have associated costs. All projects will also have associated benefits. At the outset of a project, costs will far exceed benefits. However, at some point, the benefits will start outweighing the costs. This is called the *break-even point*. The analysis that is done to figure out when this break-even point will occur is called *break-even analysis*. We can see that the break-even point comes during the first year, as shown in Table 8.1.

Calculating the break-even point in a project with multiple alternatives enables the PM to select the optimum solution. The PM will generally select the alternative with the shortest break-even point.

Return on Investment

Most organizations select projects that have a positive return on investment (ROI). The ROI, is the additional amount earned after costs are earned back. In our "buy versus not buy" PC decision discussed earlier, we can see that the ROI is quite positive during the first year, and especially during subsequent years of ownership.

The formula for ROI:

$$ROI = \frac{(Benefit - Cost)}{Cost}$$

Thus, for the first year:

$$ROI = \frac{(4500 - 1000)}{1000} = 3.5$$

ROI calculations require large amounts of accurate data, which is sometimes unavailable to the PM. Many variables need to be considered, and decisions made regarding which factors to calculate and which to ignore.

Before starting an ROI calculation, identify the following factors:

■ Know what you're measuring—Successful ROI calculators isolate their true data from other factors, including the work environment and the level of management support.
■ Don't saturate—Instead of analyzing every factor involved, pick a few. Start with the most obvious factors that can be identified immediately.
■ Convert to money—Converting data into hard monetary values is essential in any successful ROI study. Translating intangible benefits into dollars is challenging and might require some assistance from the accounting or finance departments. The goal is to demonstrate the impact on the bottom line.
■ Compare apples to apples—Measure the same factors before and after the project.

According to Berry (2001), there are a variety of ROI techniques:

1. Treetop: Treetop metrics investigate the impact on profitability for the entire company. Profitability can take the form of cost reductions because of IT's potential to reduce workforce size for any given process.
2. Pure cost: There are several varieties of pure cost ROI techniques. Total cost of ownership (TCO) details the hidden support and maintenance costs over time that provide a more concise picture of the total cost. The Gartner Group's NOW (or normalized cost of work produced) index measures the cost of one's conducting a work task compared to the cost of others doing similar work.
3. Holistic IT: This is the same as the IT scorecard, where the IT department tries to align itself with the traditional balanced scorecard performance perspective of financial, customer, internal operations, and employee learning and innovation.
4. Financial: Aside from ROI, economic value added (EVA') keeps on optimizing a company's shareholder wealth.

There are a variety of ways of calculating ROI. Davidson (1998) suggests measuring the following:

1. Productivity: Output per unit of input
2. Processes: Systems, workflow
3. Human resources: Costs and benefits for a specific initiative
4. Employee factors: Retention, morale, commitment, and skills

Phillips (1997) contends that ROI calculation is not complete until the results are converted to dollars. This includes looking at combinations of hard and soft data. Hard data includes traditional measures such as output, time, quality, and costs. In general, hard data is readily available and relatively easy to calculate. Soft data, which is harder to calculate, includes morale, turnover rate, absenteeism, loyalty, conflicts avoided, new skills learned, new ideas, successful completion of projects, etc., as shown in Table 8.2.

After the hard or soft data items have been determined, they need to be converted to monetary values:

Step 1: Focus on a single unit.
Step 2: Determine a value for each unit.
Step 3: Calculate the change in performance. Determine the performance change after factoring out other potential influences on the training results.
Step 4: Obtain an annual amount. The industry standard for an annual performance change is equal to the total change in performance data during one year.

Table 8.2   Hard Data Versus Soft Data

Hard Data	
Output	Units produced
	Items assembled or sold
	Forms processed
	Tasks completed
Quality	Scrap
	Waste
	Rework
	Product defects or rejects
Time	Equipment downtime
	Employee overtime
	Time to complete projects
	Training time
Cost	Overhead
	Variable costs
	Accident costs
	Sales expenses

Table 8.2 Hard Data Versus Soft Data (Continued)

Soft Data	
Work habits	Employee absenteeism
	Tardiness
	Visits to nurse
	Safety rule violations
Work climate	Employee grievances
	Employee turnover
	Discrimination charges
	Job satisfaction
Attitudes	Employee loyalty
	Employee self-confidence
	Employee's perception of job responsibility
	Perceived changes in performance
New skills	Decisions made
	Problems solved
	Conflicts avoided
	Frequency of use of new skills
Development and advancement	Number of promotions or pay increases
	Number of training programs attended
	Requests for transfer
	Performance appraisal ratings
Initiative	Implementation of new ideas
	Successful completion of projects
	Number of employee suggestions

Step 5: Determine the annual value. The annual value of improvement equals the annual performance change, multiplied by the unit value. Compare the product of this equation to the cost of the program using this formula: ROI = net annual value of improvement − program cost.

Net Present Value

ROI evaluates an investment's potential by comparing the magnitude and timing of expected gains to the investment costs. For example, a new initiative costs $500,000 and will deliver an additional $700,000 in increased profits. Simple ROI = (gains − investment costs)/investment costs (i.e., $700,000 − $500,000 = $200,000; $200,000/$500,000 = 40 percent). This calculation works well in situations where benefits and costs are easily known and is usually expressed as an annual percentage return.

However, technological investments frequently involve financial consequences that extend over several years. In this case, the metric has meaning only when the time period is clearly stated. Net

Present Value (NPV) recognizes the time value of money by discounting costs and benefits over a period of time, and focuses either on the impact on cash flow rather than net profit, or savings.

A meaningful NPV requires sound estimates of the costs and benefits, and use of the appropriate discount rate. An investment is acceptable if the NPV is positive. For example, an investment costing $1 million has an NPV of savings of $1.5 million. Therefore, ROI = (the NPV of savings – initial investment cost/initial investment cost (i.e., $1,500,000 – $1,000,000 = $500,000; $500,000/$1,000,000 = 50 percent). This may also be expressed as ROI = $1.5 million (NPV of savings)/$1 million (initial investment) × 100 = 150 percent.

The internal rate of return (IRR) is the discount rate that sets the net present value of the program or project to zero. Although the IRR does not generally provide an acceptable decision criterion, it does provide useful information, particularly when budgets are constrained or there is uncertainty about the appropriate discount rate.

Earned-Value Management

Most companies track the cost of a project using only two dimensions—planned costs versus actual costs. Using this particular metric, if managers spend all of the money that has been allocated to a particular project, they are right on target. If they spend less money, they have a cost underrun; a greater expenditure results in a cost overrun. Fleming (2003) contends that this method ignores a key third dimension—the value of work performed.

Earned-value management (EVM) enables you to measure the true cost of performance of long-term capital projects. Even though EVM has been in use for over 100 years, government contractors are the major practitioners of this method.

The key tracking EVM metric is the cost performance index (CPI), which has proved remarkably stable over the source of most projects, according to Fleming. The CPI shows the relationship between the value of work accomplished (earned value) and the actual costs. Fleming provides the following example to show how it works:

> If the project is budgeted to have a final value of $1 billion, but the CPI is running at 0.8 when the project is, say, one-fifth complete, the actual cost at completion can be expected to be around $1.25 billion ($1 billion/0.8). You're earning only 80 cents of value for every dollar you're spending. Management can take advantage of this early warning by reducing costs while there's still time.

Several software tools, including Microsoft Project and PMPlan (www.pmplan.com), have the capability of working with EVM.

Rapid Economic Justification

Microsoft developed the Rapid Economic Justification (REJ) framework (http://www.microsoft.com/windows/windowsmedia/Enterprise/AboutWM/BusinessValue/default.aspx) as an assessment and justification process that helps organizations align IT solutions with business requirements and then quantify the direct financial benefits of the proposed solutions. This approach combines the TCO with project substantiation.

Freedman (2003) describes the five-step REJ process as follows:

1. Understand the business—IT managers should first evaluate the company's overall strategic direction and goals along with any tactical problems and opportunities. This is done to ensure that the initiatives being considered actually do fit with the organization's overall objectives.
2. Understand the solutions—Both technical and business leaders need to work together to design possible alternative solutions to the identified problems. This often includes a "build versus buy" analysis to determine whether it is possible to solve the problem by using third-party software.
3. Understand the cost–benefit equation—This step calculates the summation of costs found under traditional TCO models. It incorporates hard financial benefits as well as intangible benefits (e.g., enhanced responsiveness).
4. Understand the risks—Standard risk analysis and development of risk mitigation strategies are performed.
5. Understand the financial metrics—Finally, the team projects the impact of the proposed IT investment in financial terms (i.e., payback, NPV, etc.) used by the specific company.

Conclusion

DeMarco (1982) suggests that the main reasons for inaccurate cost estimates are the following:

1. Many estimates for complex projects are rushed. A rough order of magnitude (ROM) estimate is provided before the requirements are really understood and defined. These estimates tend to be lower than later more accurate ones.
2. A lack of expertise on the part of the estimator and lack of data to base the estimate on.
3. The human tendency to underestimate work requirements may result from an overestimation of staff productivity capabilities or an oversight of necessary supplemental activities.
4. The push from management for competitive estimates—it must be low to win the bid!

Accurate project estimation relies on a thorough understanding of the discrete tasks that require automation. The WBS is a visual tool enabling the PM to decompose a system into a series of tasks and subtasks. From this base, the PM can use a variety of estimation techniques (i.e., COCOMO, parametric, etc.) to arrive at a dollar cost for the project. To this must be added nonhuman resources such as hardware, software, and office equipment. The total cost of a project will ordinarily be evaluated to determine whether the project is cost justified. Budgetary techniques such as ROI, cost–benefit analysis, and break-even analysis are techniques commonly used for this purpose.

Links

http://www.ispa-cost.org/newbook.htm Parametric Estimating Handbook.
http://guinness.cs.stevens-tech.edu/~lbernste/cs552-S03/Cost_EstimationTools_2001.doc Survey of Cost Estimation Tools.

References

Berry, J. (July 30, 2001). IT ROI Metrics Fall into Four Groups. *Internetweek.* 869, p. 45.

Davidson, L. (September 1, 1998). Measure What You Bring to the Bottom Line. *Workforce Magazine.* 77, pp. 34–40

DeMarco, T. (1982). *Controlling Software Projects,* New York: Yourdon Press.

Fleming Q. (September 2003). What's your project's real price tag? *Harvard Business Review.* Vol. 81, Issue 9, p20, 2p, 1c.

Freedman, R. (September 2003). Helping clients value IT investments. *Consulting to Management.* Vol. 14. No. 3, p. 33.

Phillips, J.J. (1997). *Handbook of Training Evaluation and Measurement Methods,* 3rd ed. Houston: Gulf Publishing Company.

Simmons, D. B. (November 1991). Communications: a software group productivity dominator. *Software Engineering Journal.* pp. 454–462.

Chapter 9

Project Risk

In this chapter, we will examine the concept of project risk, paying careful attention to the mitigation of risks. We will examine the different varieties of risks, e.g., risks related to business, environment, product, employee, etc.; learn how to apply probability to each risk; understand the impact of each risk; and, ultimately, learn how to devise a contingency plan for each risk.

The Proactive Risk Strategy

Project risk management addresses the following questions:

- Are we losing sight of goals and objectives as the project moves forward?
- Are we ensuring that the results of the project will improve the organization's ability to complete its mission? The result should be an improvement over the previous process.
- Are we ensuring availability of sufficient funds, including funds to address risks?
- Are we tracking implementation to ensure that "quicker/better/cheaper" objectives are being met?
- Are we applying appropriate risk management principles throughout the project?
- Are we taking corrective action to prevent or fix problems, rather than simply allocating more money and time to them?
- Have changes in the environment, such as new IT systems or leadership, created new risks that need to be managed?

A proactive risk strategy should always be adopted, as shown in Figure 9.1. It is better to plan for possible risk than have to react to it in a crisis.

Sound risk assessment and risk management planning throughout project implementation can have a big payoff. The earlier a risk is identified and dealt with, the less likely it is to negatively affect project outcomes. Risks are both more probable and more easily addressed early in a project. By contrast, risks can be more difficult to deal with and are more likely to have significant negative impact if they occur later in a project. As explained in the following sections, risk probability

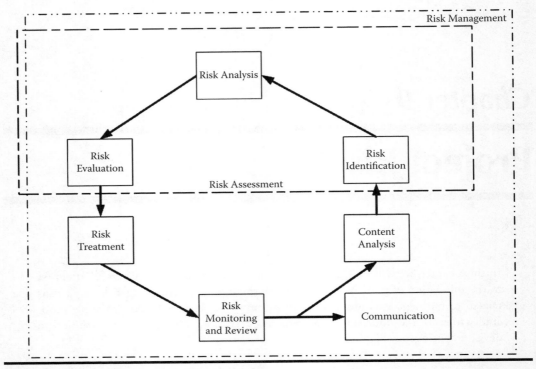

Figure 9.1   Risk management feedback loop.

is simply the likelihood that a risk event will occur. Conversely, risk impact is the result of the probability of the risk event occurring, plus the consequences of the risk event. Impact, in laymen's terms, is telling you how much the realized risk is likely to hurt.

The propensity (or probability) of project risk depends on the project's life cycle, which includes five phases: initiating, planning, executing, controlling, and closing. Although problems can occur at any time during a project's life cycle, they have a greater chance of occurring earlier, because many factors are unknown at the time.

The opposite can be said for risk impact. At the beginning of the project, the impact of a problem, assuming it is identified as a risk, is likely to be less severe than it is later in the project life cycle. This is in part because at the early stage there is much more flexibility in making changes and dealing with the risk. Additionally, if the risk cannot be prevented or mitigated, the resources invested—and potentially lost—at the earlier stages are significantly lower than those later in the project. Conversely, as the project moves into the later phases, the consequences become much more serious. This is attributed to the fact that as time passes, there is less flexibility in dealing with problems, significant resources have likely been already spent, and more resources may be needed to resolve the problem.

Risk Management

The first thing that needs to be done is identify risks. One method is to create a risk-item checklist. A typical project plan might list the following risks:

1. Customer will change or modify requirements.
2. End users will lack sophistication.
3. Delivery deadline will be tightened.
4. End users will resist the system.
5. Server may not be able to handle larger number of users simultaneously.
6. Technology will not meet expectations.
7. Number of users will be greater than the planned number.
8. End users will lack training.
9. Project team will be inexperienced.
10. System (security and firewall) will be hacked.

Keil (1998) developed a framework for identifying software project risks by interviewing experienced software project managers (PMs) in different parts of the world. The following questions are ordered by their relative importance to the ultimate success of a project:

1. Have top software and customer managers formally committed to support the project?
2. Are end users enthusiastically committed to the project and the system or product to be built?
3. Are requirements fully understood by the software engineering team and their customers?
4. Have customers been fully involved in the definition of requirements?
5. Do end users have realistic expectations?
6. Is the project scope stable?
7. Does the software engineering team have the right mix of skills?
8. Are project requirements stable?
9. Does the project team have experience with the technology to be implemented?
10. Is the number of people on the project team adequate to do the job?
11. Do all customer or user constituencies agree on the importance of the project and on the requirements for the system or product to be built?

On the basis of information uncovered from this questionnaire, we can begin to categorize risks. Software risks generally include project risks, technical risks, and business risks.

Project risks can include budgetary, staffing, scheduling, customer, requirement, and resource problems. Risks are different for each project, and risks change as a project progresses. Project-specific risks could include, for example, the following:

■ Lack of staff buy-in
■ Loss of key employees
■ Questionable vendor availability and skills
■ Insufficient time
■ Inadequate project budgets
■ Funding cuts
■ Cost overruns

Technical risks can include design, implementation, interface, ambiguity, technical obsolescence, and leading-edge problems. An example is the development of a project around a leading-edge technology that has not yet been proved.

Business risks include building a product or system no one wants (market risk), losing support of senior management (management risk), building a product that no longer fits into the strategic plan (strategic risk), losing budgetary support (budget risks), and building a product that the sales staff does not know how to sell.

Tan (2002) proposes a method of risk analysis that requires modularizing the project into measurable parts. Risk can then be calculated as follows:

1. Exposure Factor (EF) is the percentage of asset loss caused by identified threat.
2. Single Loss Expectancy (SLE) = Asset Value × EF.
3. Annualized Rate of Occurrence (ARO) is the estimated frequency a threat will occur within a year, and is characterized on an annual basis. A threat occurring ten times a year has an ARO of 10.
4. Annualized Loss Expectancy (ALE) = SLE × ARO.
5. Safeguard cost–benefit analysis = (ALE before implementing safeguard) – (ALE after implementing safeguard) – (annual cost of safeguard) = value of safeguard to the company.

Charette (1989) proposes that risks also be categorized as known, predictable, or unpredictable risks. Known risks are those that can be uncovered upon careful review of the project plan and the environment in which the project is being developed (e.g., lack of development tools, unrealistic delivery date, or lack of knowledge in the problem domain). Predictable risks can be extrapolated from past experience. For example, your past experience with the end users has not been good so it is reasonable to assume that the current project will suffer from the same problem. Unpredictable risks are hard, if not impossible, to identify in advance. For example, no one could have predicted the events of September 11, but this one event affected computers worldwide.

Once risks have been identified, most managers project these risks in two dimensions: likelihood and consequences. As shown in Table 9.1, a risk table is a simple tool for risk projection. As the first step, consult the risk-item checklist and list all risks in the first column of the table. Then in the following columns, fill in each risk's category, probability of occurrence, and assessed impact. Afterward, sort the table by probability and then by impact, study it, and define a cutoff line (i.e., the line demarking the threshold of acceptable risk).

Table 9.2 describes the generic criteria used for assessing likelihood that a risk will occur. All risks above the designated cutoff line must be managed and discussed. Factors influencing their probability and impact should be specified.

A risk mitigation, monitoring, and management plan (RMMM) is the tool to help tackle risks. Causes of the risks must be identified and mitigated. Risk-monitoring activities take place as the project proceeds, and they should be planned early. Table 9.3 describes typical criteria that can be used to determine the consequences of each risk.

Sample Risk Plan

An excerpt of a typical RMMM plan is presented in the following sections.

Table 9.1 A Typical Risk Table

Risks	Category	Probability (percent)	Impact
Risk 1	PS	70	2
Risk 2	CU	60	3

Impact values: 1 = catastrophic, 2 = critical, 3 = marginal, and 4 = negligible; category abbreviations: PS = process definition risk, CU = customer characteristics risk.

Table 9.2   Criteria for Determining Likelihood of Occurrence

Likelihood: What is the probability that the situation or circumstance will occur?	
5 (Very high)	Very likely to occur. Project's process cannot prevent this event, no alternate approaches or processes are available. Requires immediate management attention.
4 (High)	Highly likely to occur. Project's process cannot prevent this event, but a different approach or process might. Requires management attention.
3 (Moderate)	Likely to occur. Project's process may prevent this event, but additional actions will be required.
2 (Low)	Not likely to occur. Project's process is usually sufficient to prevent this type of event.
1 (Very low)	Very unlikely. Project's process is sufficient to prevent this event.

Table 9.3   Criteria for Determining Consequences

	1 (Very Low)	2 (Low)	3 (Moderate)	4 (High)	5 (Very High)
Technical	Minimum or no impact to mission or technical success, exit criteria, or margins. Same approach retained.	Minor impact to mission or technical success, or exit criteria, but can be handled within established margins. Same approach retained.	Moderate impact to mission or technical success, or exit criteria, but can be handled within established margins. Workarounds available.	Major impact to mission or technical success criteria, but minimum mission success, or exit criteria are still met; threatens established margins. Workarounds available.	Major impact to mission or technical success criteria, minimum mission or technical success, or exit criteria cannot be met. No alternatives exist.
Schedule	Minimum or no schedule impact, but can be handled within schedule reserve; no impact on critical path.	Minor schedule impact, but can be handled within schedule reserve; no impact on critical path.	Impact to critical path, but can be handled within schedule reserve; no impact on milestones.	Significant impact to critical path, and established lower-level milestone cannot be met.	Major impact to critical path and cannot meet major milestone.
Cost	Minimum or no cost impact or increase over that allocated, and can be handled within available reserves.	Minor cost impact, but can be handled within available reserves.	Causes cost impact and use of allocated reserves.	Causes cost impact, allocated reserves may be exceeded, and resources from another source may be required.	Causes major cost impact and additional budget resources from another source are required.

Scope and Intent of RMMM Activities

This project will be uploaded to a server, and this server will be exposed to the outside world, so we need to develop security protection. We will need to configure a firewall and restrict access to only authorized users through the linked Faculty database. We must know how to deal with load balance if the number of concurrent visits to the site is very large.

We will need to know how to maintain the database so as to make it more efficient, what type of database to use, who should have the responsibility of maintaining it, and who should be the administrator. Proper training of the aforementioned personnel is very important so that the database and the system contain accurate information.

Risk Management Organizational Role

The software PM must keep track of the efforts and schedules of the team. The project team must anticipate any unwelcome events that may occur during the development or maintenance stages, and establish plans to avoid these events or minimize their consequences.

It is the responsibility of everyone on the project team, with the regular input of the customer, to assess potential risks throughout the project. Communication among everyone involved is very important to the success of the project. In this way, it is possible to mitigate and eliminate possible risks before they occur. This is a proactive approach or strategy for risk management.

Risk Description

This section describes the risks that may occur during this project.

Description of Possible Risks

Business impact risk (BU): This risk occurs if the software produced does not meet the needs of the client. Also, risk has a business impact if the product no longer fits into the overall business strategy for the company.

Customer characteristics risk (CU): This risk is the customer's lack of involvement in the project, and their inability to meet with the developers in a timely manner. Also, the customer's sophistication with regard to the product being developed and their ability to use it is part of this risk.

Development risks (DEs): Risks associated with the availability and quality of the tools to be used to build the product come under this category. The equipment and software provided by the client, on which the product is run, must be compatible with the software product being developed.

Process definition risks (PSs): Does the software being developed meet the requirements originally defined by the developer and client? Did the development team follow the correct design throughout the project? These are examples of process risks.

Product size risk (PR): This risk involves the overall size of the software being built or modified. Risks involved would include the customer not providing the proper size of the product to be developed, and the software development team misjudging the size or scope of the project. The latter problem could create a product that is too small (rarely) or too large for the client, and could result in a loss of money to the development team because the cost of developing a larger product cannot be recouped from the client.

Staff size and experience risk (ST): This involves the availability of appropriate and knowledgeable programmers to code the software product, as well as the ability to ensure cooperation of the entire software project team. It would also mean that the team has enough team members who are competent and able to complete the project.

Technology risk (TE): This risk could occur if the product being developed is obsolete by the time it is ready to be sold. The opposite effect could also cause a TE; if the product is so "new" that the end users have problems using the system, they will resist the changes made. A "new" technological product could also be so new that there may be problems using it. It would also include the complexity of the design of the system being developed.

Risk Table

The following risk table provides a simple technique to view and analyze the risks associated with the project. The risks were listed and then categorized using the description of risks listed in the previous section. Then the probability of each risk was estimated, and its impact on the development process was assessed. A key to the impact values and categories appears at the end of the table.

Probability and Impact for Risk

Risks	Category	Probability (percent)	Impact
Customer will change or modify requirements	PS	70	2
End users will lack sophistication	CU	60	3
Users will not attend training	CU	50	2
Delivery deadline will be tightened	BU	50	2
End users will resist the system	BU	40	3
Server may not be able to handle larger number of users simultaneously	PS	30	1
Technology will not meet expectations	TE	30	1
Number of users will be greater than planned	PS	30	3
End users will lack training	CU	30	3
Project team will be inexperienced	ST	20	2
System (security and firewall) will be hacked	BU	15	2

Impact values: 1 = catastrophic, 2 = critical, 3 = marginal, and 4 = negligible; category abbreviations: BU = business impact risk, CU = customer characteristics risk, PS = process definition risk, ST = staff size and experience risk, and TE = technology risk.

RMMM Strategy

Each risk or group of risks should have a corresponding strategy associated with it. The RMMM strategy discusses how risks will be monitored and dealt with. Risk plans (i.e., contingency plans) are usually created in tandem with end users and managers. An excerpt of an RMMM strategy is given in the following sections.

Project Risk RMMM Strategy

The area of design and development that contributes the largest percentage to the overall project cost is the database subsystem. Our estimate for this portion does provide a small degree of buffer for unexpected difficulties (as do all estimates). This effort will be closely monitored, and coordinated with the customer to ensure that any impact, either positive or negative, is quickly identified. Schedules and personnel resources will be adjusted accordingly to minimize the effect, or maximize the advantage as appropriate.

Schedule and milestone progress will be monitored as part of routine project management, with appropriate emphasis on meeting target dates. Adjustments to parallel efforts will be made as appropriate, should the need arise. Personnel turnover will be managed through use of internal personnel matrix capacity. Our organization has a large software engineering base with sufficient numbers to support our potential demand.

Technical Risk RMMM Strategy

We are planning for two senior software engineers to be assigned to this project, both of whom have significant experience in designing and developing Web-based applications. The project progress will be monitored as part of the routine project management with appropriate emphasis on meeting target dates, and adjusted as appropriate.

Prior to implementing any core operating-software upgrades, full parallel testing will be conducted to ensure compatibility with the developed system. The application will be developed using only public application programming interfaces (APIs), and no "hidden" hooks. Although this doesn't guarantee compatibility, it should minimize any potential conflicts. Any problems identified will be quantified using cost–benefit and trade-off analysis, and then coordinated with the customer prior to implementation.

The database subsystem is expected to be the most complex portion of the application; however, it is still a relatively routine implementation. Efforts to minimize potential problems include the abstraction of the interface from the implementation of the database code to allow changing the underlying database with minimum impact. Additionally, only industry-standard SQL calls will be used, avoiding all proprietary extensions.

Business Risk RMMM Strategy

The first business risk, lower than expected success, is beyond the control of the development team. Our only potential impact is to use the current state-of-the-art tools to ensure that performance, in particular database access, meets user expectations, and graphics are designed using industry-standard look-and-feel styles.

Similarly, the second business risk, loss of senior management support, is really beyond the direct control of the development team. However, to help manage this risk, we will strive to impart a positive attitude during meetings with the customer, as well as present very professional work products throughout the development period.

Williams, Walker, and Dorofee (1989) advocate use of a risk information sheet, an example of which appears in Table 9.4.

Table 9.4   A Sample Risk Information Sheet

Risk Information Sheet
Risk id: PO2-4-32
Date: March 4, 2007
Probability: 80 percent
Impact: High
Description:
Over 70 percent of the software components scheduled for reuse will be integrated into the application. The remaining functionality will have to be custom-developed.
Refinement or context:
Certain reusable components were developed by a third party with no knowledge of internal design standards.
Certain reusable components have been implemented in a language that is not supported in the target environment.
Mitigation or monitoring:
Contact third party to determine conformance to design standards.
Check to see if language support can be acquired.
Management or contingency plan/trigger:
Develop a revised schedule assuming that 18 additional components will have to be built.
Trigger: Mitigation steps unproductive as of March 30, 2007.
Current status:
In process
Originator: Jane Manager

Risk Avoidance

Risk avoidance can be accomplished by evaluating the critical success factors (CSFs) of a business or business line. Managers are intimately aware of their missions and goals, but they don't necessarily define the processes required to achieve these goals. (In other words, "how are you going to get there?) In these cases, technologists must depart from traditional top-down methodologies and employ a bottom-up approach. They must work with the business units to discover the goal and work their way up through the policies, procedures, and technologies that will be necessary to arrive at that particular goal. For example, the goal of a fictitious business line is to be able to cut down the production–distribution cycle by a factor of 10, providing a customized product at no greater cost than that of the generic product in the past. To achieve this goal, the technology group needs to get the business managers to walk through the critical processes that must be invented or changed. It is only at this point that any technology solutions are introduced.

One technique, called Process Quality Management (PQM) uses the CSF concept. IBM originated this approach, which combines an array of methodologies to solve a persistent problem: how do you get a group to agree on goals and ultimately deliver a complex project efficiently, productively, and with a minimum of risk? (Hardaker and Ward, 1987).

PQM is initiated by gathering, preferably off-site, a team of essential staff. The team's members should represent all facets of the project. Obviously, all teams have leaders, and PQM teams are no different. The team leader chosen must have a skill mix closely attuned to the projected outcome of the project. For example, in a PQM team whose assigned goal is to improve plan productivity, the best team leader just might be an expert in process control, although the eventual solution might be in the form of enhanced automation.

Assembled at an off-site location, the first task of the team is to develop, in written form, specifically what the team's mission is. With such open-ended goals as, "determine the best method of employing technology for competitive advantage," the determination of the actual mission statement is an arduous task, best tackled by segmenting this rather vague goal into more concrete subgoals.

In a quick brainstorming session, the team lists the factors that might prevent the mission from being accomplished. This serves to develop a series of one-word descriptions. Given the ten minutes timeframe, the goal is to list as many of these inhibitors as possible without discussion and criticism.

It's at this point that the team turns to identifying the CSFs, which are the specific tasks that the team must perform to accomplish its mission. It is vitally important that the entire team reach a consensus on the CSFs.

The next step in the IBM PQM process is to make a list of all the tasks that are necessary to accomplish the CSFs. The description of each of these tasks, called *business processes*, should be declarative. Start each with an action word such as *study, measure, reduce, negotiate,* and *eliminate.*

Table 9.5 and Figure 9.2 show the resulting Project Chart and Priority Graph, respectively, which diagrammatically represent the PQM technique. The team's mission, in this example, is to introduce just-in-time (JIT) inventory control, a manufacturing technique that fosters greater efficiency by promoting stocking inventory only according to need. The team, in this example, identified six CSFs and eleven business processes labeled P1 through P11.

Table 9.5   CSF Project Chart

#	Business Process	Critical Success Factors						Count	Quality
		1	2	3	4	5	6		
P1	Measure delivery performance by suppliers	x	x					2	B
P2	Recognize or reward workers					x	x	2	D
P3	Negotiate with suppliers	x	x	x				3	B
P4	Reduce number of parts	x	x	x	x			4	D
P5	Train supervisors					x	x	2	C
P6	Redesign production line	x		x	x			3	A
P7	Move parts inventory	x						1	E
P8	Eliminate excessive inventory buildups	x	x					2	C
P9	Select suppliers	x	x					2	B
P10	Measure				x	x	x	3	E
P11	Eliminate defective parts		x	x	x			3	D

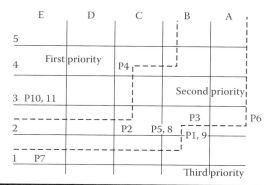

Figure 9.2   CSF Priority graph.

The Project Chart is filled out by first ranking the business processes according to their importance for the project's success. This is done by comparing each business process to the set of CSFs. A check is made under each CSF that relates significantly to the business process. This procedure is repeated until each business process has been analyzed in the same way.

The final column of the Project Chart permits the team to rank each business process relative to current performance, using a scale of A = excellent, to D = bad, and E = not currently performed.

The Priority Graph, when completed, will steer the mission to a successful, and prioritized, conclusion. The two axes of this graph are Quality, using the A through E grading scale, and Priority, represented by the number of checks each business process received. These can be lifted easily from the Project Chart for the Quality and Count columns, respectively.

The final task as a team is to decide how to divide the Priority Graph into different zones representing first priority, second priority, and so on. In this example, the team has chosen as a first priority all business processes, such as "negotiate with suppliers" and "reduce number of parts," that are ranked from a quality of "fair" degrading to a quality of "not currently performed" and having a ranking of three or greater. Most groups employing this technique will assign priorities in a similar manner.

Determining the right project to pursue is one factor in the push for competitive technology. It is equally important to be able to do the project right, which can greatly reduce risk.

Quantitative Risk Analysis

Many methods and tools are available for quantitatively combining and assessing risks. The selected method will involve a trade-off between sophistication of the analysis and its ease of use. There are at least five criteria to help select a suitable quantitative risk technique:

1. The methodology should include the explicit knowledge of project team members about the site, design, political conditions, and project approach.
2. The methodology should allow quick response to changing market factors, price levels, and contractual risk allocation.
3. The methodology should help determine project cost and schedule contingency.

4. The methodology should help foster clear communication among the project team members, and between the team and higher management, about project uncertainties and their impacts.
5. The methodology should be easy to use and understand.

Three basic risk analyses can be conducted during a project risk analysis: technical performance analysis (will the project work?), schedule risk analysis (when will the project be completed?), and cost risk analysis (what will the project cost?). Technical performance risk analysis can provide important insights into technology-driven cost and schedule growth for projects that incorporate new and unproven technology. Reliability analysis, failure modes and effects analysis (FMEA), and fault tree analysis are just a few of the technical performance analysis methods commonly used. However, this discussion of quantitative risk analysis will concentrate on cost and schedule risk analysis only (U.S. Department of Transportation [n.d.]).

At a computational level, there are two considerations about quantitative risk analysis methods. First, for a given method, what input data is required to perform the risk analysis? Second, what kinds of data, outputs, and insights does the method provide to the user?

The most stringent methods are those that require probability distributions for the various performance, schedule, and costs risks as inputs. Risk variables are differentiated depending on whether they can assume any value in a range (continuous variables), or whether they can assume only certain distinct values (discrete variables). Whether a risk variable is discrete or continuous, two other considerations are important in defining an input probability: its central tendency, and its range or dispersion. An input variable's mean and mode are alternative measures of central tendency; the mode is the most likely value across the variable's range. The mean is the value when the variable has a 50 percent chance of assuming a value that is greater, and a 50 percent chance of assuming a value that is lower.

The other key consideration when defining an input variable is its range or dispersion. The common measure of dispersion is the standard deviation, which is a measure of the breadth of values possible for the variable. Normally, the larger the standard deviation, the greater the relative risk. Finally, its shape or the type of distribution may distinguish a probability variable. Distribution shapes that are commonly continuous distributions used in project risk analysis are the normal distribution, the lognormal distribution, and the triangular distribution.

All three distributions have a single high point (the mode) and a mean value that may or may not equal the mode. Some of the distributions are symmetrical about the mean, whereas others are not. Selecting an appropriate probability distribution is a matter of choosing the distribution that is most like the distribution of actual data. When insufficient data is available to completely define a probability distribution, one must rely on a subjective assessment of the needed input variables.

The type of outputs a technique produces is an important consideration when selecting a risk analysis method. Generally speaking, techniques that require greater rigor, demand stricter assumptions, or need more input data generally produce results that contain more information and, therefore, are more helpful. Results from risk analyses may be divided into three groups according to their primary output:

1. Single-parameter output measures
2. Multiple-parameter output measures
3. Complete distribution output measures

The type of output required for an analysis is a function of its objectives. If, for example, a PM needs approximate measures of risk to help in project selection studies, simple mean values (a

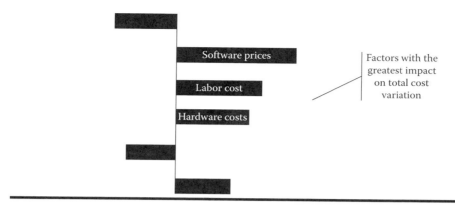

Software prices

Labor cost

Hardware costs

Factors with the greatest impact on total cost variation

Figure 9.3   A tornado diagram.

single parameter) or a mean and a variance (multiple parameters) may be sufficient. On the other hand, if a PM wishes to use the output of the analysis to aid in assigning contingency to a project, knowledge about the precise shape of the tails of the output distribution or the cumulative distribution is needed (complete distribution measures). Finally, when identification and subsequent management of the key risk drivers are the goals of the analysis, a technique that helps with such sensitivity analyses is an important selection criterion.

Sensitivity analysis is a primary modeling tool that can be used to assist in valuing individual risks, which is extremely valuable in risk management and risk allocation support. A tornado diagram is a useful graphical tool for depicting risk sensitivity or influence on the overall variability of the risk model. Tornado diagrams graphically show the correlation between variations in model inputs and the distribution of outcomes; in other words, they highlight the greatest contributors to the overall risk. Figure 9.3 is a tornado diagram for a sample project. The length of the bars on the tornado diagram corresponds to the influence of the items on the overall risk.

The selection of a risk analysis method requires an analysis of what input risk measures are available and what types of risk output measures are desired. These methods range from simple, empirical methods to computationally complex, statistical methods.

Traditional methods for risk analysis are empirically developed procedures that concentrate primarily on developing cost contingencies for projects. The method assigns a risk factor to various project elements based on historical knowledge of relative risk of various project elements. For example, documentation costs may exhibit a low degree of cost risk, whereas labor costs may display a high degree of cost risk. Project contingency is determined by multiplying the estimated cost of each element by its respective risk factors. This method is simple and does produce an estimate of cost contingency. However, the project team's knowledge of risk is only implicitly incorporated in the various risk factors. Because of the historical or empirical nature of risk assessments, traditional methods do not promote communication of the risk consequences of the specific project risks. Similarly, this technique does not support the identification of specific project risk drivers. These methods are not well adapted to evaluating project schedule risk.

Analytical methods, sometimes called second-moment methods, rely on the calculus of probability to determine the mean and standard deviation of the output (i.e., project cost). These methods use formulas that relate the mean value of individual input variables to the mean value of the variables' output. Similarly, there are formulas that relate the variance (standard deviation squared) to the variance of the variables' output. These methods are most appropriate when the output is a simple sum or product of the various input values. The following formulas show how to calculate the mean and variance of a simple sum.

For sums of risky variables, $Y = x1 + x2$. The mean value is $E(Y) = [E(x1) + E(x2)]$, and the variance is sigma sub Y squared = sigma sub x1 squared + sigma sub x2 squared.

For products of risky variables, $Y = x1 \times x2$. The mean value is $E(Y) = [E(x1) \times E(x2)]$ and the variance is sigma sub Y squared = [E(x1) squared × sigma sub x2 squared] + [E(x2) squared × sigma sub x1 squared] + (sigma sub x1 squared × sigma sub x2 squared).

Analytical methods are relatively simple to understand. They require only an estimate of the individual variable's mean and standard deviation. They do not require precise knowledge of the shape of a variable's distribution. They allow specific knowledge of risk to be incorporated into the standard deviation values. They provide for a practical estimate of cost contingency. Analytical methods are not particularly useful for communicating risks; they are difficult to apply and are rarely appropriate for risk analysis.

Simulation models, also called Monte Carlo methods, are computerized probabilistic calculations that use random number generators to draw samples from probability distributions. The objective of the simulation is to find the effect of multiple uncertainties on a value quantity of interest (such as the total project cost or project duration). Monte Carlo methods have many advantages. They can determine risk effects for cost and schedule models that are too complex for common analytical methods. They can explicitly incorporate the risk knowledge of the project team for both cost and schedule risk events. They can reveal, through sensitivity analysis, the impact of specific risk events on the project cost and schedule.

However, successfully implementing Monte Carlo methods requires knowledge and training. Input to Monte Carlo methods also requires the user to know and specify exact probability distribution information, mean, standard deviation, and distribution shape. Nonetheless, Monte Carlo methods are the most commonly used ones for project risk analysis because they provide detailed, illustrative information about risk impacts on the project cost and schedule.

Monte Carlo analysis histogram information is useful for understanding the mean and standard deviation of analysis results. The cumulative chart is useful for determining project budgets and contingency values at specific levels of certainty or confidence. In addition to graphically conveying information, Monte Carlo methods produce numerical values for common statistical parameters such as the mean, standard deviation, distribution range, and skewness.

Probability trees are simple diagrams showing the effect of a sequence of multiple events. Probability trees can also be used to evaluate specific courses of action (i.e., decisions), in which case they are known as *decision trees*. Probability trees are especially useful for modeling the interrelationships between related variables by explicitly modeling conditional probability conditions among project variables. Historically, probability trees have been used in reliability studies and technical performance risk assessments. However, they can be adapted to cost and schedule risk analysis quite easily. Probability trees have rigorous requirements for input data. They are powerful methods that allow the examination of both data and model risks. Their implementation requires significant expertise; therefore, they are used only on the most difficult and complex projects.

Risk Checklists

Checklist 1, Components of a Sound Project Plan, sets forth the key aspects of project implementation that need to be addressed and the important issues that need to be considered for each aspect. To help managers consider the wide variety of risks any project could face, Checklist 2,

Checklist 1   Framework for Project Plan

Project	
Responsible manager	
Mission	Articulate clearly the mission, goal, or vision for the project.
Objectives	Ensure that the project is feasible and will achieve its mission. Clearly define what you hope to achieve by executing the project, and make sure the project objectives are clear and measurable.
Scope	Ensure that an adequate scope statement is prepared that documents all the work of the project.
Deliverables	Ensure that all deliverables are clearly defined and measurable.
Milestones or costs	Ensure that realistic milestones are established and costs are properly supported.
Compliance	Ensure that the project meets legislative requirements, and that all relevant laws and regulations have been reviewed and considered.
Stakeholders	Identify team members, project sponsor, and other stakeholders. Encourage senior management support and buy-in from all stakeholders.
Roles and responsibilities	Clarify and document roles and responsibilities of the PM and other team members.
Work breakdown structure (WBS)	Ensure that a WBS has been developed, and that key project steps and responsibilities are specified for management and staff.
Assumptions	Articulate clearly any important assumptions about the project.
Communications	Establish main channels of communications, and plan for ways of dealing with problems.
Risks	Identify high-level risks and project constraints, and prepare a risk management strategy to deal with them.
Documentation	Ensure that project documentation is kept and is up to date.
Boundaries	Document-specific items that are not within the scope of the project, and any external constraints to achieving goals and objectives are the boundaries.
Decision-making process	Ensure that the decision-making process or processes for the project are documented.
Signatures	Key staff signature sign-off.

Examples of Common Project-Level Risks, sets forth examples of major areas in which risks can occur and examples of key risks that could arise in each area.

Monitoring will be most effective when managers consult with a wide range of team members and, to the maximum extent possible, use systematic, quantitative data on both implementation

Checklist 2   Examples of Common Project-Level Risks

Category	Risk
Scope	Unrealistic or incomplete scope definition
	Scope statement not agreed to by all stakeholders
Schedule	Unrealistic or incomplete schedule development
	Unrealistic or incomplete activity estimates
Project management	Inadequate skills and ability of the PM
	Inadequate skills and ability of business users or subject matter experts
	Inadequate skills and ability of vendors
	Poor project management processes
	Lack of, or poorly designed, change management processes
	Lack of, or poorly designed, risk management processes
	Inadequate tracking of goals or objectives throughout the implementation process
Legal	Lack of legal authority to implement project
	Failure to comply with all applicable laws and regulations
Personnel	Loss of key employees
	Low availability of qualified personnel
	Inadequate skills and training of personnel
Financial	Inadequate project budgets
	Cost overruns
	Funding cuts
	Unrealistic or inaccurate cost estimates
Organizational/business	Lack of stakeholder consensus
	Changes in key stakeholders
	Lack of involvement by project sponsor
	Loss of project sponsor during project
	Changes in office leadership
	Changes in organizational structure
Business	Poor timing of product releases
	Unavailability of resources and materials
	Poor public image of the organization
External	Congressional input or interest
	Changes in related systems, programs, etc.
	Labor strikes or work stoppages
	Seasonal or cyclical events
	Lack of vendor and supply availability

Checklist 2   Examples of Common Project-Level Risks (Continued)

Category	Risk
	Financial instability of vendors and suppliers
	Contractor or grantee mismanagement
Internal	Unavailability of business or technical experts
Technical	Complex technology
	New or unproven technology
	Unavailability of technology
Performance	Unrealistic performance goals
	Unmeasurable performance standards
Cultural	Resistance to change
	Cultural barriers or diversity issues
Quality	Unrealistic quality objectives
	Unmet quality standards

progress and project objectives. Checklist 3, Ongoing Risk Management Monitoring for Projects, provides a useful framework for ongoing risk management monitoring of individual projects. Checklist 4, To Ensure Risks Adequately Addressed in Project Plan, is useful for ensuring that risks are discussed in detail.

Checklist 3   Ongoing Risk Management Monitoring for Projects

Review period: _____ [a]				
Section 1: Progress and Performance Indicators				
Project Implementation or Outcome Objective	Progress or Performance Indicator	Status of Indicator	Are Additional Actions Needed?	Notes
A				
B				
C				
D				
Section 2: Reassessment of Risks				
Identified Risk	Actions to Be Taken	Status and Effectiveness of Actions	Are Additional Actions Needed?	Notes
1				
2				
3				
4				

[a] Managers should establish timeframes for periodic reviews in addition to ongoing monitoring of program data.

Checklist 4 To Ensure Risks Are Adequately Addressed in Project Plan

Risk Management Action	Project Design		Project Implementation		Comments
	Yes	No	Yes	No	
In developing the project plan, were stakeholders and experts outside the responsible project office consulted about their needs?					
Does the project plan address both internal and external hazards that could impede implementation or performance (see Checklist 2)?					
Have all relevant laws and regulations been considered?					
Have all safety or security concerns been considered (patient safety, animal safety, data and property security, etc.)?					
Has a strategy been implemented to prevent or mitigate all identified risks?					
Is reliable, up-to-date data available to allow tracking of project implementation and performance so that problems can be identified early?					
If not, has an expectation been set that this will be done?					
Are expectations clear and reasonable for the project and for each team member (what, when, and how), and consistent with available resources?					
Are mechanisms in place to ensure effective communication with responsible officials—both within the team and with other stakeholders, as necessary?					
If problems occur, can decisions be made quickly?					
Does the project have clear goals and objectives that are being continually tracked to ensure they are being achieved?					
Is there a clear statement of how the new process or system will be an improvement over the current process or system?					
Is there clear and accurate baseline data for comparing the new process to the old process?					
Is there a lessons-learned component so that we can use and share the good and bad lessons from the project?					

Conclusion

Risk is inherent in all projects. The key to project success is to identify risk and deal with it. Doing this requires the PM to identify as many risks as possible, categorize them, and then develop a contingency plan to deal with each risk. Project plans should always contain a risk analysis.

Links

http://www.perceptek.com.au/kteam/docs/rmmm.html RMMM sample.
http://www.sei.cmu.edu/risk/risk.faq.html Risk Management FAQ.
http://www.rmahq.org/ Risk Management Association.
http://www.riskworld.com/SOFTWARE/SW5SW001.HTM.
http://www.sei.cmu.edu/risk/main.html Software Engineering Institute's Risk Management Overview.
http://www.theirm.org/ The Institute of Risk Management.
http://www.risksig.com/ Risk Management Sig.
http://www.cs.usask.ca/resources/tutorials/csconcepts/1999_5/tutorial/risks/rmmm_i_ntroduction.html
    RMMM tutorial.

References

Charette, R. N. (1989). *Software Engineering Risk Analysis and Management*. New York: McGraw-Hill/Intertext.
Hardaker, M. and Ward, B. (November/December 1987). How to make a team work. *Harvard Business Review*. Vol. 65 Issue 6, p112, 6 pp.
Keil, M. (November 1998). A Framework for Identifying Software Project Risks. *CACM*. 41(11), pp. 76–83.
U.S. Department of Transportation (n.d.). Risk Assessment and Allocation. Retrieved from http://international.fhwa.dot.gov/riskassess/risk_hcm06_04.htm.
Tan, D. (2002, December). Quantitative Risk Analysis Step-By-Step. Retrieved from: http://www.sans.org/reading_room/whitepapers/auditing/849.php.
Williams, R. C., Walker, J. A., and Dorofee, A. J. (May 1997). Putting Risk Management into Practice. *IEEE Software*, pp. 75–81.

Chapter 10

Procurement Management

In this chapter, we will examine the concept of procurement management, need for a procurement plan, and the issue of outsourcing.

Outsourcing

Outsourcing is a three-phase process:

Phase 1: Analysis and evaluation
Phase 2: Needs assessment and vendor selection
Phase 3: Implementation and management

Phase 1: Analysis and Evaluation

To understand the services that need to be outsourced, organizational goals need to be identified, particularly the core competencies. Once the goals and core competencies are identified, information related to these activities is gathered to compare the cost of performing the functions in-house with the cost of outsourcing them. This enables the company to answer nonfinancial questions such as "how critical are these functions or activities?" or "what are the dependencies on these activities?" or "will this activity become mission-critical?" These questions will help organizations take decisions about whether or not to outsource. Long-term cost and investment implications, work morale, and support should also be considered.

Phase 2: Needs Assessment and Vendor Selection

The objective of this phase is to develop a detailed understanding of the needs of the organization and the capabilities of possible solution providers. In this phase, a request for a proposal (RFP) is developed and delivered to applicable vendors. The RFPs need to be structured in a manner

Table 10.1   Pugh Matrix

Criterion	Weight	Concepts *(Step 2)*	
(Step 1)	:	Generate score (step 3)	
	:		
:			:
:			:
Total +			
Total –			
Overall total		Generate totals (step 4)	
Weighted total			

that facilitates assessment and comparison of the various vendors. The RFP should contain the complete requirements such as a problem that needs to be resolved, desired functionalities, etc. A clearly structured and documented RFP also helps vendors understand and evaluate what a company is looking for, and helps them assess whether they can provide the required service.

When evaluating the vendor proposals, the organization should look not only at the technological capability of the vendor but also at factors such as the vendor's financial stability, track record, and customer support reputation. Contacting the vendors' existing and previous clients would give the organization a good idea of each vendor's abilities. A matrix, such as the one shown in Table 10.1, can be used to aid the decision-making process.

1. Choose or develop the criteria for comparison and the weight (importance) of each concept.
2. Select the alternatives to be compared.
3. Generate scores; for each comparison, the product should be evaluated as being better (+), the same (S), or worse (–).
4. Compute the total score.

Four scores will be generated: the number of plus scores, minus scores, the overall total, and the weighted total. The overall total is the number of plus scores less the number of minus scores. The weighted total is found by multiplying the scores by their respective weighting factors, and then adding up the products. The totals should only be treated as a rough guide in the decision-making process. If the two top scores are very close or very similar, they should be examined more closely to make a more informed decision.

Once a vendor is selected, the organization needs to ensure that a fair and reasonable contract, beneficial to the organization, is negotiated. It is imperative that the organization clearly define service levels and the consequences of not meeting them. Both parties should ensure that they understand the performance measurement criteria.

Phase 3: Implementation and Management

The final phase in the outsourcing decision process is the implementation. During this phase a clear definition of the task needs to be identified, and establishing a timeframe would be very helpful. Mechanisms need to be established to monitor and evaluate performance during the vendor's developmental process. This is important even after implementation to make sure that the outsourced tasks are being delivered by the vendor as per predetermined specifications. The ability to identify, communicate, and resolve issues promptly and fairly will help the company and the vendor achieve mutual benefits and make a relationship successful.

Depending on the size of the outsourcing contract, the manager responsible for the program's delivery and integration may be responsible for all of the processes, or only some. These are the horizontal and vertical factors of outsourcing management. A manager of the horizontal process is often involved in the decision to outsource, and is then responsible for defining the work, selecting and engaging the vendor, and managing the delivery and completion of the program. This manager normally handles all day-to-day negotiations. With larger programs, particularly those on a global scale, often a decision is taken at senior levels to outsource. A negotiation team is appointed to work through the complex agreements, usually under strict confidentiality, until the agreement is finalized and announced. It is then the role of the manager of the vertical component to implement and manage the ongoing program. Part of this role is the interpretation of the agreement, and identification of areas not covered by the agreement.

Procurement Planning

Procurement planning, which encompasses the outsourcing decision, should be every bit as rigorous as project planning. Once you've made a decision to go outside the organization, a procurement plan should be created. Although all companies do things differently, some common elements can be identified in any procurement plan. A sample plan will be described in this section.

Description of the Project

The description provides an overview of the proposed procurement request. The project itself should be described. At minimum, the project plan should be referenced. Companies practicing configuration management will have the benefit of a standardized policy for configuration identification. Configuration identification incrementally establishes and maintains the definitive current basis for control and status accounting of a system and its configuration items (CIs) throughout their life cycle. The configuration identification process ensures that all processes have common sets of documentation as the basis for developing a new system, or modifying an old one. Hence, a project plan in this environment would have a unique identifying number and would be easily referenced.

The description should also indicate whether the project requires commercial off-the-shelf (COTS), modified off-the-shelf (MOTS), or custom software development. The percentage of each should be calculated.

Other questions that should be answered in this section are the following:

1. Does the project require integration, or is the project a stand-alone system with minimum integration?
2. What is the system maintenance strategy?
3. Which databases or legacy systems are required to be used or created?

Market Research

Market research, which is a marketing term, is related to the research one typically does when performing a feasibility study. Research needs to be done to determine what is available on the market, who the vendors are, and what their products or services are. It is advisable to request meetings with customers of each product, preferably in a related industry. At minimum, you will want to conduct a reference check, detailing your findings as shown in Table 10.2.

Most importantly, you will want to assess the stability of the vendor company itself. How long has the company been in business? Is it in danger of being acquired or merged with another company? You then need to request a price estimate from interested bidders or sources.

Table 10.2 Reference-Check Statements

#	Bidder Name: _____ Statement	Did the Response Meet Expectations?					
		RC1		RC2		RC3	
		Yes	No	Yes	No	Yes	No
1	Effectiveness of contractor collaboration with the on-site project manager						
2	Ability of contractor to facilitate discussions with other stakeholders						
3	Ability of the contractor to integrate easily with other project staff						
4	Overall satisfaction with contractor method of introducing issues or problems encountered on project						
5	Speed with which contractor brought forward identified issues						
6	Did contractor bring forward feasible solutions at the same time they presented issues or problems?						
7	Was the assignment of staff personnel stable?						
8	Were deliverables timely and in conformance with contract specifications?						
9	What was your overall satisfaction with contractor?						

The procurement plan should describe this effort in terms of approach to the market survey, functional requirements of the product or services to be acquired, prospective sources, and competitive environment.

Acquisition Methodology Steps

In this section of the procurement plan, the proposed acquisition methodology should be described. Describe why this will be a competitive or noncompetitive bid. If consultants are being used, explain why in-house staff can't be used.

Describe how sources for competition will be sought, promoted, and sustained throughout the acquisition. If competition is not contemplated or achievable, discuss the basis of that decision. Justify why the requirements cannot be modified to take advantage of competition.

Describe the proposed procurement steps. For example, an RFP can be structured using all or a combination of a request for information (RFI), conceptual, technical, draft, and final proposal methodologies. Discuss key deliverables, including management plans and reports, which will be used to monitor the contractor's performance.

For best-value solicitations, describe the evaluation factors and values (percent or points) assigned for the functional or technical requirements. As shown in Table 10.3, the evaluation factors must be based on functional requirements.

Discuss the evaluation factors and scoring methodology. If appropriate, include additional scoring or evaluation worksheets as appendices, as shown in Tables 10.4 and 10.5. Discuss mandatory and desirable requirements and indicate if reference checks will be performed. If weighted scores are used, indicate how the weighted score is computed, and how the weighting is applied. Indicate why the weights were chosen, as shown in Table 10.6.

Table 10.3   Sample Evaluation Factors and Values

Evaluation Factor	Value Assigned (e.g., percent or points)
Development and conversion	45 percent
Training tasks and deliverables	25 percent
Costs	30 percent

Table 10.4   Mandatory Requirements

REQMT #	Description of Requirement	Score

Table 10.5   Weighted Desirable Requirements

REQMT #	Description of Requirement	Weight	Score	Weighted Score

Table 10.6   Scoring Values

Score	Description
0	No value: Fails to address the component, or the bidder does not describe any experience related to the component.
1	Poor: Addresses the component superficially, but one or more major considerations of the component are not addressed. Low degree of confidence in the bidder's response or proposed solution.
2	Fair: The response addresses the component adequately, but minor considerations may not be addressed. Acceptable degree of confidence in the bidder's response or proposed solution.
3	Good: The response fully addresses the component and provides a good-quality solution. Good degree of confidence in the bidder's response or proposed solution.
4	Very good: All considerations of the component are addressed with a high degree of confidence in the bidder's response or proposed solution.
5	Excellent: All considerations of the component are addressed with the highest degree of confidence in the bidder's response or proposed solution. The response exceeds the requirements in providing a superior solution.

Procurement Risk Management

In this section, methods to protect the company's investment and ensure adequate contractor performance are described. Protections might include the following:

1. Payment holdbacks
2. Performance bond requirements
3. Warranty provisions
4. Liquidated damage provisions

Similar to everything else in project management, procurement risks must be managed. This can be done similarly to project risk management, as discussed in Chapter 9. One of the most popular techniques is to include language in the Statement of Work (SOW) that requires deliverables to be accepted by the company before it will pay the vendor's invoice. The vendor should be required to take timely and appropriate measures to correct or remediate the reasons for nonacceptance, and demonstrate that the vendor has successfully completed the scheduled work for each deliverable before payment is made.

Contract Management Approach

In this section of the procurement plan, the project's specific approach, tools, and processes should be described, including the following:

1. Contract Management Plan
2. Issue and Action Item Process
3. Problem Tracking Process
4. Status Reporting Process
5. System Acceptance Process
6. Invoice Process

7. Deficiency Management Process
8. Dispute Resolution Process
9. Deliverable Management Process

Describe the tools used to manage the contract, contractual requirements, and deliverables (e.g., Microsoft Project and IBM's Rational RequisitePro). The status-reporting approach, including written reports and meetings, should also be documented. Discuss how meeting minutes, issues, and action items are recorded, tracked, and resolved. Detail specific approaches to monitor and manage contractor performance, and how performance problems and issues, including the dispute process and payment withholds or liquidated damages, will be resolved.

Perhaps the best way to manage risk is to prevent problems from happening in the first place. Keeping a tight rein over outsider contracts is critically important. Status meetings, walkthroughs, quality assurance, and other software engineering and project management techniques should be used.

Conclusion

Procurement in many organizations is a hit-or-miss affair. Project managers need to recognize that this is an important aspect of the project, as selecting the correct vendor (and solution) can make or break a project. The process of procurement management needs to be standardized, as does the process of project management. In all cases, a procurement plan should be created that details the steps taken to research and then select the most cost-effective technologies or services.

Links

http://www-306.ibm.com/software/awdtools/reqpro/ IBM Rational RequistePro.
http://www.gatherspace.com/ Agile software development requirements management tool.

Chapter 11

Project Termination

In this chapter, we will examine project termination. Particular attention will be given to the steps for project completion, the concept of change control, configuration management, and the project audit report.

All Good Things Must Come to an End

All good things must come to an end—projects do as well. For the most part, project termination is a carefully controlled process in which the artifacts of the effort are evaluated and the resulting system is turned over to production. However, not all projects actually make it that far.

The best possible termination for a system is successful completion and transfer to production. From a systems development life cycle (SDLC) perspective, this means the following:

1. The system is thoroughly tested (e.g., unit, system, integration, parallel, and acceptance testing), and ultimately, accepted by the end users. Many companies have quality assurance (QA) departments that are responsible for testing.
2. Procedure manuals are written, published, and distributed to appropriate stakeholders. These include manuals for end users (i.e., how to use the system) and operators (i.e., how to run the system).
3. End users are trained.
4. The system is turned over to the systems operations group for placement on the production computers. Computer systems are typically developed on a development computer to ensure that the programming bugs that often plague systems-in-progress do not negatively impact end-user systems. As a one-time programmer, the author was personally responsible for "bringing down" computers on a weekly basis. Indeed, among programmers, it is a badge of honor to have one's bug bring down a computer. The process of turning over a system for placement in production requires paperwork to be filled out specifying the program modules, databases, and other files to be moved from the development computer to the production computer.

5. Project completion reports are written and submitted to management. Depending on the project, management might engage the marketing or public relations department to announce the introduction of the system to the organization's clients, suppliers, and the public.
6. Project documentation is stored, usually in an online repository.
7. Project staff are reassigned. If contractors are used, these resources are reassigned or terminated as per the organization's contractual obligations.
8. Other project resources are reassigned (e.g., equipment).
9. System monitoring is put into place. These are metrics that measure the quality and productivity of the system.
10. Once a system goes into production, it must be maintained. Because it is quite common that a project placed in production already has a list of requested changes waiting for it, a maintenance team is assigned to the system (i.e., change control). Often, members of the original development team are assigned this job.

However, not all projects are successful. A systems developer once worked on a project to bring voice recognition to the floor of a major stock exchange. They were not able to get the technology to distinguish voices from background noise on the floor of the exchange. This project, then, was a failure. Project termination in the event of failure requires the project manager (PM) to do the following:

1. Prepare a preliminary report and meet with management and end users.
2. Reassign resources after evaluating the performance of each human resource.
3. Terminate contracts in consultation with attorneys.
4. Dispose of equipment.
5. Close out financial documents and audit final charges and costs.
6. Prepare final report, including information from the preceding steps.
7. Work with public relations, if necessary, to put the best possible face on a bad situation.
8. Update appropriate Lessons Learned databases.

Figure 11.1 provides an overview of the close-out processes. Snedaker (2005) stresses that inputs to the final project closeout are the final project deliverables as well as the most current project plan. The course of action in this closeout phase is to update project data and documentation to ensure that deliverables are formally accepted and ongoing operations and support processes are in place.

It should also be noted that not all systems end in *success or failure*. Sometimes a project is terminated midstream. There are a number of possible reasons for this:

1. Requirements change.
2. Regulations change.
3. New technologies are introduced.
4. Technologies in use are deemed obsolete.
5. Functionality is outsourced to or merged into another department or company.
6. Employee illness, vacations, departure, and unanticipated developer-related difficulties in developing the system.

Any of these problems might lead to premature project termination.

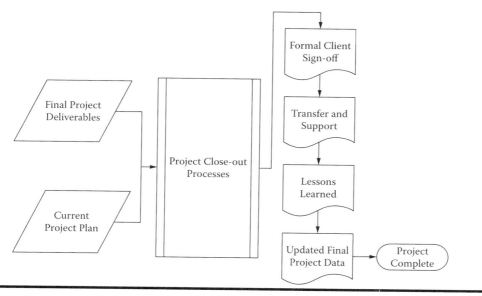

Figure 11.1 Closeout steps.

The Project Audit

Deciding whether or not to terminate a project midstream is not always easy. In fact, there are often mitigating factors that complicate the decision-making process. Lockheed, a major avionics company, continued with the development of the L1011 Tri-Star aircraft although the project accumulated enormous losses. Lockheed never really expected to earn a profit from it. Instead, they saw the L1011 as their reentry into commercial aviation. The same can be said for Digital Equipment Corporation's (DEC's) AltaVista search engine. AltaVista was one of the first search engines on the Internet. Development and maintenance was costly, but Digital saw it as a vehicle for modernizing their company and improving their image. (Note: DEC was bought by Compaq, which itself was bought out by Hewlett-Packard. AltaVista is now owned by Overture.)

As we've discussed, most projects are not clear successes or failures. What this means is that a particular project might reach a point where it is not really obvious to its stakeholders whether the project will ultimately be a success or a failure or whether it should be continued or terminated. Therefore, management should continually monitor all projects. In Chapter 4, we talked about project tracking and control. However, this is usually done from within the project team. A project audit is a form of project tracking and control that is performed by people external to the project team.

The project audit reviews a large number of variables, including the following:

1. Schedule
2. Costs, including ongoing or annual costs
3. Technology
4. Risk
5. Probability of success
6. Investment return
7. Degree of innovation
8. Degree of linkage with other projects

9. Degree of management support
10. Degree of staff support
11. Resource use
12. Personnel
13. Information assets
14. Future trends

Shtub (1994) discusses a series of questions designed to provide management with a methodology for reaching the termination decision. They are as follows:

1. Have the organization's goals changed sufficiently that the original project definition is now inconsistent with the current goals?
2. Does management still support the project?
3. Is the project's budget consistent with the organizational budget?
4. Are technological, cost, and scheduling risks acceptable?
5. Is the project still innovative? Is it possible to achieve the same results with current technology faster and at lower cost without completing the project?
6. How is the project team's morale?
7. Can the team complete the project successfully?
8. Is the project still profitable and cost-effective?
9. Can the project be easily integrated into the organization's functional units?
10. Is the project still current? Do sufficient environmental or technological changes make the project obsolete?
11. Are there opportunities to use the project's resources elsewhere that would prove more cost-effective or beneficial?

These questions need to be asked repeatedly throughout the project's life cycle. The responses to these questions, in conjunction with analysis of project and budgetary reports, should give management the ammunition it needs to decide whether to give the red or green flag to the project.

Lessons Learned

Once management decides to terminate a project or a project successfully terminates on its own, a plan must be developed for project closure. The introductory section of this chapter discusses the steps one takes when terminating a project, or closing it out. In addition to these steps, many project teams hold a Lessons Learned session. The goal of this usually off-site meeting is to uncover just what went right or wrong in this particular project.

The process is fairly straightforward. The first step is to appoint a facilitator and a scribe. These two session leaders should not be part of the original project team, as an objective perspective is required for this process to be done successfully. Participants should include project staff—including planning, design, development, and testing staff members. The discussion agenda should be preplanned and include a comprehensive list of topics. These topics could include project phases, deliverables, training, team composition, stakeholder cooperation, etc. One technique commonly used is "sticky" notes, which permit a degree of anonymity in responses.

Once the session is completed, the scribe should organize the information into a Lessons Learned document, which should be stored with the project documentation, and also circulated among organizational staff for continuing educational purposes.

Change Control

Change is inevitable. Once a system has been completed, it will inevitably need to be modified. Change control combines human procedures and automated tools to provide a mechanism for the control of change that can rapidly lead a project to chaos if uncontrolled. The change control process begins with a change request, leads to a decision to accept or reject the request, and culminates with a controlled update of the software that is to be changed.

An organization is made up of many departments such as marketing, sales, finance, etc. All of these departments are called end-user departments and may make requests of the IT department. These requests for service may be for new systems or maintenance of an existing system, i.e., change requests.

Most organizations have policies and procedures to control the flow of requests made to the IT department. End users are often required to fill out one or more forms that specify the type of change and the reason for the work request.

It is critically important to provide detailed instructions for the following:

1. Identifying changes
2. Requesting changes
3. Classifying changes
4. Documenting requests for changes
5. Change impact assessment
6. Change approval

The Maintenance Process

As the new system is implemented and users begin to work with it, errors occur or changes are needed. Just as in the development of a new system, maintenance requires that care be taken in making changes or fixing errors. In the event of an error, this can be even more critical. Each step of the maintenance process is similar to steps in the SDLC, as shown in Figure 11.2. This is a logical extension of the development process, as changes being made to the system can affect the whole system and need to be controlled carefully.

The first step in this process is to obtain a maintenance request from a user. Many organizations use a System Service Request form that spells out the problem or need. Once the request has been received, it can be translated into changes that can then be implemented, following design and testing.

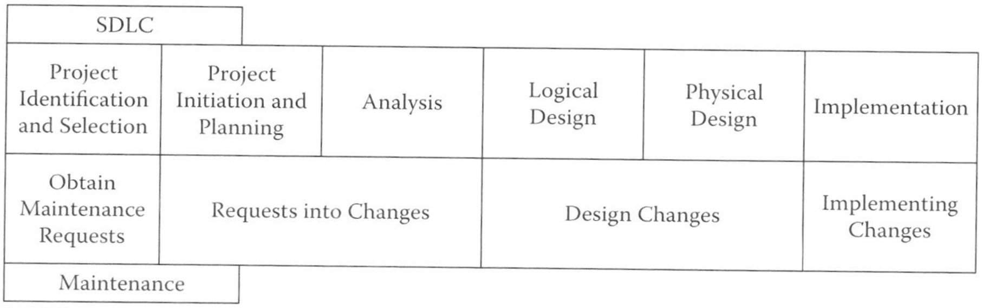

SDLC					
Project Identification and Selection	Project Initiation and Planning	Analysis	Logical Design	Physical Design	Implementation
Obtain Maintenance Requests	Requests into Changes		Design Changes		Implementing Changes
Maintenance					

Figure 11.2 The maintenance life cycle compared to the systems development life cycle (SDLC).

Categorizing the types of maintenance required is helpful in organizing and prioritizing user requests. There is more to software maintenance than fixing mistakes. Maintenance activities can be broken down into four subactivities:

Corrective maintenance: This involves fixing bugs or errors in the system as they are discovered. Corrective maintenance is the type of error most users are familiar with because it is also the most annoying to them. This maintenance usually receives top priority as bugs and errors can paralyze the functioning of the organization, if not identified and fixed.
Major skills required for corrective maintenance:
  ■ Good diagnostic skills
  ■ Good testing skills
  ■ Good documentation skills
Adaptive maintenance: This maintenance is performed to make a computer program usable in a changed environment. For example, the computer on which the software runs may use a new operating system. Thus, the system will require some adaptive tweaking. Adaptive maintenance is typically part of a new release of the code or part of a larger development effort.
Perfective maintenance: Also known as enhancement, this refers to improving the software's functionality as a result of end-user requests to improve product effectiveness. It includes the following:
  – Adding additional functionality
  – Making the product run faster
  – Improving maintainability
It is the most time-consuming maintenance.
Preventive maintenance: Also known as reengineering, this refers to performing "premaintenance" to prevent system problems. It is different from corrective maintenance, which is performed to correct an existing problem. Preventive maintenance is similar to maintaining a car: you change the oil and air filter, not in response to some problem but to prevent a problem from occurring in the first place.

Maintenance Costs

As computers and information systems become more widely used, the need for maintenance grows. When these systems age, maintenance becomes more critical and time consuming. Since the early 1980s, it is estimated that maintenance costs have skyrocketed from 40 percent of the IT budget to 75–80 percent. The reason for this increase stems from the aging of once newly designed systems. This shift from development to maintenance is a natural occurrence because organizations avoid the high cost of new systems and prefer to maintain their existing systems.

Many factors affect the cost, in terms of time and money expended, of system maintenance. One of the most costly factors is design defects. The greater the number of defects in the system, the greater the time spent identifying and fixing them. If a system was designed and tested properly, most defects should have been eliminated. But in the case of poor design or limited testing, defects can cause system downtime, and downtime costs the organization in terms of lost efficiency, and perhaps, lost sales.

The number of users can also affect the cost of system maintenance. The greater the number of users, the greater the time spent on changes to the system. More importantly, the greater the number of platforms the system is installed on, the higher the cost of maintenance. If a single system requires a change, the time taken to change it is limited. But if that system resides on platforms across the country, as is the case in many branch offices of corporations, then the cost increases significantly.

The quality of documentation can also affect the overall cost of maintenance. Poor documentation can result in many lost hours spent searching for an answer that should have been explained in the documentation in the first place. The documentation is a kind of road map to the system, and when the map is well defined, finding your way through the system and understanding it become much easier.

The quality of the employees of an IT department and their skill level also impact the maintenance costs. An inexperienced or overloaded programmer can increase the cost of maintenance in two ways. First, the programmer can waste hours learning on the job at the IT department's expense. Second, if the programmer is overwhelmed with projects, he or she may skip steps in the maintenance process and thus make mistakes that cost time and money to fix.

Tools can save maintenance personnel many hours of work. Using automation tools, such as CASE tools, debuggers, and other automation tools, can help the programmer pinpoint problems faster or make changes more easily.

A Model for Maintenance

The structure of the software can also contribute to maintenance costs. If software is built in a rational and easy-to-follow manner, making changes will be much easier and faster, saving time and resources. Software maintenance costs can be reduced significantly if the software architecture is well defined, clearly documented, and creates an environment that promotes design consistency through the use of guidelines and design patterns.

Harrison and Cook (n.d.) have developed a new model of software maintenance that is based on an objective decision rule which determines whether a given software module can be effectively modified, or if it should instead be rewritten. Their take is that completely rewriting a module can be expensive. However, it can be even more expensive if the module's structure has been severely degraded over successive maintenance activities. A module that is likely to experience significant maintenance activity is called *change prone*. Their paper suggests early identification of change-prone modules through the use of change measures across release cycles, which can be an effective technique for efficient allocation of maintenance resources.

In maintenance requests for non-change-prone modules, the process flow is as follows:

Analyze code and identify change → Implement change and update documentation → Apply metric analysis → Compare with baseline → Check to see if it exceeds the threshold → If yes, then declare module to be change prone, otherwise declare module to be non-change-prone.

The process for maintenance requests for a change-prone module is as follows:

Identify the highest-level artifact affected by the request → Regenerate artifact ‡ Identify artifacts that can be reused → Iterate through "Development" → Declare module to be non-change-prone.

Managing Maintenance Personnel

As systems age and demand increases for maintenance personnel, there has been a loud debate over just who should be doing the maintaining. Should it be the original developers? Or should it be a separate maintenance department? Many have argued that the people who developed the system should maintain it. The logic here is that they best understand the system and are better able to change it. This logic is correct but hard to implement because developers want to keep building new stuff and consider maintenance a less desirable function. IT professionals view maintenance as fixing someone else's mistakes. One solution to this problem has been tried recently and involves rotating the IT personnel from development to maintenance and back to allow everyone to share in the valued as well as disdained functions of the department.

Measuring Effectiveness

An important part of managing maintenance is understanding and measuring the effectiveness of the maintenance process. As a system is implemented, service requests may be quite high as bugs are still being worked out and needs for change are being discovered. If the maintenance process is operating properly, an immediate decrease in failures should be seen. Good management of maintenance should include the recording of failures over time and analyzing these for effectiveness. If a decrease is not noticed, the problem should be identified and resolved.

Another measure of success of the maintenance process is the time between failures. The longer the time between failures, the more the time that can be spent on improving the system and not just fixing the existing system. Failures will occur, but more expensive is the time spent fixing even the simplest failure.

Recording the type of failure is important to understand how the failure occurred and can help prevent failures in the future. Because this information is recorded and maintained as a permanent record of the system, solutions can be developed to fix the root cause of a variety of failures.

Controlling Maintenance Requests

As problems arise or the need for change is discovered, the flow of these requests must be handled in a methodical way. As requests have different priority and arrive at the PM's desk at various times, a system to process them has been developed by most IT departments. This system provides a logical path for the approval of requests and prioritizes and organizes the approved ones. The PM has the job of categorizing the requests and passing them on to the "priority board," which decides if the request is within the business model and what, if any, priority to give the change. As decisions are made by the board, they are passed back to the PM for action. It is for the PM to then report the decision back to the user and to act on the change, depending on the priority given.

The type of change and severity help decide what priority to give the change. If the change is important enough, it may be placed at the top of the queue for immediate action. If several changes occur in a single module, a batch change may be requested. A batch change involves making changes to an entire module at once to avoid working on the same module several times. This also allows users to view the changes made as a single update that may alter the use of a module because of screen changes or changes in functionality.

The queue of changes is a valuable tool in controlling the work that needs to be done. Items high in the queue receive the immediate attention they deserve, and those of lesser importance may never be acted on (because of a change in needs or the use of a new system that solves the problem).

Configuration Control or Enhanced Change Control

Configuration control is part of the broader engineering discipline called software configuration management (SCM, or just CM). It is the process of controlling changes to the software developed within an organization or purchased by it. Essentially, it is a more formal, systematized version of change control during maintenance. It is a set of tracking and control activities that do the following:

1. Identify the change.
2. Control the process of change.
3. Ensure that change is properly architected and implemented (i.e., audit).
4. Report changes to others who may have an interest.

The benefits of the process should be obvious, but are often overlooked. ANSI/EIA-649 summarizes the benefits of CM from an industry point of view, as follows:

1. Product attributes are defined: Provides measurable performance parameters. Both buyer and seller have a common basis for acquisition and use of the product.
2. Product configuration is documented and a known basis for making changes is established: Decisions are based on correct, current information. Production repeatability is enhanced.
3. Products are labeled and correlated with their associated requirements, design, and product information: The applicable data (such as for procurement, design, or servicing the product) is accessible, avoiding guesswork and trial and error.
4. Proposed changes are identified and evaluated for impact prior to making change decisions: Downstream surprises are avoided. Cost and schedule savings are realized.
5. Change activity is managed using a defined process: Costly errors of ad hoc, erratic change management are avoided.
6. Configuration information, captured during the product definition, change management, product build, distribution, operation, and disposal processes, is organized for retrieval of key information and relationships, as needed: Timely, accurate information precludes costly delays and product downtime, ensures proper replacement and repair, and decreases maintenance costs.
7. Actual product configuration is verified against the required attributes. Incorporation of changes to the product is verified and recorded throughout the product life: A high level of confidence in the product information is established.

In the absence of CM, or where it is ineffectual, the following may occur:

1. Failures due to incorrect installation or modification
2. Schedule delays and increased costs due to unanticipated changes
3. Operational delays due to mismatches with support assets
4. Maintenance problems, downtime, and increased maintenance cost due to inconsistencies between equipment and its maintenance instructions
5. Numerous other circumstances that decrease operational effectiveness and add cost

SCM requires the organization to do the following:

1. Uniquely identify each work product that is produced when developing the software.
2. Establish detailed procedures for version control and change control.
3. Audit the process to ensure that quality is maintained as changes are made.

4. Provide a reporting mechanism to make sure that those who need to know are informed about changes.

Everyone involved in the software engineering process is also involved with SCM to some extent, but sometimes, specialized support positions are created to manage the SCM process. There will be change coordinators (i.e., project leaders), and there will be deployment coordinators, who are involved in deploying and controlling the software versions. Developers will be responsible for updating the software configuration item (SCI) with the changes they perform. Documentation is done by a group of people who are also involved in report audit or report generation for the SCI.

A change control form usually contains the following information:

1. Originator of request
2. Department requesting change
3. Title of change
4. Description of change
5. Need for change
6. Urgency of change
7. Effect of change
8. Estimated net total costs/savings
9. Authorizing signatures

A change control form using proper SCM methodology would contain the following additional information:

1. Baseline affected. Configuration baselines are established to identify the currently approved documents.
2. List of specifications affected, including their document numbers.
3. Configuration item (CI) nomenclature of the item to be modified. The basis of SCM is a tightly controlled documentation system that requires item numbers for all components of a system: hardware, software, documentation, etc.
4. Nomenclature of all affected lower-level items (e.g., CI of affected items).

Typical Configuration Management Plan

Tasks associated with CM planning and management include in the following:

1. Identifying the scope and constraints of the project
2. The creation of a written plan
3. Implementation procedures
4. Training
5. Measurements

A typical CM plan will consist of, at minimum, the following components [http://www.sei.cmu. edu/legacy/scm/papers/CM_Plans/CMPlans.Chapter3.html#RTFToC1]:

1. INTRODUCTION
    1.1 Scope
    1.2 Definitions
    1.3 References
    1.4 Tailoring

2. SOFTWARE CONFIGURATION MANAGEMENT (SCM)
   2.1 SCM organization
   2.2 SCM responsibilities
   2.3 Relationship of CM to the software process life cycle
       2.3.1 Interfaces to other organizations on the project
       2.3.2 Other project organizations' CM responsibilities
3. SOFTWARE CONFIGURATION MANAGEMENT (SCM) ACTIVITIES
   3.1 Configuration identification
       3.1.1 Specification identification
   - Labeling and numbering scheme for documents and files
   - How identification between documents and files relate
   - Description of identification tracking scheme
   - When a document/file identification number enters controlled status
   - How the identification scheme addresses versions and releases
   - How the identification scheme addresses hardware, application software, system software, COTS products, support software (e.g., test data and files), etc.

       3.1.2 Change control form identification
   - Numbering scheme for each of the forms used

       3.1.3 Project baselines
   - Identify various baselines for the project
   - For each baseline created, provide the following information:
     - How and when it is created
     - Who authorizes and who verifies it
     - The purpose
     - What goes into it (software and documentation)

       3.1.4 Library
   - Identification and control mechanisms used
   - Number of libraries and the types
   - Backup and disaster plans and procedures
   - Recovery process for any type of loss
   - Retention policies and procedures
   - What needs to be retained, for whom, and for how long
   - How the information is retained (online, offline, media type, and format)

   3.2 Configuration control
       3.2.1 Procedures for changing baselines (procedures may vary with each baseline)
       3.2.2 Procedures for processing change requests and approvals-change classification scheme
   - Change reporting documentation
   - Change control flow diagram

       3.2.3 Organizations assigned responsibilities for change control
       3.2.4 Change control boards (CCBs)—describe and provide the following information for each
   - Charter
   - Member
   - Role
   - Procedure
   - Approval mechanism

3.2.5 Interfaces, overall hierarchy, and the responsibility for communication between multiple CCBs, when applicable

3.2.6 Level of control—identify how it will change throughout the life cycle, when applicable

3.2.7 Document revisions—how they will be handled

3.2.8 Automated tools used to perform change control

3.3 Configuration status accounting

3.3.1 Storage, handling, and release of project media

3.3.2 Types of information needed to be reported and the control over this information that is needed

3.3.3 Reports to be produced (e.g., management reports, QA reports, etc.), the audience for each report, and the information needed to produce each report

3.3.4 Release process to include the following information:
- What is in the release
- Whom the release is being provided to and when
- The media the release is on
- Any known problems in the release
- Any known fixes in the release
- Installation instructions

3.3.5 Document status accounting and change management status accounting that needs to occur

3.4 Configuration auditing

3.4.1 Number of audits to be done and when they will be done (internal audits as well as configuration audits); for each audit provide the following:
- Which baseline is it tied to, if applicable?
- Who performs the audit?
- What is audited?
- What is the CM role in the audit, and what are the roles of other organizations in the audit?
- How formal is the audit?

3.4.2 All reviews that CM supports; for each provide the following:
- The materials to be reviewed
- CM responsibility in the review and the responsibilities of other organizations

4. CM MILESTONES

4.1 Define all CM project milestones (e.g., baselines, reviews, audits)

4.2 Describe how the CM milestones tie into the software development process

4.3 Identify what the criteria are for reaching each milestone

5. TRAINING

5.1 Identify the types and duration of training (e.g., orientation, tools)

Conclusion

A project may be terminated for many reasons. Determining whether or not a project should be terminated can be decided through use of a project audit, which is generally done externally to the project team. Whatever the reason for termination, it is important that project closeout be planned and methodologically executed. Closeout steps include staff reassignment, project reporting, meetings, and project rolldowns via a Lessons Learned brainstorming session.

If a project has been terminated via a successful completion, the system will then move into maintenance mode, where changes to the system must be managed and controlled. The best methodology for managing system development and system change is through CM. CM provides the means to manage software processes in a structured, orderly, and productive manner. It spans all areas of the software life cycle and impacts all data and processes. Hence, the maximum benefit is derived when CM is viewed as an engineering discipline rather than an art form, which, unfortunately, is how many developers view CM.

Links

http://www.sei.cmu.edu/legacy/scm/scmHomePage.html Software Engineering Institute on Configuration Management.
http://www.rspa.com/apm/umtask04.html Roger Pressman on Configuration Management.
http://www.maxwideman.com/pmglossary/PMG_P15.htm Project Management Glossary.
http://www.4pm.com/articles/pmtalk8-2-00.pdf The Lessons Learned Review.
http://www.rochester.edu/ORPA/resource/page16box1.html Project Closeout Checklist.
http://www.cmiiug.com Configuration Management Users Group.

References

Harrison, W. & Cook, C. (n.d.). *Insights on Improving the Maintenance Process Through Software Measurement*. Retrieved from http://web.cecs.pdx.edu/~warren/papers/CSM.htm.
Shtub, A. (1994). *Project Management: Engineering, Technology, and Implementation*. New York: Prentice Hall.
Snedaker, S. (2005). *How to Cheat at IT Project Management*. Rockland, MA: Syngress Publishing.

REFERENCE GUIDES

REFERENCE GUIDES

Reference A: Traditional IT Metrics Reference

The following dismal statistics prove that metrics are an absolute requirement:

- Over half (53 percent) of IT projects overrun their schedules and budgets, 31 percent are cancelled, and only 16 percent are completed on time. (Source: Standish Group, publication date: 2000.)
- Of those projects that failed in 2000, 87 percent went more than 50 percent over budget. (Source: KPMG Information Technology, publication date: 2000.)
- 45 percent of failed projects in 2000 did not produce the expected benefits, and 88–92 percent went over schedule. (Source: KPMG Information Technology, publication date: 2000.)
- Half of new software projects in the United States will go significantly over budget. (Source: META Group, publication date: 2000.)
- The average cost of a development project for a large company is $2,322,000; for a medium company it is $1,331,000; and, for a small company, it is $434,000. (Source: Standish Group, publication date: 2000.)
- $81 billion was the estimated cost for cancelled projects in 1995. (Source: Standish Group, publication date: 1995.)
- Over half (52.7 percent) of projects were projected to cost over 189 percent of their original estimates. (Source: Standish Group, publication date: 2000.)
- As many as 88 percent of all U.S. projects are over schedule, over budget, or both. (Source: Standish Group, publication date: 2000.)
- The average time overrun on projects is 222 percent of original estimates. (Source: Standish Group, publication date: 2000.)

Why should we care about productivity and quality? There are several reasons. First and foremost, our customers and end users require a working, quality product. Measuring the process as well as the product tells us whether we've achieved our goal. However, there are other reasons why we need to measure productivity and quality:

The development of systems is becoming increasingly complex. Unless we measure, we will never know whether or not our efforts have been successful.

Occasionally, new technology is used just for its own sake. This is not an effective use of technology. Measuring the effectiveness of an implementation assures us that our decision has been cost-effective.

We measure productivity and quality to quantify the project's progress as well as to quantify the attributes of the product. A metric enables us to understand and manage the process as well as to measure the impact of changes to the process, i.e., new methods, training, etc. The use of metrics also enables us to know when we've met our goals (i.e., usability, performance, test coverage, etc.)

In measuring software systems, we can create metrics based on the different parts of a system—e.g., requirements, specifications, code, documentation, tests, training, etc., For each of these components we can measure its attributes, which include usability, maintainability, extendibility, size, defect level, performance, and completeness.

Although the majority of organizations use metrics found in books such as this one, it is possible to generate metrics specific to a particular task. Characteristics of metrics dictate that they have the following attributes:

1. Collectibility
2. Reproducibility
3. Pertinence
4. System independence

Typical IT Metrics

Sample product metrics include the following:

1. Size: lines of code, pages of documentation, number and size of test, token count, and function count
2. Complexity: decision count, variable count, number of modules, size or volume, and depth of nesting
3. Reliability: count of changes required by phase, count of discovered defects, defect density (number of defects/size), and count of changed lines of code

Sample process metrics include the following:

1. Complexity: time to design, code and test, defect discovery rate by phase, cost to develop, number of external interfaces, and defect fix rate
2. Methods and tools used: number of tools used and why, project infrastructure tools, and tools not used and why
3. Resource metrics: years of experience with team, years of experience with language, years of experience with type of software, MIPS (million instructions per second) per person, support personnel to engineering personnel ratio, nonproject time to project time ratio
4. Productivity: Percentage of time to redesign, percentage of time to redo, variance of schedule, and variance of effort

Once the organization determines the slate of metrics to be implemented, it must develop a methodology for reviewing the results of the metrics program. Metrics are useless if they don't result in improved quality or productivity. At minimum, the organization should take the following measures:

1. Determine the metric and measuring technique.
2. Measure to understand where you are.
3. Establish worst, best, and planned cases.

4. Modify the process or product depending on results of measurement.
5. Remeasure to see what's changed.
6. Iterate.

Developing an IT Assessment Program

A four-stepped procedure (Linkman and Walker, 1991) is outlined for establishing targets and means for IT system development assessment. The procedure is not focused on any particular set of metrics; rather, it selects metrics on the basis of goals. This procedure is suitable for setting up goals for either the entire project deliverables or for any partial product created in the software life cycle.

1. Define measurable goals: The project goals establishment process is similar to the development process for project deliverables. Software projects usually start with abstract problem concepts, and the final project deliverables are obtained by continuously partitioning and refining the problem into tangible and manageable pieces. Final quantified goals can be transformed from initial intangible goals by following the same divide-and-conquer method for software deliverables. Three sources of information are helpful in establishing the targets:
   - Historical data under the assumptions that data is available, development environment is stable, and projects are similar in terms of type, size, and complexity.
   - Synthetic data such as modeling results, is useful if models used are calibrated to the specific development environment.
   - Expert opinions.
2. Maintain balanced goals: The measurable goals are usually established on the basis of the following four factors—cost, schedule, effort, and quality. It is feasible to achieve just a single goal, but it is always a challenge to deliver a project with the minimum staff and resources on time and within budget. It needs to be kept in mind that trade-off is always involved, and all issues should be addressed to reach a set of balanced goals.
3. Set up intermediate goals: A project should never be measured at its endpoint only. Checkpoints should be set up to provide confidence that the project is running on course. The common practice involves setting up quantifiable targets for each phase, measuring the actual values against the targets, and establishing a plan to make corrections for any deviations. All four earlier-mentioned factors (cost, schedule, effort, quality) should be broken down into phases or activities for setting up intermediate targets. Measurements for cost and effort can be divided into machine and human resources according to the software life-cycle phase so that expenditures can be monitored, to ensure that the project is running within budget. Schedules should always be defined in terms of milestones or checkpoints to ensure that intermediate products will be evaluated and final product can be delivered on time. The quality of intermediate products should always be measured to guarantee that the final deliverable will meet its target goal.
4. Establish the means of assessment: This activity involves two aspects: data collection and data analysis. Based on the project characteristics such as size, complexity, level of control, etc., a decision should be made in terms of whether a manual or an automated data collection process should be used. If a nonautomated process is applied, then the availability of the

collection medium at the right time should be emphasized. The following two types of data analyses should be considered:

- Project analysis—This type of analysis, consisting of checkpoint analysis and continuous analysis (trend analysis), is concerned with verifying whether the intermediate targets are being met, to ensure that the project is on the right track.
- Component analysis—This type of analysis concentrates on the finer level of detail of the end product, and is concerned with identifying those components in the product that may require special attention and action. The complete process includes deciding on the set of measures to be analyzed, identifying the components detected as anomalous using measured data, finding out the root cause of the anomalies, and taking corrective actions.

Traditional Configuration Management Metrics

The following metrics are typically used by those measuring the CM process:

1. Average rate of variance from scheduled time.
2. Rate of first-pass approvals.
3. Volume of deviation requests, categorized by cause.
4. The number of scheduled, performed, and completed configuration management audits by each phase of the life cycle.
5. The rate at which new changes are released and the rate at which changes are verified as they are completed. The history compiled from successive deliveries is used to refine the scope of the expected delivery rate.
6. The number of completed versus scheduled (stratified by type and priority) actions.
7. Person-hours per project.
8. Schedule variances.
9. Tests per requirement.
10. Change category count.
11. Changes by source.
12. Cost variances.
13. Errors per thousand lines of code (KSLOC).
14. Requirements volatility.

IEEE Process for Measurement

Using the IEEE methodology (IEEE, 1989), the measurement process can be described in nine stages. These stages may overlap or occur in different sequences depending on organization needs. Each stage in the measurement process is designed to ensure that the delivered product will have high reliability. Other factors influencing the measurement process include the following:

1. A firm management commitment to continually assess product and process maturity, or stability, or both during the project
2. Use of trained personnel who can apply measures to the project in a useful way
3. Software support tools
4. A clear understanding of the distinctions between errors, faults, and failures

Product measure subcategories include the following:

1. Errors, faults, and failures—The count of defects with respect to human cause, program bugs, and observed system malfunctions
2. Mean time to failure, failure rate—A derivative measure of defect occurrence and time
3. Reliability growth and projection—Assessment of change in failure-freeness of the product under testing or operation
4. Remaining product faults—Assessment of fault-freeness of the product in development, testing, or maintenance
5. Completeness and consistency—Assessment of the presence and integration of all necessary software system parts
6. Complexity—Assessment of complicating factors in a system

Process measures include the following:

1. Management control measures address the number and distribution of errors and faults, and an estimate of cost necessary for defect removal.
2. Coverage measures allow one to monitor the ability of developers and managers to guarantee the completion of all the activities of the life cycle, and support the definition of corrective actions.
3. Risk, benefit, and cost evaluation measures support delivery decisions based both on technical and cost criteria.
4. Risk can be assessed on the basis of residual faults present in the product at delivery and the cost of the associated support activity.

The nine stages in the measurement process using the IEEE methodology consist of the following:

Stage 1: Plan the organizational strategy. Initiate a planning process. Form a planning group and review reliability constraints and objectives, giving consideration to user needs and requirements. Identify the reliability characteristics of a software product necessary to achieve these objectives. Establish a strategy for measuring and managing software reliability. Document practices for conducting measurements.

Stage 2: Determine software reliability goals. Define the reliability goals for the software being developed so that reliability can be optimized in light of realistic assessments of project constraints, including size, scope, cost, and schedule.

Review the requirements for the specific development effort, so that the desired characteristics of the delivered software can be determined. For each characteristic, identify specific reliability goals that can be demonstrated by the software or measured against a particular value or condition. Establish an acceptable range of values. Consideration should be given to user needs and requirements. Also, establish intermediate reliability goals at various points in the development effort.

Stage 3: Implement the measurement process. Establish a software reliability measurement process that best fits an organization's needs. Review the rest of the process, and select those stages that best lead to optimum reliability. Add to or enhance these stages as needed. Consider the following suggestions:

1. Select appropriate data collection and measurement practices designed to optimize software reliability.
2. Document the measures required, the intermediate and final milestones when measurements are taken, the data collection requirements, and the acceptable values for each measure.
3. Assign responsibilities for performing and monitoring measurements, and support these activities across the internal organization.
4. Initiate a measure selection and evaluation process.
5. Prepare educational material for training personnel in concepts, principles, and practices of software reliability and reliability measures.

Stage 4: Select potential measures. Identify potential measures that would be helpful in achieving the reliability goals established in Stage 2.

Stage 5: Prepare a data collection and measurement plan for the development and support effort. For each potential measure, determine the primitives needed to perform the measurement. Data should be organized so that information related to events during the development effort can be properly recorded in a database and retained for historical purposes.

For each intermediate reliability goal identified in Stage 2, identify the measures needed to achieve it. Identify the points during development when the measurements are to be taken. Establish acceptable values or a range of values to assess whether the intermediate reliability goals are being achieved.

Include in the plan an approach for monitoring the measurement effort itself. The responsibility for collecting and reporting data, verifying its accuracy, computing measures, and interpreting the results should be described.

Stage 6: Monitor the measurements. Once the data collection and reporting begins, monitor the measurements and the progress made during development, so as to manage the reliability and thereby achieve the goals for the delivered product. The measurements assist in determining whether the intermediate reliability goals are achieved and whether the final goal is achievable. Analyze the measure and determine if the results are sufficient to satisfy the reliability goals. Decide whether a measure helps affirm the reliability of the product or process being measured. Take corrective action.

Stage 7: Assess reliability. Analyze measurements to ensure that the reliability of the delivered software satisfies the reliability objectives and the measured reliability is acceptable. Identify assessment steps that are consistent with the reliability objectives documented in the data collection and measurement plan. Check the consistency of acceptance criteria and the sufficiency of tests to satisfactorily demonstrate that the reliability objectives have been achieved. Identify the organization responsible for determining final acceptance of the reliability of the software. Document the steps in assessing the reliability of the software.

Stage 8: Use software. Assess the effectiveness of the measurement effort and perform necessary corrective action. Conduct a follow-up analysis of the measurement effort to evaluate reliability assessment and development practices, to record the lessons learned and to evaluate user satisfaction with the software's reliability.

Stage 9: Retain software measurement data throughout the development and operation phases for use by future projects. This data provides a baseline for reliability improvement and an opportunity to compare the same measures across completed projects. This information can assist in the development of future guidelines and standards.

Metrics as a Component of the Process Maturity Framework

Pfleeger (1990) has suggested a set of metrics for which data must be collected and analyzed for the improvement of software engineering productivity. This set of metrics is based on a process maturity framework developed at the Software Engineering Institute (SEI) at Carnegie Mellon University. The SEI framework divides organizations into five levels on the basis of how mature (i.e., organized, professional, aligned to software tenets, etc.) the organization is. The five levels range from an initial, or ad hoc, environment to an optimizing environment. Pfleeger recommends that metrics be divided into five levels as well. Each level is based on the amount of information made available to the development process. As the development process matures and improves, additional metrics can be collected and analyzed.

Level 1: Initial Process. This level is characterized by an ad hoc approach to software development. Inputs to the process are not well defined, but the outputs are as expected. Preliminary baseline project metrics should be gathered at this level to form a basis for later comparison as improvements are made and maturity increases. This can be accomplished by comparing new project measurements with the baseline ones.

Level 2: Repeatable Process. At this level the process is repeatable in much the same way that a subroutine is repeatable. The requirements act as input, the code as output, and constraints are budget, schedule, etc. Even though proper inputs produce proper outputs, there is no way to discern easily how the outputs are actually produced. Only project-related metrics make sense at this level, because the activities within the actual transitions from input to output are not available to be measured. Measures at this level can include the following:

1. Amount of effort needed to develop the system
2. Overall project cost
3. Software size: noncommented lines of code, function points, and object and method count
4. Personnel effort: actual person-months of effort and related reports
5. Person-months of effort
6. Requirements volatility: requirements changes

Level 3: Defined Process. At this level the activities of the process are clearly defined. This additional structure means that the input to and output from each well-defined functional activity can be examined, which permits a measurement of the intermediate products. Measures include the following:

1. Requirements complexity: number of distinct objects and actions addressed in requirements
2. Design complexity: number of design modules, cyclomatic complexity, and McCabe design complexity
3. Code complexity: number of code modules and cyclomatic complexity
4. Test complexity: number of paths to test (for object-oriented development, this includes the number of object interfaces to test)
5. Quality metrics: defects discovered, defects discovered per unit size (defect density), requirements faults discovered, design faults discovered, and fault density for each product
6. Pages of documentation

Level 4: Managed Process. At this level, feedback from early project activities are used to set priorities for later project activities. Activities are readily compared and contrasted; the effects of changes in one activity can be tracked in the others. At this level measurements can be made across activities, and they are used to control and stabilize the process so that productivity and quality can match expectations. The following types of data are recommended to be collected. Metrics at this stage, although derived from the following data, are tailored to the individual organization.

1. Process type: What process model is used and how does it correlate to positive or negative consequences?
2. Amount of producer reuse: How much of the system is designed for reuse? This includes reuse of requirements, design modules, test plans, and code.
3. Amount of consumer reuse: How much does the project reuse components from other projects? This includes reuse of requirements, design modules, test plans, and code. (By reusing tested and proven components, effort can be minimized and quality can be improved.)
4. Defect identification: How and when are defects discovered? Knowing this will indicate whether those process activities are effective.
5. Use of defect density model for testing: To what extent does the number of defects determine when testing is complete? This controls and focuses testing as well as increases the quality of the final product.
6. Use of configuration management: Is a configuration management scheme imposed on the development process? This permits traceability, which can be used to assess the impact of alterations.
7. Module completion over time: At what rates are modules being completed? This reflects the degree to which the process and development environment facilitates implementation and testing.

Level 5: Optimizing Process. At this level measures from activities are used to change and improve the process. This process change can affect both the organization and the project. Studies by SEI report that 85 percent of organizations are at Level 1, 14 percent at Level 2, and 1 percent at level 3. None of the firms surveyed had reached levels 4 or 5. Therefore, the authors have not recommended a set of metrics for Level 5.

Steps in Using Metrics

1. Assess the process and determine the level of process maturity.
2. Determine the appropriate metrics to collect.
3. Recommend metrics, tools, and techniques.
4. Estimate project cost and schedule.
5. Collect appropriate level of metrics.
6. Construct project database of metrics data that can be used for analysis and to track value of metrics over time.
7. When the project is complete, evaluate the initial estimates of cost and schedule for accuracy. Determine which of the factors may account for discrepancies between predicted and actual values.
8. Form a basis for future estimates.

IEEE-Defined Metrics

The IEEE standards (1988) were written with the objective of providing the software community with defined measures, which are currently used as indicators of reliability. By emphasizing early reliability assessment, this standard supports methods through measurement to improve product reliability.

This section presents a subset of the IEEE standard that can be easily adapted by the general IT community.

1. Fault density: This measure can be used to predict the remaining faults, by comparison with the expected fault density; determine if sufficient testing has been completed; and establish standard fault densities for comparison and prediction.

$$F_d = F/KSLOC$$

where:

F = total number of unique faults found in a given interval resulting in failures of a specified severity level

KSLOC = number of source lines of executable code and nonexecutable data declarations in thousands

2. Defect density: This measure can be used after design and code inspections of new development or large block modifications. If the defect density is outside the norm after several inspections, it is an indication of a problem.

$$DD = \frac{\sum_{i=1}^{I} D_i}{KSLOD}$$

where:

D_i = total number of unique defects detected during the *i*-th design or code inspection process

I = total number of inspections

KSLOD = in the design phase this is the number of source lines of executable code and nonexecutable data declarations in thousands

3. Cumulative failure profile: This is a graphical method used to predict reliability, estimate additional testing time to reach an acceptable reliable system, and identify modules and subsystems that require additional testing. A plot is drawn of cumulative failures versus a suitable time base.

4. Fault-days number: This measure represents the number of days that faults spend in the system from their time of creation to their removal. For each fault detected and removed, during any phase, the number of days from its creation to its removal is determined (fault-days). The fault-days are then summed for all faults detected and removed, to get the fault-days number at the system level, including all faults detected and removed up to the delivery date. In those cases where the creation date of a fault is not known, the fault is assumed to have been created at the middle of the phase in which it was introduced.

5. Functional or modular test coverage: This measure is used to quantify a software test coverage index for a software delivery. From the system's functional requirements, a cross-reference listing of associated modules must first be created.

FUNCTIONAL (MODULAR) TEST COVERAGE INDEX = $\dfrac{FE}{FT}$

where:

FE = number of the software functional (modular) requirements for which all test cases have been satisfactorily completed

FT = total number of software functional (modular) requirements

6. Requirements traceability: This measure aids in identifying requirements that are either missing from, or have been added to, the original requirements.

$$TM = \frac{R1}{R2} \times 100\%$$

where:

R1 = number of requirements met by the architecture

R2 = number of original requirements

7. Software maturity index: This measure is used to quantify the readiness of a software product. Changes from previous baselines to the current baselines are an indication of the current product stability.

$$SMI = \frac{M_T - \left(F_a + F_c + F_{del}\right)}{M_T}$$

where:

SMI = maturity index

M_T = number of software functions (modules) in the current delivery

F_a = number of software functions (modules) in the current delivery that are additions to the previous delivery

F_c = number of software functions (modules) in the current delivery that include internal changes from a previous delivery

F_{del} = number of software functions (modules) in the previous delivery that are deleted in the current delivery

The Software Maturity Index may be estimated in the following manner:

$$SMI = \frac{M_T - F_c}{M_T}$$

8. Number of conflicting requirements: This measure is used to determine the reliability of a software system resulting from the software architecture under consideration, as represented by a specification based on the entity-relationship-attributed model. What is required is a list of the systems inputs, outputs, and a list of the functions performed by each program.

The mappings from the software architecture to the requirements are identified. Mappings from the same specification item to more than one differing requirement are examined for requirements inconsistency. Additionally, mappings from more than one specification item to a single requirement are examined for specification inconsistency.

9. Cyclomatic complexity: This measure is used to determine the complexity of a coded module. The use of this measure is designed to limit the complexity of the module, thereby promoting understandability of the module.

$$C = E - N + 1$$

where:
   C = complexity
   N = number of nodes (sequential groups of program statements)
   E = number of edges (program flows between nodes)

10. Design structure: This measure is used to determine the simplicity of the detailed design of a software program. The values determined can be used to identify problem areas within the software design.

$$DSM = \sum_{i=1}^{6} W_i\, D_i$$

where:

   DSM = design structure measure
      P1 = total number of modules in program
      P2 = number of modules dependent on input or output
      P3 = number of modules dependent on prior processing (state)
      P4 = number of database elements
      P5 = number of nonunique database elements
      P6 = number of database segments
      P7 = number of modules not single-entrance or single-exit
   The design structure is the weighted sum of six derivatives determined by using the primitives aforementioned.
      D_1 = design organized top-down
      D_2 = module dependence (P2/P1)
      D_3 = module dependent on prior processing (P3/P1)
      D_4 = database size (P5/P4)
      D_5 = database compartmentalization (P6/P4)
      D_6 = module single-entrance or single-exit (P7/P1)
   The weights (W_i) are assigned by the user based on the priority of each associated derivative. Each W_i has a value between 0 and 1.

11. Test coverage: This is a measure of the completeness of the testing process from the perspectives of both developer and user. The measure relates directly to the development, integration, and operational test stages of product development.

$$TC \text{ (in percent)} = \frac{\text{implemented capabilities}}{\text{required capabilities}}$$

$$\times \frac{\text{program primitives tested}}{\text{total program primitives}} \times 100 \text{ percent}$$

where:

program functional primitives are either modules, segments, statements, branches, or paths; data functional primitives are classes of data; and requirement primitives are test cases or functional capabilities

12. Data or information flow complexity: This is a structural complexity or a procedural complexity measure that can be used to evaluate the following: the information flow structure of large-scale systems, the procedure and module information flow structure, the complexity of interconnections between modules, the degree of simplicity of relationships between subsystems, and the correlation of total observed failures and software reliability with data complexity.

$$\text{Weighted IFC} = \text{length} \times (\text{fan-in} \times \text{fan-out})^2$$

where:

IFC = information flow complexity

fan-in = local flows into a procedure + number of data structures from which the procedures retrieve data

fan-out = local flows from a procedure + number of data structures that the procedure updates

length = number of source statements in a procedure (excluding comments)

The flow of information between modules or subsystems needs to be determined either through the use of automated techniques or charting mechanisms. A local flow from module A to module B exists if one of the following occurs:

   a. A calls B.
   b. B calls A, and A returns a value to B that is passed by B.
   c. Both A and B are called by another module that passes a value from A to B.

13. Mean time to failure: This measure is the basic parameter required by most software reliability models. Detailed record keeping of failure occurrences, which accurately tracks the times (calendar or execution) at which the faults manifest themselves is essential.

14. Software documentation and source listings: The objective of this measure is to collect information to identify the parts of the software maintenance products that may be inadequate for use in a software maintenance environment. Questionnaires are used to examine the format and content of the documentation and source code attributes from a maintainability perspective.

The questionnaires examine the following product characteristics:

   a. Modularity
   b. Descriptiveness
   c. Consistency
   d. Simplicity
   e. Expandability

f. Testability

Two questionnaires, the Software Documentation Questionnaire and the Software Source Listing Questionnaire, are used to evaluate the software products in a desk audit.

For the software documentation evaluation, the resource documents should include those that contain the program design specifications, program testing information and procedures, program maintenance information, and guidelines used in preparation of the documentation. Typical issues addressed in the questionnaire include the following:

a. The documentation indicates that data storage locations are not used for more than one type of data structure.

b. Parameter inputs and outputs for each module are explained in the documentation.

c. Programming conventions for I/O processing have been established and followed.

d. The documentation indicates that the resource (storage, timing, tape drives, disks, etc.) allocation is fixed throughout program execution.

e. The documentation indicates that there is a reasonable time margin for each major time-critical program function.

f. The documentation indicates that the program has been designed to accommodate software test probes to aid in assessing processing performance.

The software source listings evaluation reviews either high-order language or assembler source code. Multiple evaluations using the questionnaire are conducted for the unit level of the program (module). The modules selected should represent a sample size of at least 10 percent of the total source code. Typical evaluation topics include the following:

a. Each function of the module under consideration is an easily recognizable block of code.

b. The number of comments does not detract from the legibility of the source listings.

c. Mathematical models described or derived in the documentation correspond to the mathematical equations used in the source listing.

d. Esoteric (clever) programming is avoided in the module under consideration.

e. The size of any data structure that affects the processing logic of the module under consideration is parameterized.

f. Intermediate results within the module can be selectively collected for display without code modification.

IT Developer's List of Metrics

McCabe's Complexity Metric (1976): McCabe's proposal for a cyclomatic complexity number was the first attempt to objectively quantify the "flow of control" complexity of software.

The metric is computed by decomposing the program into a directed graph that represents its flow of control. The cyclomatic complexity number is then calculated using the following formula:

$$V(g) = edges - nodes + 2$$

In its shortened form, the cyclomatic complexity number is a count of decision points within a program with a single entry and a single exit plus one.

Halstead Effort Metric (1977): In the 1970s Maurice Halstead developed a theory regarding the behavior of software. Some of his findings evolved into software metrics. One of these is referred to as "Effort" or just "E," and is a well-known complexity metric. The Effort measure is calculated using the following formula:

$$E = Volume/Level$$

where Volume is a measure of the size of a piece of code and Level is a measure of how abstract the program is. The level of abstraction varies from almost 0 (low level) to almost 1 (high level).

References*

Halstead, M. (1977). *Elements of Software Science.* New York: Elsevier.

IEEE Guide for the Use of IEEE Standard Dictionary of Measures to Produce Reliable Software (June 12, 1989). Standard 982.2-1988. IEEE Standards Department. Piscatawy, NJ.

IEEE Standard of Measures to Produce Reliable Software. Standard 982.1-1988. IEEE Standards Department. Piscataway, NJ.

Linkman, S.G. and Walker, J.G. Controlling programs through measurement. Information and Software Technology, Vol. 33, No 1 (1991), pp. 93–102.

McCabe, T. (December 1976). A complexity measure. *IEEE Transactions on Software Engineering.* 308–320.

Pfleeger, S.L. and C. McGowan (1990). Software Metrics in the Process Maturity Framework. *Journal of Systems Software.* Vol 12. pp. 255–261.

---

* The information contained within the IEEE standards metrics section is copyrighted information of the IEEE, extracted from IEEE Std. 982.1-1988, IEEE Standard Dictionary of Measures to Produce Reliable Software. This information was written within the context of IEEE Std 982.1-1988 and the IEEE takes no responsibility for or liability for damages resulting from the reader's misinterpretation of said information resulting from the placement and context of this publication.

Reference B: Value Measuring Methodology[1]

The purpose of the Value Measuring Methodology (VMM) is to define, capture, and measure value associated with electronic services, but unaccounted for in traditional return-on-investment (ROI) calculations; to fully account for costs; and to identify and assess risk. Developed in response to the changing definition of value brought about by the advent of the Internet and advanced software technology, VMM incorporates aspects of numerous traditional business analysis theories and methodologies, as well as newer hybrid approaches.

VMM was designed to be used by organizations across the federal government to steer the development of an E-government initiative, to assist decision makers in choosing among investment alternatives, to provide the information required to manage effectively, and to maximize the benefit of an investment to the government.

VMM is based on public and private sector business and economic analysis theories and best practices. It provides the structure, tools, and techniques for comprehensive quantitative analysis and comparison of value (benefits), cost, and risk at the appropriate level of detail.

This reference provides a high-level overview of the four steps that constitute the VMM framework. The terminology used to describe the steps should be familiar to those involved in developing, selecting, justifying, and managing an IT investment. The steps are as follows:

Step 1: Develop a decision framework
Step 2: Perform alternatives analysis—estimate value, costs, and risk
Step 3: Pull the information together
Step 4: Communicate and document

Step 1: Develop a Decision Framework

A decision framework provides a structure for defining the objectives of an initiative, analyzing alternatives, and managing and evaluating ongoing performance. Just as an outline defines a document's organization before it is written, a decision framework creates an outline for designing, analyzing, and selecting an initiative for investment, and then, managing that investment.

The framework facilitates the establishment of consistent measures for evaluating existing or proposed initiatives. Program managers may use the decision framework as a tool to understand and prioritize the needs of customers and the organization's business goals. In addition, it

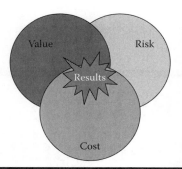

Figure B.1   The decision framework.

encourages early consideration of risk and thorough planning practices directly related to effective E-government initiative implementation.

The decision framework should be developed as early as possible in the development of a technology initiative. Employing the framework at the earliest phase of development makes it an effective tool for defining the benefits that an initiative will deliver, the risks that are likely to jeopardize its success, and the anticipated costs that must be secured and managed. The decision framework is also helpful later in the development process as a tool to validate the direction of an initiative or to evaluate an initiative that has already been implemented.

The decision framework consists of value (benefits), cost, and risk structures, as shown in Figure B.1. Each of these three elements must be understood to plan, justify, implement, evaluate, and manage an investment.

The tasks and outputs involved in creating a sound decision framework include the following:

	Tasks	Outputs
1.	Identify and define value structure	Prioritized value factors Defined and prioritized measures within each value factor
2.	Identify and define risk structure	Risk factor inventory (initial) Risk tolerance boundary
3.	Identify and define cost structure	Tailored cost structure
4.	Begin documentation	Initial documentation of basis of estimate of cost, value, and risk

Task 1: Identify and Define Value Structure

The value structure describes and prioritizes benefits in two layers. The first layer considers an initiative's ability to deliver value within each of the five value factors (User Value, Social Value, Financial Value, Operational and Foundational Value, and Strategic Value). The second layer delineates the measures to define those values.

By defining the value structure, managers gain a prioritized understanding of the stakeholder's needs. This task also requires the definition of metrics and targets critical to the comparison of alternatives and performance evaluation.

Value Factor	Definitions and Examples
Direct Customer (User)	Benefits to users or groups associated with providing a service through an electronic channel *Example: Convenient Access*
Social (non-User/Public)	Benefits to society as a whole *Example: Trust in government*
Gov't/Operational Foundational	Improvements in Government operations and enablement of future initiatives *Example: Cycle Time; Improved Infrastructure*
Strategic/Political	Contributions to achieving strategic goals, priorities and mandates *Example: Fulfilling the organizational mission*
Government Financial	Financial benefits to both sponsoring and other agencies *Example: Reduced cost of correcting errors*

Figure B.2   Value factors.

Direct User Value Factor		
Concise, Illustrative Name		
24/7 Access to Real-Time Information & Services, Anytime & Anywhere		
Brief Description		
Are customers able to access real-time electronic travel services and policy information from any location 24 hours a day?		
Metrics and Scales		
	% of remote access attempts that are successful (10 points for every 10%)	
	% of travel services available electronically 10 points = 25% 90 points = 75% (threshold requirement) 100 points = 100%	
	Is data updated in the system in real time? No = 0 Yes = 100	

Figure B.3   An example of a value factor, with associated metrics.

The value factors consist of five separate, but related, perspectives on value. As defined in Figure B.2, each factor contributes to the full breadth and depth of the value offered by the initiative. Because the value factors are usually not equal in importance, they must be weighted according to their importance to executive management.

Identification, definition, and prioritization of measures of success must be performed within each value factor, as shown in Figure B.3. Valid results depend on project staff working directly with representatives of user communities to define and array the measures in order of importance. These measures are used to define alternatives, and also serve as a basis for alternatives analysis, comparison, and selection, as well as ongoing performance evaluation.

In some instances, measures may be defined at a higher level to be applied across a related group of initiatives, such as organizationwide or across a focus-area portfolio. These standardized measures then facilitate "apples-to-apples" comparison across multiple initiatives. This comparison provides a standard management yardstick against which to judge investments.

Whether a measure has been defined by project staff or at a higher level of management, it must include the identification of a metric, a target, and a normalized scale. The normalized scale provides a method for integrating objective and subjective measures of value into a single decision metric. The scale used is not important; what is important is that the scale remain consistent. The measures within the value factors are prioritized by representatives from the user and stakeholder communities during facilitated group sessions.

Task 2: Identify and Define Risk Structure

The risk associated with an investment in a technology initiative may degrade performance, impede implementation, or increase costs. Risk that is not identified cannot be mitigated or managed, causing a project to fail in the pursuit of funding or, more dramatically, during implementation. The greater the attention paid to mitigating and managing risk, the greater the probability of success.

The risk structure serves a dual purpose. First, the structure provides the starting point for identifying and inventorying potential risk factors that may jeopardize an initiative's success and ensures that plans for mitigating their impact are developed and incorporated into each viable alternative solution. Second, the structure provides management the information it needs to communicate its organization's tolerance for risk. Risk tolerance is expressed in terms of cost (what is the maximum acceptable cost creep beyond the projected cost) and value (what is the maximum tolerable performance slippage).

Risks are identified and documented during working sessions with stakeholders. Issues raised during preliminary planning sessions are discovered, defined, and documented. The result is an initial risk inventory.

To map risk tolerance boundaries, selected knowledgeable staff are polled to identify at least five data points that will define the highest acceptable level of risk for cost and value.

Task 3: Identify and Define the Cost Structure

A cost structure is a hierarchy of elements created specifically to accomplish the development of a cost estimate, and is also called a cost element structure (CES). The most significant objective in the development of a cost structure is to ensure a complete and comprehensive cost estimate and to reduce the risk of missing costs or double counting. An accurate and complete cost estimate is critical for an initiative's success. Incomplete or inaccurate estimates can result in exceeding the budget for implementation, thus requiring justification for additional funding or a reduction in scope. The cost structure developed in this step will be used during Step 2 to estimate the cost for each alternative.

Ideally, a cost structure will be produced early in development, before defining alternatives. However, a cost structure can also be developed after an alternative has been selected or, in some cases, in the early stage of implementation. Early structuring of costs guides refinement and improvement of the estimate during planning and implementation.

Task 4: Begin Documentation

Documentation of the elements leading to the selection of a particular alternative is the "audit trail" for that decision. The documentation of assumptions, the analysis, the data, and the decisions and rationale behind them is the foundation for the business case and the record of information required to defend a cost estimate or value analysis.

Early documentation will capture the conceptual solution, the desired benefits, and the attendant global assumptions (e.g., economic factors such as the discount and inflation rates). The documentation also includes project-specific drivers and assumptions derived from tailoring the structures.

The basis for the estimate, including assumptions and business rules, should be organized in an easy-to-follow manner that links to all other analysis processes and requirements. This will provide easy access to information supporting the course of action and will also ease the burden associated with preparing investment justification documents. As an initiative evolves through the life cycle, becoming better defined and more specific, the documentation will also mature in specificity and definition.

Step 2: Alternatives Analysis—Estimate Value, Costs, and Risk

An alternatives analysis is an estimation and evaluation of all value, cost, and risk factors (see Figure B.4 for risk categories) leading to the selection of the most effective plan of action to address a specific business issue (e.g., service, policy, regulation, business process, or system). An alternative that must be considered is the *base case*. The base case is the alternative where no change is made to existing practices or systems. All other alternatives are compared against the base case as well as with one another.

In alternatives analysis, a rigorous process that considers the range of possible actions to achieve the desired benefits is required. The process yields the data required to justify an investment or course of action. It also provides the information required to support the completion of the budget justification documents. The process produces a baseline of anticipated value, costs, and risks to guide the management and ongoing evaluation of an investment.

An alternatives analysis must consistently assess the value, cost, and risk associated with more than one alternative for a specific initiative. Alternatives must include the base case and accommodate specific parameters of the decision framework. VMM, properly used, is designed to avoid "analysis paralysis."

The estimation of cost and projection of value uses ranges to define the individual elements of each structure. Those ranges are then subject to an uncertainty analysis (see Note 1 in this reference). The result is a range of expected values and cost. Next, a sensitivity analysis (see Note 2 in this reference) identifies the variables that have a significant impact on this expected value and cost. The analyses will increase confidence in the accuracy of the cost and predicted performance estimates (see Figure B.5 on predicting performance). However, a risk analysis is critical

Defining Risk

In the assessment of an e-Travel initiative, risks were bundled into five categories: cost, technical, schedule, operational, and legal.

The following sample table demonstrates how a single "risk factor" is likely to impact multiple risk categories. Note the level of detail provided in the description. Specificity is critical to distinguish among risks and avoid double counting.

Selected e-Travel Initiative Risks by Risk Category	Cost	Tech	Shc.	Op.	Legal
Different agencies have different levels and quality of security mechanisms, which may leave government data vulnerable. Web-enabled system will have increased points of entry for unauthorized internal or external users and pose greater security risks.	X	X			
The e-Travel concept relies heavily on technology. Although, the private sector has reduced travel fees and operational costs by implementing e-Travel services, the commercial sector has not yet widely adopted/developed end-to-end solutions that meet the broad needs (single end-to-end electronic system) articulated by the e-Travel initiative. The technology and applications may not be mature enough to provide all of the functionality sought by the e-Travel initiative managers.	X	X	X	X	
Resistance to change may be partially due to fear of job loss, which may lead to challenges from unions.			X	X	X

Figure B.4   Risk can be bundled across categories.

VMM in Action

Predicting Performance

Example 1: This measure was established for an e-Travel initiative in the Direct User Value Factor.

Value	10	20	30	40	50	60	70	80	90	100
Average # hours from receipt of customer feedback message to response	48.00	44.67	41.33	38.00	34.67	31.33	28.00	24.67	21.33	18.00

Analysts projected the low, expected, and high performance for that measure.

	Low	Expected	High
Average # hours from receipt of customer feedback message to response	38	24	18

The model translated those projections onto the normalized scale.

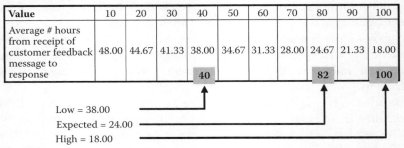

Example 2: This measure was established for Alternative 2 in the Direct User Value Factor. The normalized scale set for this measure was binary.

Normalized Value Scale

Value Points	0	10	20	30	40	50	60	70	80	90	NO
Duplicate Entry of Data	Yes										

Figure B.5   Predicting performance.

to determine the degree to which other factors may drive up expected costs or degrade predicted performance.

An alternatives analysis must be carried out periodically throughout the life cycle of an initiative. The following list provides an overview of how the business value resulting from an alternatives analysis changes depending on where in the life cycle the analysis is conducted.

1. Strategic planning (predecisional)
   a. How well will each alternative perform against the defined value measures?
   b. What will each alternative cost?
   c. What is the risk associated with each alternative?
   d. What will happen if no investment is made at all (base case)?
   e. What assumptions were used to produce the cost estimates and value projections?
2. Business modeling and pilots
   a. What value is delivered by the initiative?

    b. What are the actual costs to date? Do estimated costs need to be reexamined?

    c. Have all risks been addressed and managed?

3. Implementation and evaluation

    a. Does the initiative deliver the predicted value? What is the level of value delivered?

    b. What are the actual costs to date?

    c. Which risks have been realized, how do they affect costs and performance, and how are they being managed?

The tasks and outputs involved in conducting an alternatives analysis include the following:

	Tasks	Outputs
1.	Identify and define alternatives	Viable alternatives
2.	Estimate value and cost	Cost and value analyses
3.	Conduct risk analysis	Risk analyses
4.	Ongoing documentation	Tailored basis of estimate documenting value, cost, and risk factors and assumptions

Task 1: Identify and Define Alternatives

The challenge for this task is to identify viable alternatives that have the potential to deliver an optimum mix of both value and cost efficiency. Decision makers must be given, at minimum, two alternatives in addition to the base case to make an informed investment decision.

The starting point for developing alternatives should be the information in the value structure and preliminary drivers that were identified in the initial basis of estimate (see Step 1). Using this information will help to ensure that the alternatives, and ultimately, the solution chosen, accurately reflect a balance of performance, priorities, and business imperatives. Successfully identifying and defining alternatives requires cross-functional collaboration and discussion among the stakeholders.

The base case explores the impact of identified drivers on value and cost if an alternative solution is not implemented. That may mean that existing processes and systems are kept in place or that organizations will build a patchwork of incompatible, disparate solutions. A base case should always be included in the analysis of alternatives.

Task 2: Estimate Value and Cost

Comparison of alternatives, justification for funding, creation of a baseline against which ongoing performance may be compared, and development of a foundation for more detailed planning requires an accurate estimate of an initiative's cost and value. The more reliable the estimated value and cost of the alternatives, the greater the confidence one can have in the investment decision.

The first activity to pursue when estimating value and cost is the collection of data. Data sources and detail will vary depending on an initiative's stage of development. Organizations should recognize that more detailed information may be available at a later stage in the process and should provide the best estimates in the early stages rather than delaying the process by continuing to search for information that is likely not available.

To capture cost and performance data, and conduct the VMM analyses, a VMM model should be constructed. The model facilitates the normalization and aggregation of cost and value, as well as the performance of uncertainty, sensitivity, and risk analyses.

Analysts populate the model with the dollar amounts for each cost element and the projected performance for each measure. These predicted values, or the underlying drivers, will be expressed in ranges (e.g., low, expected, or high). The range between the low and high values will be determined on the basis of the amount of uncertainty associated with the projection.

Initial cost and value estimates are rarely accurate. Uncertainty and sensitivity analyses increase confidence that likely cost and value have been identified for each alternative.

Task 3: Conduct Risk Analysis

The only risks that can be managed are those that have been identified and assessed. A risk analysis considers the probability and potential negative impact of specific factors on an organization's ability to realize projected benefits or estimated cost, as shown in Figure B.6.

Even after diligent and comprehensive risk mitigation during the planning stage, some level of residual risk will remain that may lead to increased costs and decreased performance. A rigorous risk analysis will help an organization to better understand the probability that a risk will occur and the level of impact the occurrence of the risk will have on both cost and value. Additionally, risk analysis provides a foundation for building a comprehensive risk management plan.

Task 4: Ongoing Documentation

Inherent in these activities is the need to document the assumptions and research that compensate for gaps in information or understanding. For each alternative, the initial documentation of the high-level assumptions and risks will be expanded to include a general description of the alternative being analyzed, a comprehensive list of cost and value assumptions, and assumptions regarding the risks associated with a specific alternative. This often expands the initial risk inventory.

VMM In Action

Assessing Probability and Impact

Below are excerpts from tables developed for the risk analysis of an e-Authentication initiative. Note that the impact and probability of risk were assessed for both cost and value.

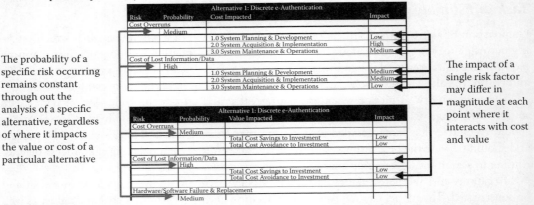

Figure B.6   Assessing probability and impact.

Step 3: Pull Together the Information

As shown in Figure B.7, the estimation of cost, value, and risk provide important data points for investment decision making. However, when analyzing an alternative and making an investment decision, it is critical to understand the relationships between them.

	Tasks	Outputs
1.	Aggregate the cost estimate	Cost estimate
2.	Calculate the return on investment	Return-on-investment metrics
3.	Calculate the value score	Value score
4.	Calculate the risk scores (cost and value)	Risk scores (cost and value)
5.	Compare value, cost, and risk	Comparison of cost, value, and risk

Task 1: Aggregate the Cost Estimate

A complete and valid cost estimate is critical to determining whether or not a specific alternative should be selected. It is also used to assess how much funding must be requested. Understating cost estimates to gain approval, or not considering all costs, may create doubts regarding the veracity of the entire analysis. An inaccurate cost estimate might lead to cost overruns, create the need

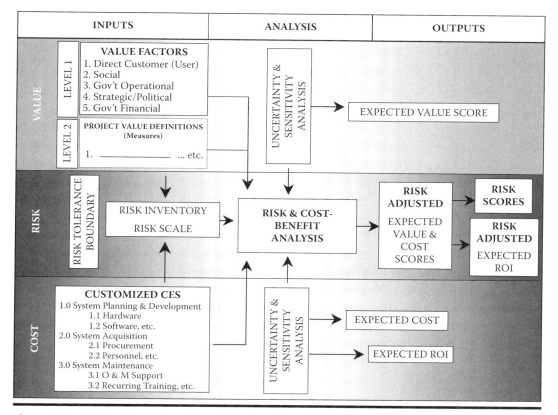

Figure B.7   Risk and cost–benefit analysis.

to request additional funding, or reduce scope. The total cost estimate is calculated by aggregating expected values for each cost element.

Task 2: Calculate the ROI

ROI metrics express the relationship between the funds invested in an initiative and the financial benefits the initiative will generate. Simply stated, it expresses the financial "bang for the buck." Although it is not considered the only measure on the basis of which an investment decision should be made, ROI is, and will continue to be, a critical data point for decision making.

Task 3: Calculate the Value Score

The value score quantifies the full range of value that will be delivered across the five value factors as defined against the prioritized measures within the decision framework. The interpretation of a value score will vary depending on the level from which it is being viewed. At the program level, the value score will be viewed as a yardstick of how alternatives performed against a specific set of measures. These measures will be used to make an "apples-to-apples" comparison of the value delivered by multiple alternatives for a single initiative.

For example, the alternative that has a value score of 80 will be preferred over the alternative with a value score of 20, if no other factors are considered. At the organizational or portfolio level, value scores are used as data points for the selection of initiatives to be included in an investment portfolio. As the objectives and measures associated with each initiative will vary, decision makers at the senior level use value scores to determine what percentage of identified value an initiative will deliver. For example, an initiative with a value score of 75 is providing 75 percent of the possible value that it has the potential to deliver. To understand what exactly is being delivered, the decision maker will have to look at the measures of the value structure.

Consider the value score as a simple math problem. The scores projected for each of the measures within a value factor should be aggregated according to their established weights. The weighted sum of these scores is a factor's value score. The sum of the factors' value scores, aggregated according to their weights, is the total value score.

Task 4: Calculate the Risk Scores

After considering the probability and potential impact of risks, risk scores are calculated to represent a percentage of overall performance slippage or cost increase.

Risk scores provide decision makers with a mechanism to determine the degree to which value and cost will be negatively affected and whether that degree of risk is acceptable on the basis of the risk tolerance boundaries defined by senior staff. If a selected alternative has a high-cost or high-value risk score, program management is alerted to the need for additional risk mitigation, project definition, or more detailed risk management planning. Actions to mitigate the risk may include establishment of a reserve fund, a reduction of scope, or refinement of the alternative's definition. Reactions to excessive risk may also include reconsideration of whether it is prudent to invest in the project at all, given the potential risks, the probability of their occurrence, and the actions required to mitigate them.

Task 5: Compare Value, Cost, and Risk

Tasks 1–4 of Step 3 analyze and estimate the value, cost, and risk associated with an alternative. In isolation, each data point does not provide the depth of information required to ensure sound investment decisions.

Before the advent of VMM, only financial benefits could be compared to investment costs through the development of an ROI metric. When comparing alternatives, the consistency of the decision framework allows the determination of how much value will be received for the funds invested. Additionally, the use of risk scores provides insight into how all cost and value estimates are affected by risk.

By performing straightforward calculations, it is possible to model the relationships among value, cost, and risk as follows:

1. The effect risk will have on estimated value and cost.
2. The financial ROI.
3. If comparing alternatives, the "bang for the buck" value (total value returned compared to total required investment).
4. If comparing initiatives to be included in the investment portfolio, senior managers can look deeper into the decision framework, moving beyond overall scores to determine the scope of benefits through an examination of the measures and their associated targets.

Step 4: Communicate and Document

Regardless of the projected merits of an initiative, its success will depend heavily on the ability of its proponents to generate internal support, to gain buy-in from targeted users, and to foster the development of active supporters of the leadership (champions). Success or failure may depend as much on the utility and efficacy of an initiative as it does on the ability to communicate its value in a manner that is meaningful to stakeholders who have diverse definitions of value. The value of an initiative can be expressed to address the diverse definitions of stakeholder value in funding justification documents and in materials designed to inform and enlist support.

Using VMM, the value of a project is decomposed according to the different value factors. This gives project-level managers the tools to customize their value proposition according to the perspective of their particular audience. Additionally, the structure provides the flexibility to respond accurately and quickly to project changes requiring analysis and justification.

The tasks and outputs associated with Step 4 are as follows:

	Tasks	Outputs
1.	Communicate value to customers and stakeholders	Documentation, insight, and support For communicating initiatives value
2.	Prepare budget justification documents	For Exhibit 300 data and analytical needs
3.	Satisfy ad hoc reporting requirements	Change and ad hoc reporting requirements
4.	Use lessons learned to improve processes	To develop results-based management controls For improving decision making and performance measurement through Lessons Learned

Task 1: Communicate Value to Customers and Stakeholders

Leveraging the results of VMM analysis can facilitate relations with customers and stakeholders. VMM makes communication with diverse audiences easier by incorporating the perspectives of all potential audience members from the outset of analysis. Because VMM calculates the potential value that an investment could realize for all stakeholders, it provides data pertinent to each of those stakeholder perspectives, which can then be used to bolster support for the project. It also fosters substantive discussion with customers regarding the priorities and detailed plans of the investment. These stronger relationships not only prove critical to the long-term success of the project, but can also lay the foundation for future improvements and innovation.

Task 2: Prepare Budget Justification Documents

Many organizations require comprehensive analysis and justification to support funding requests. IT initiatives may not be funded if they have not proved the following:

1. Their applicability to executive missions
2. Sound planning
3. Significant benefits
4. Clear calculations and logic justifying the amount of funding requested
5. Adequate risk identification and mitigation efforts
6. A system for measuring effectiveness
7. Full consideration of alternatives
8. Full consideration of how the project fits within the confines of other government entities and current law

After completion of the VMM, one will have data required to complete or support completion of budget justification documents.

Task 3: Satisfy Ad Hoc Reporting Requirements

Once a VMM model has been built to assimilate and analyze a set of investment alternatives, it can easily be tailored to support ad hoc requests for information or other reporting requirements. In the current rapidly changing political and technological environment, project managers often need to be able to perform rapid analysis. For example, funding authorities, agency partners, market pricing fluctuations, or portfolio managers might impose modifications on the details (e.g., the weighting factors) of a project investment plan; many of these parties are also likely to request additional investment-related information later in the project life cycle. VMM's customized decision framework makes such adjustments and reporting feasible under short time constraints.

Task 4: Use Lessons Learned to Improve Processes

Lessons learned through the use of VMM can be a powerful tool when used to improve overall organizational decision-making and management processes. For example, in the process of identifying metrics, one may discover that adequate mechanisms to collect critical performance information are not in place. Using this lesson to improve measurement mechanisms will give an organization improved capabilities to gauge the project's success and mission fulfillment, demonstrate progress to stakeholders and funding authorities, and identify shortfalls in performance that could be remedied.

Note 1: Uncertainty Analysis

Conducting an uncertainty analysis requires the following:

1. Identify the variables: Develop a range of values for each variable. This range expresses the level of uncertainty about the projection. For example, an analyst may be unsure whether an Internet application will serve a population of 100 or 100,000. It is important to be aware of and express this uncertainty when developing the model so that the reliability of the model in predicting results can be accurately defined.
2. Identify the probability distribution for the selected variables: For each variable identified, assign a probability distribution. There are several types of probability distributions. A triangular probability distribution is frequently used for this type of analysis. In addition to establishing the probability distribution for each variable, the analyst must also determine whether the actual amount is likely to be high or low.
3. Run the simulation: Once the variables' level of uncertainty has been identified and each one has been assigned a probability distribution, run the Monte Carlo simulation. The simulation provides the analyst the information required to determine the range (low to high) and expected results for both the value projection and cost estimate. As shown in Figure B.8, the output of the Monte Carlo simulation produces a range of possible results and defines the mean (the point at which there is an equal chance that the actual value or cost will be higher or lower). The analyst then surveys the range and selects the expected value.

VMM In Action

Uncertainty Results

Below is a sample generated by running an automated Monte Carlo simulation on the VMM Model.

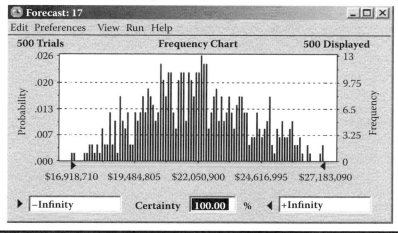

Figure B.8   Output of the Monte Carlo simulation.

Build 5/6 Schedule Slip	.95			▓▓▓▓▓▓▓▓▓▓▓▓▓▓▓
Build 4.0/4.1 Schedule Slip	.17			▓▓
Development-Application S/W OSD Contra	.12			▓
Development: Support Contractors	.07			▓
Development-PRC CLIN 0004 FTE	.04			▓
OSO-NCF	−.03			▓
L82	.03			▓
Development-Tech Support: OSD	.02			▓
CLIN 0101	.02			▓
Development-Application S/W: OSD	.02			▓
Deployment-PRC PM	.02			▓
Deployment: Support Contractors	.00			▓

Figure B.9   A sample sensitivity chart.

Note 2: Sensitivity Analysis

Sensitivity analysis is used to identify the business drivers that have the greatest impact on potential variations of an alternative's cost and its returned value. Many of the assumptions made at the beginning of a project's definition phase will be found to be inaccurate later in the analysis. Therefore, one must consider how sensitive a total cost estimate or value projection is to changes in the data used to produce the result. Insight from this analysis allows stakeholders not only to identify variables that require additional research to reduce uncertainty, but also to justify the cost of that research.

The information required to conduct a sensitivity analysis is derived from the same Monte Carlo simulation used for the uncertainty analysis. Figure B.9 shows a sample sensitivity chart. On the basis of this chart, it is clear that "Build 5/6 Schedule Slip" is the most sensitive variable.

Definitions

analytic hierarchy process (AHP): A proven methodology that uses comparisons of paired elements (comparing one against the other) to determine the relative importance of criteria mathematically.

benchmark: A measurement or standard that serves as a point of reference by which process performance is measured.

benefit: A term used to indicate an advantage, profit, or gain attained by an individual or organization.

benefit-to-cost ratio (BCR): The computation of the financial benefit-to-cost ratio, given by the following formula: benefits ÷ cost.

cost element structure (CES): A hierarchical structure created to facilitate the development of a cost estimate. May include elements that are not strictly products to be developed or produced, e.g., travel, risk, program management reserve, life-cycle phases, etc. Samples include the following:

1. System planning and development
   1.1 Hardware
   1.2 Software
       1.2.1 Licensing fees
   1.3 Development support
       1.3.1 Program management oversight
       1.3.2 System engineering architecture design
       1.3.3 Change management and risk assessment
       1.3.4 Requirements definition and data architecture
       1.3.5 Test and evaluation
   1.4 Studies
       1.4.1 Security
       1.4.2 Accessibility
       1.4.3 Data architecture
       1.4.4 Network architecture
   1.5 Other
       1.5.1 Facilities
       1.5.2 Travel
2. System acquisition and implementation
   2.1 Procurement
       2.1.1 Hardware
       2.1.2 Software
       2.1.3 Customized software
   2.2 Personnel
   2.3 Training
3. System maintenance and operations
   3.1 Hardware
       3.1.1 Maintenance
       3.1.2 Upgrades
       3.1.3 Life-cycle replacement
   3.2 Software
       3.2.1 Maintenance
       3.2.2 Upgrades
       3.2.3 License fees
   3.3 Support
       3.3.1 Help desk
       3.3.2 Security
       3.3.3 Training

cost estimate: The estimation of a project's life-cycle costs, time-phased by fiscal year, based on the description of a project's or system's technical, programmatic, and operational parameters. A cost estimate may also include related analyses such as cost–risk analyses, cost–benefit analyses, schedule analyses, and trade studies.

commercial cost-estimating tools:
    PRICE S (PRICE Software) – A parametric model used to estimate software size, development cost, and schedules, along with software operations and support costs. Software size estimates can be generated for source lines of code, function points, or

predictive objective points. Software development costs are estimated on the basis of input parameters reflecting the difficulty, reliability, productivity, and size of the project. These parameters are used to generate operations and support costs. Monte Carlo risk simulation can be generated as part of the model output. Government agencies (e.g., NASA, IRS, U.S. Air Force, U.S. Army, U.S. Navy, etc.) as well as private companies have used PRICE S.

PRICE H (PRICE Hardware) – HL (PRICE Hardware Life Cycle), M (PRICE Electronic Module and Microcircuit Model) – A suite of hardware parametric cost models used to estimate hardware development, production, and operations and support costs. These hardware models provide the capability to generate a total ownership cost to support program management decisions. Monte Carlo risk simulation can be generated as part of the model output. Government agencies (e.g., NASA, U.S. Air Force, U.S. Army, U.S. Navy, etc.) as well as private companies have used the PRICE suite of hardware models.

SEER-SEM (System Evaluations and Estimation of Resources-Software – Estimating Model) – A parametric modeling tool used to estimate software development costs, schedules, and staff resource requirements. On the basis of the input parameters provided, SEER-SEM can be used to develop cost, schedule, and resource requirement estimates for a given software development project.

SEER-H (System Evaluations and Estimation of Resources-Hybrid) – A hybrid cost-estimating tool that combines analogous and parametric cost-estimating techniques to produce models that accurately estimate hardware development, production, and operations and maintenance cost. SEER-H can be used to support a program manager's hardware life-cycle cost estimate, or provide an independent check on vendor quotes or estimates developed by third parties. SEER-H is part of a family of models from Galorath Associates, including SEER-SEM (which estimates the development and production costs of software) and SEER-DFM (used to support design for manufacturability analyses).

data sources (by phase of development):

1. Strategic planning
   1.1 Strategic and performance plans
   1.2 Subject matter expert input
   1.3 New and existing user surveys
   1.4 Private/public sector best practices, lessons learned, and benchmarks
   1.5 Enterprise architecture
   1.6 Modeling and simulation
   1.7 Vendor market survey
2. Business modeling and pilots
   2.1 Subject matter expert input
   2.2 New and existing user surveys
   2.3 Best practices, lessons learned, and benchmarks
   2.4 Refinement of modeling and simulation
3. Implementation and evaluation
   3.1 Data from phased implementation
   3.2 Actual spending/cost data
   3.3 User group/stakeholder focus groups
   3.4 Other performance measurement

internal rate of return (IRR): The discount rate that sets the net present value of the program or project to zero. Although IRR does not generally provide an acceptable decision criterion, it does provide useful information, particularly when budgets are constrained or there is uncertainty about the appropriate discount rate.

life-cycle costs: The overall estimated cost for a particular program alternative over the time period corresponding to the life of that program, including direct and indirect initial costs plus any periodic or continuing costs of operation and maintenance.

Monte Carlo simulation: A simulation is any analytical method that is meant to model a real-life system, especially when other analyses are too mathematically complex or too difficult to reproduce. Spreadsheet risk analysis uses both a spreadsheet model and simulation to analyze the effect of varying inputs on the outputs of the modeled system. One type of spreadsheet simulation is the Monte Carlo simulation, which randomly generates values for uncertain variables repeatedly to simulate a model. (Monte Carlo simulation was named for Monte Carlo, Monaco, where the primary attractions are casinos hosting games of chance.) Analysts identify all key assumptions for which the outcome is uncertain. For the life cycle, numerous inputs are each assigned one of several probability distributions. The type of distribution selected depended on the conditions surrounding the variable. During simulation, the value used in the cost model is selected randomly from the defined possibilities.

net present value (NPV): Defined as the difference between the present value of benefits and the present value of costs. The benefits referred to in this calculation must be quantified in cost or financial terms to be included. NPV is expressed by the following formula: Net Present Value = [PV(Internal Project Cost Savings, Operational) + PV (Mission Cost Savings)] – PV(Initial Investment).

polling tools:

option finder – A real-time polling device that permits participants, using handheld remotes, to vote on questions and have the results displayed immediately—with statistical information such as degree of variance—and discussed.

group systems – A tool that allows participants to answer questions using individual laptops. The answers to these questions are then displayed to all participants, anonymously, to spur discussion and free-flowing exchange of ideas. Group systems also have a polling device.

return-on-investment (ROI): A financial management approach used to explain how well a project delivers benefits in relation to its cost. Several methods are used to calculate a return on investment. Refer to internal rate of return (IRR), net present value (NPV), and savings-to-investment ratio (SIR).

risk: A term used to define the class of factors that have a measurable probability of occurring during an investment's life cycle, have an associated cost or effect on the investment's output or outcome (typically an adverse effect that jeopardizes the success of an investment), and have alternatives from which the organization may choose.

risk categories:

1. Project resources/financial – Risk associated with cost creep, misestimation of life-cycle costs, reliance on a small number of vendors without cost controls, and (poor) acquisition planning.

2. Technical/technology – Risk associated with immaturity of commercially available technology, reliance on a small number of vendors, technical problems/failures with applications, and its ability to provide planned and desired technical functionality.
3. Business/operational: Risk associated with business goals, the proposed alternative's failure to produce process efficiencies and streamlining, the inability to achieve business goals of the program or initiative, and the inability to achieve program effectiveness targeted by the project.
4. Organizational and change management: Risk associated with organizational/agency/governmentwide cultural resistance to change and standardization; risk associated with bypassing, lack of use, or improper use or adherence to new systems and processes, due to organizational structure and culture; inadequate training planning.
5. Data/information: Risk associated with the loss/misuse of data or information, and risk of increased burdens on citizens and businesses due to data collection requirements if the associated business processes or the project requires access to data from other sources (federal, state, or local agencies).
6. Security: Risk associated with the security/vulnerability of systems, Web sites, information, and networks; risk of intrusion and connectivity to other (vulnerable) systems; and risk associated with the misuse (criminal/fraudulent) of information. Must include level of risk (high, medium, basic) and what aspect of security determines the level of risk, e.g., need for confidentiality of information associated with the project/system, availability of the information or system, or reliability of the information or system.
7. Strategic: Risk that the proposed alternative fails to result in the achievement of the goals or in making contributions to their achievement.
8. Privacy: Risk associated with the vulnerability of information collected on individuals, or risk of vulnerability of proprietary information on businesses.

risk analysis: A technique to identify and assess factors that may jeopardize the success of a project or achievement of a goal. This technique also helps define preventive measures to reduce the probability of occurrence of these factors and identify countermeasures to successfully deal with these constraints when they develop.

savings-to-investment ratio (SIR): Represents the ratio of savings to investment. The "savings" in the SIR computation are generated by internal operational savings and mission cost savings. The flow of costs and cost savings into the SIR formula is shown in Figure B.10.

sensitivity analysis: An analysis of how sensitive outcomes are to changes in the assumptions. The assumptions that deserve the most attention should depend largely on the dominant benefit and cost elements and the areas of greatest uncertainty of the program or process being analyzed.

stakeholder: An individual or group with an interest in the success of an organization, in relation to its delivering intended results and maintaining the viability of its products and services. Stakeholders influence programs, products, and services.

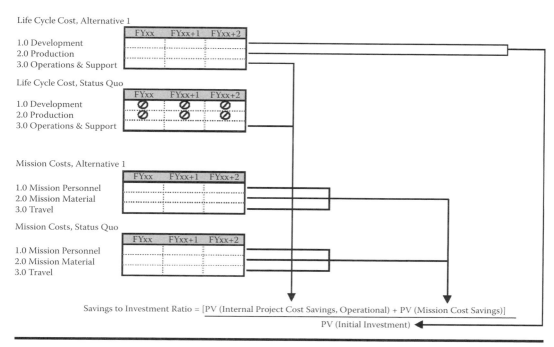

Figure B.10   Savings-to-investment ratio.

Endnote

1. This reference is based on the Value Measuring Methodology — How-To-Guide. (The U.S. Chief Information Officers Council. http://www.cio.gov/archive/ValueMeasuring_Methodology_HowTo Guide_Oct_2002.pdf).

Reference C: Establishing a Software Measurement Program[1]

This reference provides an overview of software measurement and an infrastructure for establishing a software measurement program. It is recommended to start small and build on the successes achieved. It is also recommended to combine a software measurement program with a software process improvement initiative so that the measurement program is sustainable. As far as possible, establish automated mechanisms for measurement data collection and analysis. Automated methods should be a resource supporting the measurement process rather than defining it. Collect the core measurements and additional measurements specific to the local goals in the organization regularly. Plan and schedule the resources that will be required to collect and analyze the measurement data within the organization's overall software process improvement efforts and the organization's specific projects. Evolve the measurement program according to the organization's goals and objectives. Provide a mechanism for project teams and the organization's software process improvement group to consolidate software project measurements. The following four steps illustrate a comprehensive process for establishing a software measurement program:

Step 1: Adopt a Software Measurement Program Model.
1. Identify resources, processes, and products.
2. Derive core measurement views.

Step 2: Use a Software Process Improvement Model.
1. Establish a baseline assessment of the project or organization.
2. Set and prioritize measurable goals for improvement.
3. Establish action plan with measures.
4. Accomplish actions and analyze results.
5. Leverage improvements through measurement.

Step 3: Identify a Goal-Question-Metric (GQM) Structure.
1. Link software goals with corporate goals.
2. Derive measures from attribute questions.
3. Establish success criteria for measurement.

Step 4: Develop a Software Measurement Plan and Case.
1. Plan addresses questions such as what, why, who, how, and when.
2. Case addresses measurement evidence and analysis results.

An organization may decide to implement a subset of the aforementioned activities. Organizations should tailor their use of the activities as required to meet organizational and project goals and objectives. Each of these four major activities is described in the following sections.

Adopt a Software Measurement Program Model

An organization or a project must understand what to measure, who is interested in the results, and why. To assist in understanding these questions, it is recommended that a software measurement program model, such as the one illustrated in Figure C.1, be adopted.

The measurement program model provides a simple framework for specifically identifying what software attributes of potential interest are to be measured, who the various customers of measurement results might be, and why such measurement results are of interest to those customers. The measurement program model includes the general software objects of measurement interest such as resources, processes, and products. The measurement customers include the end user, software organization and project management, and software application personnel. These customers need software measures for different reasons. Their viewpoints drive the eventual measurement selection priorities, and therefore, must be integrated and consistent to be most effective.

To establish a successful measurement program (e.g., one that is used for organizational or project decision making and lasts for more than two years), it is necessary to have a basic understanding of measurement. The following subsections provide an introduction to attributes of resources, processes, and products that might be useful for measurement, and some software measurement terminology that relates to the software measurement program.

Resources, Processes, and Products

Software objects such as resources, processes, and products have attributes that characterize software projects and are therefore of interest to measure. A software measure is an objective assignment of a number (or symbol) to a software object to characterize a specific attribute (Fenton, 1991).

Resources are inputs to processes. Such inputs specifically include personnel, materials, tools, and methods. Resources for some processes are products of other processes. An attribute of great

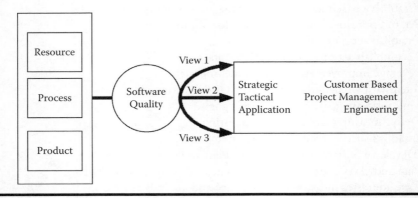

Figure C.1   Software measurement program model.

interest that is relevant to all of these types of resources is *cost*. Cost is dependent on the number of resources and the market price of each resource. For personnel, the cost is dependent upon the effort expended during the process and the market price value of each person assigned to the process.

Processes are any software-related activities such as requirements analysis, design activity, testing, formal inspections, and project management. Processes normally have *time and effort* as attributes of interest, as well as the number of incidents of a specified type arising during the process. Certain incidents may be considered to be *defects in the process* and may result in *defects or faults in products*.

Products are any artifacts, deliverables, or documents that are produced by software processes. Products include specifications, design documentation, source code, test results, and unit development folders. Products normally have *size and inherent defects* as attributes of interest.

Direct and Indirect Software Measurement

Direct measurement of a software attribute does not depend on the measurement of any other attribute. Measures that involve counting, such as number of source lines of code (SLOC) and number of staff hours expended on a process, are examples of a direct measure.

Indirect or derived measurement involves more than one attribute. Rates are typically indirect measures because they involve the computation of a ratio of two other measures. For example, software failure rate is computed by dividing the count of the failures observed during execution by the execution time of the software. Productivity is also an indirect measure as it depends on the amount of product developed divided by the amount of effort or time expended.

Two other very important aspects of the measurement assignment are preservation of attribute properties and mapping uniqueness. The mapping should preserve natural attribute properties (e.g., order and interval size). If another assignment mapping of the attribute is identified, there should be a unique relationship between the first and the second mappings. It is very difficult to ensure that measures satisfy these preservation and uniqueness properties. This document will not consider these issues in any detail.

Views of Core Measures

The three views—strategic, tactical, and application—of the core measures illustrated in Figure C.1 identify important attributes from the viewpoints of the customer, project management, and applications engineers, respectively. It is extremely important for the measurement program to be consistent across the three views of core measures. There must be agreement and consistency on what measures mean, which measures are important, and how measures across the three views relate to and support one another.

Strategic view: This view is concerned with measurement for the long-term needs of the organization and its customers. Important measures include product cost (effort), time to market (schedule), and the trade-offs among such quality measures as functionality, reliability, usability, and product support. It may be critical to an organization to establish new customers and solidify old ones through new product capabilities with limited reliability and usability, but with a well-planned support program. Time to market is usually a critical measure, and may become one of upper management's most important measures.

Tactical view: This view is concerned with short- and long-term needs of each individual project's management goals. It should be possible to aggregate the project measures that support the tactical view to show a relationship with the organization's strategic goals. If not, then individual projects will appear to be out of sync with the organization. The primary measures of interest to project management are schedule progress and labor cost.

Application view: This view is concerned with the immediate resource, process, and product engineering needs of the project. Resources (e.g., personnel and support equipment) are of some interest in this view, but the engineer is primarily interested in the process activities because they are critical to producing a high-quality product. The engineering definitions of process and product quality should be consistent with those of project management or upper-level organization management. Product size, complexity, reliability, and inherent defect measures are important to the engineers because they indicate achievement of functional and performance requirements.

Use a Software Process Improvement Model

For a software measurement program to be successful, the measurement activities should be conducted within the environment of continuous software process improvement. Without such an environment, measures will not be seen as value-added and the measurement program will not be sustainable. Two models are important to a software process improvement initiative and the integration of software measurement, as illustrated in Figure C.2. The IDEAL model (McFeeley, 1996) provides an organization with an approach to continuous process improvement. The CMM (Capability Maturity Model; Paulk et al., 1993) can be used to establish a measurement baseline.

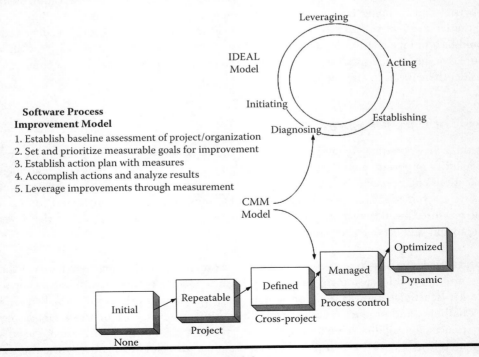

Software Process Improvement Model
1. Establish baseline assessment of project/organization
2. Set and prioritize measurable goals for improvement
3. Establish action plan with measures
4. Accomplish actions and analyze results
5. Leverage improvements through measurement

Figure C.2 Software Process Improvement Models.

The IDEAL Model

The IDEAL model (McFeeley, 1996) provides a framework for conducting process improvement activities at both the organization and the project levels. The IDEAL model is similar to the Plan-Do-Check-Act model identified in Deming (1986).

Organization software measurement: During the Initiate stage, the organization's goals and measures for improvement are defined along with success criteria. The Diagnose stage includes baselining the organization's current process capability (e.g., using the SEI CMM during a Software Process Assessment) in accordance with the measures inherent in the assessment process. The Establish stage focuses on identifying specific improvements that will be accomplished by action teams, and the measures for those improvements. Prioritized improvement actions are determined, and action teams are formed to develop specific plans that address the high-priority improvements. The Act stage includes implementation of the action team plan, including collection of measurements to determine if the improvement has been (or can be) accomplished. The Leverage stage includes documenting the results of the improvement effort and leveraging the improvement across all applicable organization projects.

Project software measurement: During the Initiate stage, the project goals and measures for success are defined along with success criteria. A project software measurement plan should be developed or included as part of the software project management information (e.g., referenced as an appendix to a software development plan). The Diagnose stage includes documenting and analyzing the project's measures as a measurement case during the project life cycle in accordance with the measures in the measurement plan. The Establish stage focuses on identifying specific project or organization improvements that might be accomplished.

Prioritized improvement actions are determined and assigned to project or organization level, as appropriate. For more mature organizations, project teams can accomplish the improvements during the project. For less mature organizations, the identified improvements will serve as lessons learned for future projects. Action teams are formed (by the project or organization) and a plan developed to address the high-priority improvements. The Act and Leverage stages for the project are limited to making midcourse project corrections based on the measurement information. Such measurement data and the actions taken are recorded in the measurement case. The project's measurement case then becomes the complete documentation of the project management and engineering measures, of any changes to project direction based on measurement analysis, and of the lessons learned for future projects.

SEI CMM

The SEI CMM serves as a guide for determining what to measure first, and how to plan an increasingly comprehensive improvement program. The measures suggested for different levels of the CMM are illustrated in Table C.1. The set of core measures described in this document primarily addresses Level 1, 2, and 3 issues.

Table C.1   Relationship of Software Measures to Process Maturity

Maturity Level	Measurement Focus	Applicable Core Measures
1	Establish baselines for planning and estimating project resources and tasks	Effort, schedule progress (pilot or selected projects)
2	Track and control project resources and tasks	Effort, schedule progress (project by project basis)
3	Define and quantify products and processes within and across projects	Products: size, defects Processes: effort, schedule (compare the aforementioned measures across projects)
4	Define, quantify, and control subprocesses and elements	Set upper and lower statistical control boundaries for core measures. Use estimated versus actual comparisons for projects, and compare across projects
5	Dynamically optimize at the project level, and improve across projects	Use statistical control results dynamically within the project to adjust processes and products for improved success

Level 1 measures provide baselines for later comparisons as an organization starts improving. Measurement occurs at a project level without good organization control, or perhaps on a pilot project with better controls.

Level 2 measures focus on project planning and tracking. Applicable core measures are the staff effort and schedule progress. Size and defect data are necessary to understand measurement needs for levels 3 and 4, and to provide a database for future evaluations. Individual projects can use the measurement data to set process entry and exit criteria.

Level 3 measures become increasingly directed toward measuring and comparing the intermediate and final products produced across multiple projects. The measurement data for all core measures is collected for each project and compared to the organization's project standards.

Level 4 measures capture characteristics of the development process to gain control of the individual activities of the process. This is usually done through techniques such as statistical process control where upper and lower bounds are set for all core measures (and any useful derived measures). Actual measure deviation from the estimated values is tracked to determine whether the attributes being measured are within the statistically allowed control bounds. A decision process is put into place to handle projects that do not meet the statistical control boundaries. Process improvements can be identified the on the basis of the decision process.

At Level 5, processes are mature enough and managed carefully enough so that the statistical control process measurements from Level 4 provide immediate feedback to individual projects based on integrated decisions across multiple projects. Decisions concerning dynamically changing processes across multiple projects can then be optimized while the projects are being conducted.

Identify a Goal-Question-Metric Structure

One of the organization's or project's most difficult tasks is to decide what to measure. The key is to relate any measurement to organization and project goals. One such method is the Basili and Weiss (1984) Goal-Question-Metric (GQM) paradigm, illustrated in Figure C.3 with a partial example related to software reliability.

This method links software goals to corporate goals and derives the specific software measures that provide evidence of whether the goals are met. Because such measures are linked directly to organization goals, it is easier to show the value of the measurement activity and establish success criteria for measurement.

The GQM approach to software measurement uses a top-down approach with the following steps:

1. Determine the goals of the organization or project in terms of what is wanted, who wants it, why it is wanted, and when it is wanted.
2. Refine the goals into a set of questions that require quantifiable answers.
3. Refine the questions into a set of measurable attributes (measures for data collection) that attempt to answer the question.
4. Develop models relating each goal to its associated set of measurable attributes.

GOAL QUESTION METRIC

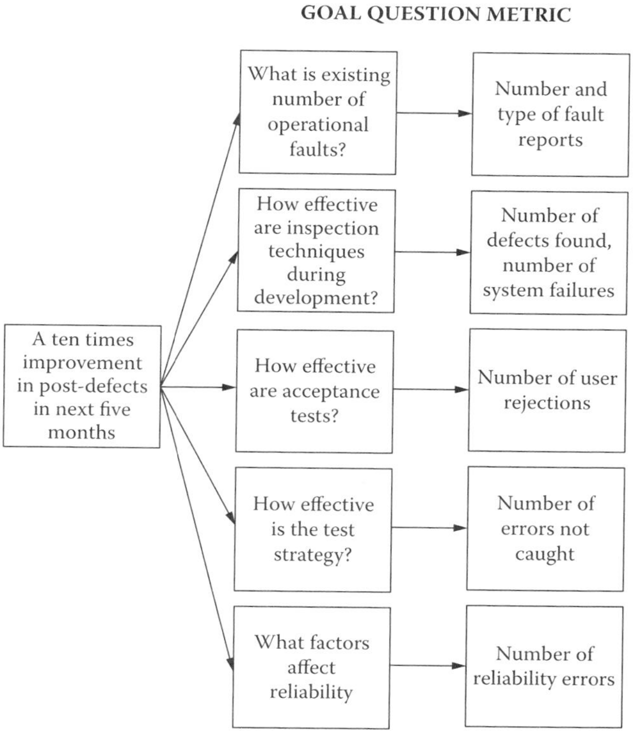

Figure C.3 Goal-Question-Metric (GQM) Paradigm.

Some attributes of software development, such as productivity, are dependent on many factors that are specific to a particular environment. The GQM method does not rely on any standard measure, and the method can cope with any environment.

This activity may be conducted concurrently with any other software measurement activities, and may be used to iteratively refine the software measurement program model, core measurement views, and process improvement efforts.

Develop a Software Measurement Plan and Case

The software measurement program activities provide organization- and project-specific planning information, and a variety of measurement data and analysis results. These plans, data, and results should be documented through the use of a software measurement plan and software measurement case.

A software measurement plan defines the following:

- What measurement data is to be collected
- How the data is to be analyzed to provide the desired measures
- The representation forms that will describe the measurement results

Such a plan also provides information as to who is responsible for the measurement activities, and when the measurement activities are to be conducted. A software measurement plan should be developed at an organization level to direct all measurement activity, and at a project level to direct specific project activity. In most cases a project's software measurement plan can be a simple tailoring of the organizational plan. The organization's software measurement plan can be a separate document or an integrated part of the organization's Software Management Plan or Software Quality Plan.

A software measurement plan at either the organization or project level should relate goals to specific measures of the resource, process, and product attributes that are to be measured. The GQM method can be used to identify such measures. Improvement in accordance with the SEI CMM key process areas should be an integral part of the derivation. The identified measures may be a core measure or may be derived from one or more core measures.

The following activities are critical to developing a software measurement plan:

1. **Establish program commitment:** Define why the program is needed, obtain management approval, and identify ownership.
2. **Determine goals and expected results:** Use software process assessment results to set the improvement context.
3. **Select project measurements:** Apply the GQM method to derive project measures.
4. **Develop measurement plan:** Document the measures to be collected; data collection, analysis, and presentation methods; and establish the relationship to an overall improvement program.

The software measurement case documents the actual data, analysis results, lessons learned, and presentations of information identified in an associated software measurement plan. The following activities are key to developing a software measurement case:

1. **Implement measurement plan:** Collect and analyze data, provide project feedback, and modify project or program as necessary.
2. **Analyze measurement results:** Store project measurement results, and analyze results against historical project results.
3. **Provide measurement feedback:** Report the results of analysis as project lessons learned, update measurement and process improvement programs, and repeat the process of developing or updating a measurement plan and case.

Summary of Recommendations

Specific software measurement actions on individual projects and within organizations depend on existing software capability and initiatives. The following recommendations summarize the guidelines in this reference:

Software Measurement Program

Adopt a measurement model appropriate to the organization. Identify core measures of product, process, and resource attributes as a baseline model. Integrate measurement as a part of a process improvement program. Baseline current process and measurement practices using a model such as the SEI CMM. Initiate process improvement activities following a model such as the SEI IDEAL model. Use the GQM approach to link organization goals to software measures. Use the CMM and the core measures to link the software measures to process improvement. Develop organization and project measurement plans, and document measurement evidence as standard activities. Use the measurement evidence to influence organizational and project decision making.

Core Measures

Define and collect the four core measures of size, effort, progress to schedule, and defects for all projects.

Size: Some of the more popular and effective measures of software size are physical SLOC (noncomment, nonblank source statements), logical source statement (instructions), function points (or feature points), and counts of logical functions or computer software units (i.e., modules). Size measurements can be used to track the status of code from each production process, and to capture important trends. It is recommended that projects adopt physical SLOC or function points as the principal measure for size.

Effort: Reliable measures for effort are prerequisites to dependable measures of software cost. By tracking human resources assigned to individual tasks and activities, effort measures provide the principal means for managing and controlling costs and schedules. It is recommended that projects adopt staff hours as the principal measure for effort.

Progress to schedule: Schedule and progress are primary project management concerns. Accordingly, it is important for managers to monitor adherence to intermediate milestone dates. Early schedule slips often foreshadow future problems. It is also important to have objective and timely measures of progress that accurately indicate status, and that can be used to project completion dates for future milestones.

At minimum, the following information should be planned for and tracked:

- Major milestone completion progress—estimates and actuals of requirements, design, implementation, test, delivery
- Intermediate milestone completion progress—estimates and actuals of modules coded, modules integrated
- Estimated size progress—estimates and actuals of date completed
- Exit or completion criteria—associated with each milestone date

Defects: The number of problems and defects associated with a software product varies inversely with perceived quality. Counts of software problems and defects are among the few direct measures for software processes and products. These counts allow qualitative description of trends in detection and repair activities. They also allow the tracking of progress in identifying and fixing process and product imperfections. In addition, problem and defect measures are the basis for quantifying other software quality attributes such as reliability, correctness, completeness, efficiency, and usability.

Automated Methods

To make the software measurement program as efficient as possible, it is recommended to establish automated mechanisms for measurement data collection and analysis. Automated methods should be a support resource of the measurement process rather than a definition of the process. Regularly collect the core measurements and additional measurements specific to the local goals in your organization.

Example Measurement Plan Standard

Abstract

This document contains an example of a standard defining the contents and structure of a software measurement plan for each project of an organization. The term *Measurement Plan* will be used throughout.

Table of Contents

1. Introduction

This standard provides guidance on the production of a Measurement Plan for individual software projects.

1.1. Scope

This standard is mandatory for all projects. Assistance in applying it to existing projects will be given by the organization measures coordinator.

2. *Policy*

It is the policy to collect measures to assist in the improvement of the following:

- Accuracy of cost estimates
- Project productivity
- Product quality
- Project monitoring and control

In particular, each project manager will be responsible for identifying and planning all activities associated with the collection of these measures. The project manager is responsible for the definition of the project's objectives for collecting measures, analyzing the measures to provide the required presentation results, and documenting the approach in an internally approved Measurement Plan. The project manager is also responsible for capturing the actual measurement information and analysis results. The form of this actual measurement information could be appended to the Measurement Plan or put in a separate document called a Measurement Case.

3. *Responsibility and Authorities*

The project leader or project manager shall be responsible for the production of the project Measurement Plan at the start of the project. Advice and assistance from the Organization Measures Coordinator shall be sought when needed.

The Measurement Plan shall be approved by the project leader or project manager (if not the author of the plan), product manager, organization measures coordinator, and project quality manager.

4. *General Information*

4.1. Overview of Project Measures Activities

The collection and use of measures must be defined and planned in a project during the start-up phase. The haphazard collection of measures is more likely to result in the collection of a large amount of inconsistent data that will provide little useful information to the project management team, or for future projects.

The following activities shall be carried out at the start of the project:

- Define the project's objectives for collecting measures.
- Identify the users of the measures-derived information, as well as any particular requirements they may have.
- Identify the measures to meet these objectives or provide the information. Most, if not all, of these measures should be defined at the organization level.

- Define the project task structure, e.g., work breakdown structure (WBS).
- Define, in terms of the project task structure, when each measure is to be collected.
- Define how each measure is to be collected (in terms of preprinted forms or tools), who will collect it, and where or how it will be stored.
- Define how the data will be analyzed to provide the required information, including the specifications of any necessary algorithms and the frequency with which this will be done.
- Define the organization (including the information flow) within the project required to support the measures collection and analyses activities.
- Identify the standards and procedures to be used.
- Define which measures will be supplied to the organization as a whole.

4.2. Purpose of the Measurement Plan

The project's Measurement Plan is produced as one of the start-up documents to record the project's objectives for measures collection and how the program is intended to be carried out. The plan has the following functions also:

- The plan ensures that activities pertinent to the collection of project measures are considered early in the project, and are resolved in a clear and consistent manner.
- The plan ensures that project staff are aware of the measures activities, and provides an easy reference to them.

The Measurement Plan complements the project's quality and project plans, highlighting matters specifically relating to measures. The Measurement Plan information can be incorporated into the quality or project plans. Information and instructions shall not be duplicated in these plans.

4.3. Format

Section 5 defines a format for the Measurement Plan in terms of a set of headings that are to be used, and the information required to be given under each heading. The front pages shall be the minimum requirements for a standard configurable document.

4.4. Document Control

The Measurement Plan shall be controlled as a configurable document.

4.5. Filing

The Measurement Plan shall be held in the project filing system.

4.6. Updating

The Measurement Plan may require updating during the course of the project. Updates shall follow any changes in requirements for collecting measures, or any change to the project that results in a change to the project WBS. The project leader or project manager shall be responsible for such updates or revisions.

5. Contents of Measurement Plan

This section details what is to be included in the project's Measurement Plan. Wherever possible, the Measurement Plan should point to the existing organization standards, rather than duplicating the information. The information required in the plan is detailed under appropriate headings in the following text.

For small projects, the amount of information supplied under each topic may amount to only a paragraph or so, and may not justify the production of the Measurement Plan as a separate document. Instead, the information may form a separate chapter in the Quality Plan, with the topic headings forming the sections or paragraphs in that chapter. On larger projects, a separate document will be produced, with each topic heading becoming a section in its own right.

Thematic Outline for a Measurement Plan

Section 1: Objectives for Collecting Measures

The project's objectives for collecting measures shall be described here. These will also include the relevant organization objectives. Where the author of the Measurement Plan is not the project leader or project manager, project management agreement to these objectives will be demonstrated by the fact that the project manager is a signatory to the plan.

Section 2: Use and Users of Information

Information provided here includes the following:

Who will be the users of the information derived from the measures.

Why the information is needed.

Required frequency of the information.

Section 3: Measures to be Collected

This section describes the measures to be collected by the project. As far as possible the measures to be collected should be a derivative of the core measures. If organization standards are not followed, justification for the deviation should be provided. Project-specific measures shall be defined in full here in terms of the project tasks.

A GQM approach should be used to identify the measures from the stated project objectives. The results of the GQM approach should also be documented.

Section 4: Collection of Measures

Information provided here includes the following:

Who will collect each measure.

The level within the project task against which each measure is to be collected.

At what time each measure is to be collected in terms of initial estimate, reestimates, and actual measurement.

How the measures are to be collected, with reference to proformas, tools, and procedures, as appropriate.

Validation to be carried out, including details of the project-specific techniques if necessary, and by whom.

How and where the measures are to be stored—includes details of electronic database or spreadsheet or filing cabinet as appropriate, how the data is amalgamated and when it is archived, who is responsible for setting up the storage process, and who is responsible for inserting the data into the database.

When, how, and what data is provided to the Organization Measures database.

Section 5: Analysis of Measures

Information provided here includes the following:

How the data is to be analyzed, giving details of project-specific techniques if necessary, any tools required, and how frequently it is to be carried out.

The information to be provided by the analysis.

The person who will carry out the analysis.

Details of project-specific reports, their frequency of generation, and how and by whom they are generated.

Section 6: Project Organization

Describe the organization within the project that is required to support the measurement activities. Identify roles and the associated tasks and responsibilities. These roles combined with other roles within the project may constitute complete jobs for individual people. The information flow between these roles and the rest of the project should also be described.

Section 7: Project Task Structure

Describe or reference the project task structure. It should be noted that the project's measurement activities should be included in the project task structure.

Section 8: Standards

The measurement standards and procedures used by the project must be described, indicating which are organization standards and which are project specific. These standards will have been referenced throughout the plan, as required. If it is intended not to follow any of the organization standards completely, this must be clearly indicated in the relevant section of the Measurement Plan, and a note must be made in this section.

Example Project Core Measures

This section provides examples, summarized in Table C.2, that illustrate the use of the recommended core measures (with some minor variations) for a variety of software projects.

References

Basili, V. and Weiss, D.M., (November 1984). A Methodology for Collecting Valid Software Engineering Data, *IEEE Transactions on Software Engineering*, Vol. SE-10, No. 6.

Deming, W. E. (1986). *Out of the Crisis,* MIT Press, Cambridge, MA, 1986.

Fenton, N. E. (1991). *Software Metrics: A Rigorous Approach*, Chapman & Hall, London.

McFeeley, B. (February 1996). *IDEAL: A User's Guide for Software Process Improvement* (CMU/SEI-96-HB-001), Software Engineering Institute, Pittsburgh, PA.

Paulk, M.C., Curtis, B., Chrissis, M.B., and Weber, C.V. (1993). *Capability Maturity Model for Software, Version 1.1* (CMU/SEI-93-TR-024), Software Engineering Institute, Pittsburgh, PA.

Table C.2   Core Measures for Example Projects

Core Measures	Project A: Large Embedded Development	Project B: Commercial Purchase	Project C: Information System Development	Project D: Simulation Analysis Code Support	Project E: Graphical User Interface Small Development
Size	SLOC (reused and new)	Disk space (utilized)	Function points (reused and new)	SLOC (total, new, and modified for each release)	Function points (reused and new)
Effort	Staff hours (development)	Staff hours (installation and updates)	Staff hours (development)	Staff hours (total, change request for each release)	Staff hours (development)
Progress to schedule	Total months (estimated and actual) Task months (estimated and actual) Task completion ratio per reporting period	Installation time (estimated and actual for initial release and updates)	Total months (estimated and actual) Task months (estimated and actual) Task completion ratio per reporting period	Total months (estimated and actual for each release) Task months (estimated and actual for each release) Task completion ratio per reporting period	Total months (estimated and actual) Task months (estimated and actual) Task completion ratio per reporting period
Defects	Inspection defects (major and minor) Test failures (major and minor) Operational problem reports (all)	Operational failures (all) Operational problem reports (all)	Inspection defects (major and minor) Test failures (major and minor) Operational problem reports (all)	Inspection defects (major and minor) Test failures (major and minor total and in modified code) Operational problem reports (all and for modified code)	Test failures (major and minor) Operational problem reports (all)

Endnote

1. This reference has been adapted from Software Quality Assurance Subcommittee of the Nuclear Weapons Complex Quality Managers. U.S. Department of Energy Albuquerque Operations Office (April 1997). Guidelines for Software Measurement, Quality Report SQAS97-001. http://cio.doe.gov/ITReform/sqse/download/sqas97_1.doc.

Reference D: Selected Performance Metrics[1]

Types of Performance Measures

Process metrics	Increase capability level (i.e., SEI CMM[a] levels)
	Do more with less (shorter schedule, less resources)
	Improve quality (less defects, less rework)
Project metrics	Track project progress
	Assess project status
	Award contract fees
Product metrics	Determine product quality
	Identify defect rates
	Ensure product performance

[a] Software Engineering Institute Capability Maturity Model.

Typical Metric Categories

Schedule	Actual versus planned:
	Schedule and progress
Budget	Actual versus planned:
	Resources and cost
Functionality	Delivered versus planned:
	Product characteristics
	Technology effectiveness
	Process performance
	Customer satisfaction

Measures versus Indicators

Basic measures:
   Number of requirements reviewed
   Number of reviewers involved
   Number of defects found
   Effort expended
	Indicators of efficiency:
	   Number reviewed per effort
	   Number reviewed per time
	   Number found per effort, time
	Indicators of Effectiveness:
	   Percentage found of those expected
	   Percentage escaped

Note: The table provides an example of finding defects in products (e.g., a Requirements Document).

The following table provides examples of performance measures that are typical for many IT projects. Although the Category and Metrics columns are fairly representative of those used in IT projects in general, the Measure of Success column will vary greatly and should be established for each individual project, as appropriate.

Examples of Performance Measures

Category	Metrics	Purpose	Measure of Success
Schedule performance	Tasks completed versus tasks planned at a point in time	Assess project progress; Apply project resources	100 percent completion of tasks on critical path; 90 percent on all others
	Major milestones met versus milestones planned	Measure time efficiency	90 percent of major milestones met
	Revisions to approved plan	Understand and control project churn	All revisions reviewed and approved
	Changes to customer requirements	Understand and manage scope and schedule	All changes managed through approved change process
	Project completion date	Reward or penalize (depending on contract type)	Project completed on schedule (per approved plan)
Budget performance	Revisions to cost estimates	Assess and manage project cost	100 percent of revisions are reviewed and approved
	Dollars spent versus dollars budgeted	Measure cost efficiency	Project completed within approved cost parameters
	Return on investment (ROI)	Track and assess performance of project investment portfolio	ROI (positive cash flow) according to plan
	Acquisition cost control	Assess and manage acquisition dollars	All applicable acquisition guidelines followed

Examples of Performance Measures (Continued)

Category	Metrics	Purpose	Measure of Success
Product quality	Defects identified through quality activities	Track progress in, and effectiveness of, defect removal	90 percent of expected defects identified (e.g., via peer reviews, inspections)
	Test-case failures versus number of cases planned	Assess product functionality and absence of defects	100 percent of planned test cases executed successfully
	Number of service calls	Track customer problems	75 percent reduction after three months of operation
	Customer satisfaction index	Identify trends	95 percent positive rating
	Customer satisfaction trend	Improve customer satisfaction	5 percent improvement each quarter
	Number of repeat customers	Determine if customers are using the product multiple times (could indicate satisfaction with the product)	"x" percent of customers used the product "x" times during a specified time period
	Number of problems reported by customers	Assess quality of project deliverables	100 percent of reported problems addressed within 72 hours
Compliance	Compliance with enterprise architecture model requirements	Track progress toward departmentwide architecture model	Zero deviations without proper approvals
	Compliance with interoperability requirements	Track progress toward system interoperability	Product works effectively within system portfolio
	Compliance with standards	Alignment, interoperability, consistency	No significant negative findings during architecture assessments
	For Web site projects, compliance with style guide	Ensure standardization of Web site	All Web sites have the same look and feel
	Compliance with Section 508	To meet regulatory requirements	Persons with disabilities may access and utilize the functionality of the system

Examples of Performance Measures (Continued)

Category	Metrics	Purpose	Measure of Success
Redundancy	Elimination of duplicate or overlapping systems	Ensure return on investment	Retirement of 100 percent of identified systems
	Decreased number of duplicate data elements	Reduce input redundancy and increase data integrity	Data elements are entered once and stored in one database
	Consolidate help desk functions	Reduce dollar spent on help desk support	Approved consolidation plan by June 30, 2002
Cost avoidance	System is easily upgraded	Take advantage of, e.g., commercial off-the-shelf (COTS) upgrades	Subsequent releases do not require major "glue code" project to upgrade
	Avoid costs of maintaining duplicate systems	Reduce IT costs	100 percent of duplicate systems have been identified and eliminated
	System is maintainable	Reduce maintenance costs	New version (of COTS) does not require "glue code"
Customer satisfaction	System availability (uptime)	Measure system availability	100 percent of requirement met (e.g., 99 percent M–F, 8 am to 6 pm, and 90 percent S & S, 8 am to 5 pm)
	System functionality (meets customer's/user's needs)	Measure how well customer needs are being met	Positive trend in customer satisfaction surveys
	Absence of defects (that impact customer)	Measure number of defects removed during project life cycle	90 percent of defects expected were removed
	Ease of learning and use	Measure time to becoming productive	Positive trend in training surveys
	Time taken to answer calls for help	Manage/reduce response times	95 percent of severity-one calls answered within three hours
	Rating of training course	Assess effectiveness and quality of training	90 percent of responses of "good" or better

Examples of Performance Measures (Continued)

Category	Metrics	Purpose	Measure of Success
Business goals/ mission	Functionality tracks reportable inventory	Validate system supports program mission	All reportable inventory tracked in system
	Turnaround time in responding to Congressional queries	Improve customer satisfaction and national interests	Improved turnaround time from two days to four hours
	Maintenance costs	Track reduction of costs to maintain system	Reduced maintenance costs by 2/3 over three-year period.
	Standard desktop platform	Reduce costs associated with upgrading user's systems	Reduced upgrade costs by 40 percent
Productivity	Time taken to complete tasks	Evaluate estimates	Completions within 90 percent of estimates
	Number of deliverables produced	Assess capability to deliver products	Improved product delivery 10 percent during each of the next three years

The following set of questions is designed to stimulate ideas to determine performance measures that are appropriate for a given project or organization.

Project/process measurement questions

What options are available if the schedule is accelerated by four months to meet a tight market window?

How many people must be added to get two months of schedule compression and how much will it cost?

How many defects are still in the product and when will it be good enough so that it can be shipped as a reliable product and have satisfied customers?

What impact does requirements growth have on schedule, cost, and reliability?

Is the current forecast consistent with the company's performance history?

Organizational measurement questions

What is the current typical cycle time and cost of the organization's development process?

What is the quality of the products the organization produces?

Has the organization's development process got more or less effective and efficient?

How does the organization stack up against the competition?

How does the organization's investment in process improvement compare with the benefits that have been achieved?

What impact do environmental factors such as requirements volatility and staff turnover have on the process productivity?

What level of process productivity should be assumed for the next development project?

Endnote

1. Adapted from Basic Performance Measures for Information Technology Projects. (2002, January), Department of Energy (DOE). Retrieved from http://www.cio.energy.gov/PE-WI-V3-011502.doc.

Reference E: Introduction to Software Engineering

There are more than a few project managers (PMs) who are not really familiar with software engineering techniques. It is nearly impossible to be an effective IT manager without having a good grasp of architectural, database, and programming techniques. This reference provides a brief overview of the processes and artifacts involved in software engineering and is based on the *Software Engineering Handbook* (Keyes, 2002).

System Types

Computer systems come in all shapes and sizes. There are systems that process e-mail and those that process payroll. There are also systems that monitor space missions and systems that monitor student grades. No matter how diverse the functionality of these systems, they have several features in common:

1. All systems have end users: It is for these end users that the system has been created. These end users have a vested interest in seeing that this system does what it is supposed to do, correctly and efficiently. You might say that these end users have a "stake" in ensuring that the system is successful. Sometimes, these end users are referred to as stakeholders. There are different types of stakeholders. A good systems analyst is careful to make sure that he or she doesn't leave out any stakeholders. This is indeed what happened when the post office started developing the automated system that you now see in use at all post offices. This system was developed "in a vacuum." What this means is that only higher-level employees were involved in system development. The clerks who actually man the windows were left out of the process. When the time came for this system to be deployed, the lack of involvement of this critical set of stakeholders almost led to an employee mutiny.

2. All systems are composed of functions and data: All of us like to get our payroll checks. Creating a payroll check requires the definition of several functions (sometimes called *processes*). For example, there may be functions for (a) obtaining employee information, (b) calculating payroll taxes, (c) calculating other deductions, and (d) printing the check. Systems analysts are neither payroll clerks nor accountants. A typical systems analyst does not have the information to create a payroll processing system without the involvement of stakeholders. He or she needs to utilize several analytical techniques—including interviewing and observation—to obtain the details on how to perform these processes. However, functions are only

225

one half of the equation; the other half is the data. Sometimes, the data will already be available to the systems analyst—i.e., via a corporate database or file. However, sometimes the systems analyst will have to create a new database for the application. For this particular task, he or she will usually work with a database administrator (DBA) or data administrator. This person has the expertise and authority to create or modify a database for use with the new or enhanced application.

3. All systems use hardware and software: A systems analyst has many decisions to make. He or she has to decide on which platform to run this system: (a) PC only; (b) mainframe only; (c) client/server (c/s; i.e., PC client and mainframe or workstation server), etc. The analyst has to also decide whether or not to use any third-party software (i.e., Excel, SAP, etc.). He or she may even have to decide on the programming language and type of database to use.

4. All systems are written using programming languages: If the IT department is filled with COBOL programmers, it may not be a wise decision to use Java. If Java is mandatory, then the systems analyst has to plan for this by either training existing staff or outsourcing the development effort to a consulting firm. This information is contained within the Requirements Document. In this reference, this document will be called the System Requirements Specification (SRS).

5. All systems are designed using a methodology and proper documentation techniques: There are many developmental methodologies; the two main generic categories are structured and object-oriented (OO). The tools and techniques surrounding these methodologies are part and parcel of software engineering. A properly developed system is carefully analyzed and then designed. Some of the main steps in the SDLC (systems development life cycle) are (1) the plan, (2) the SRS, (3) the design document, (4) implementation, (5) testing, and (6) deployment.

IT Job Descriptions

I started out in this field as a programmer. In those days (several aeons ago!) there were real barriers between the different types of jobs one could do. If you were a programmer, you didn't do analysis work, and vice versa. In fact, most analysts back then knew very little about programming.

That has all changed now. Typically, you still start out as a programmer, but then the sky's the limit. A programmer is a person who knows one or more programming languages (e.g., Java, C++, etc.). His or her job is to read a programming specification, which is usually written by the systems analyst, and then translate that specification into program code.

In most companies, the programmer works within project teams managed by a project leader (PL), who in turn is managed by a PM. Each project team has one or more programmers, and probably, one or more systems analysts. The programmer works on the code and seldom, if ever, interacts with the end users. The systems analysts, on the other hand, work directly with the end users to develop the requirements and specifications for the system being designed.

Although a programmer can lack all the social graces, because few "outsiders" deal with this person, the systems analyst is on the front lines. He or she needs to be articulate, friendly, and a good listener. The analyst must also have the ability to pay a great deal of attention to detail and the creativity to come up with techniques for uncovering hidden information. For example, when developing the FOCUS system, I had to uncover hundreds of mathematical formulas that could be used to analyze the financial forms. I also had to design dozens of screens that could be utilized efficiently by the end users. Instead of designing the screens myself (those were the pre-Internet days), I asked the end users to work with a word-processing programmer and list the information they wanted to see and where they wanted to see it. This method is called JAD (joint application development).

When I first starting working for the New York Stock Exchange, I was responsible for building a computer system that processed a series of financial forms such as tax forms that were required to be filled out by the exchange's numerous member firms, (e.g., Merrill Lynch). These forms contained hundreds of financial items.

My job as an analyst was to work with the people in the regulatory department who understood how to process these forms—these people were the end users. Our job was hard because of the complexity of the forms. However, the end users were accountant types with vast experience in interpreting these forms. The reason for the development of this system was to determine whether the firm (i.e., Merrill Lynch) was financially healthy—a very important job.

As the systems analyst on the job, I had to regularly meet with these end users and try to "pick their brains." We met several times a week to work on the project. There was lots of yelling and screaming and tons of pizza. In the end, however, we developed a document that was quite detailed, describing everything that the system—called FOCUS—was supposed to do.

Once this document was completed, it was turned over to the programmers whose job it was to turn the document into a complete working system.

As can be seen from the description, I've left out a few job titles. That is because each organization is structured a bit differently. For the most part, when one develops a system, there are at least two departments involved. One is the end-user department (e.g., marketing, operations). The end users require a system to be developed or modified. They approach the computer department, sometimes called IS (information systems), MIS (management information systems), or IT (information technology), to help them turn this need into a working system.

The end-user department is composed of experts who do a particular task. They may be in accounting or in marketing—they are experts at what they do. They are managed, just as IS people, by managers. We can refer to these managers as business managers, just as we refer to a computer manager as an IS manager. Although most systems analysts work directly with those who report to the business manager, this manager still plays a critical role. He or she has to be approached if some information is needed from the entire department or something that only the business manager can direct needs to be done.

The SDLC

The development of computer systems involves many phases: analysis, design, etc. These phases in their entirety are called the SDLC.

Why do we call this a life cycle? A system has a life of its own. It starts out as an idea, progresses until this idea germinates, and then is born. Eventually, when the system ages and becomes obsolete, it is discarded or "dies." So, *life cycle* is an apt term.

The idea phase of the SDLC is the point at which the end user, systems analyst, and various managers meet for the first time. This is where the scope and objectives of the system are fleshed out in a very-high-level document.

Next, a team composed of one or more systems analysts and end users tries to determine whether the system is feasible. There are many reasons for lack of feasibility: expense too great, technology not yet available, and not enough experience to create it. These are just some of the reasons why system development will not be undertaken.

Once the system has been determined feasible, systems analysis is initiated. This is the point when the analysts put on their detective hats and try to ferret out all the system's rules and regulations. What are the inputs? What are the outputs? How will the online screens be? What types of reports will there be? Will paper forms be required? Will any hookups to external files or companies be required? How shall this information be processed? As you can see, there is much work to be done at this point and many questions to be answered. In the end, all of the answers to these questions will be fully documented in a requirements document.

Once all the unknowns have been identified and fully documented, the systems analyst can "put flesh on the skeleton" by creating both high-level, and later, detailed designs. This is usually called a specification and can be hundreds of pages long. The document contains flowcharts, file and database definitions, and detailed instructions for writing each program.

Along the way, the accuracy of all of these documents is checked and verified by having the end users and analysts meet with one another. In fact, most approaches to system development involve the creation of a project team that consists of both end users and IS staff. This team meets regularly to work on the project and verify its progress.

Once a complete working specification has been delivered to the programmers, implementation can get under way. For the FOCUS system, we turned the specification over to a team of about 20 programmers. The systems analyst, PL, and PM were all responsible for ensuring that the implementation effort went smoothly. Code was written and tested by programmers. This first level (unit testing) of testing was followed by several other phases of testing, including systems testing, parallel testing, and integration testing. Many companies have QA (quality assurance) departments, which use automated tools to test the accuracy of systems being implemented.

Once the system has been fully tested, it is turned over to production (changeover). Usually, just before this, the end-user departments (not just the team working on the project) are trained and manuals distributed. The entire team is usually on call during the first few weeks after changeover, because errors often crop up and it can take several weeks for the system to stabilize.

Once the system has been stabilized, it is evaluated for correctness. At this point, a list of faults to remedy as well as a "wish list" of features that were not included in the first phase of the system are created and prioritized. The team, which consists of technical and end-user staff, usually is retained and works on the future versions of the system.

The Feasibility Study

It never pays to just jump into developing a system. Usually, it's a good idea to do a feasibility study first. The easiest part of the feasibility study is determining whether the system is technically feasible. Sometimes, however, it may not be feasible because the company doesn't have the technical expertise to do the job. A good systems analyst will go one step further and see if it is feasible to outsource (i.e., let someone else do it) the project to people who can do it. Sometimes, you'll find that the technology is just not robust enough. For example, many years ago I wanted to deliver voice recognition devices to the floor of the New York Stock Exchange. The technology at that time was just too primitive, so the entire project was deemed infeasible.

A layer of complexity is added to the problem when you discover that the project is feasible from a technical perspective but will require vast organizational changes (e.g., creation of new end-user departments). This would make the project organizationally infeasible.

Also, the project may be too expensive. Cost calculation will require a cost–benefit analysis (take out those spreadsheets). This analysis will require a cost estimation for everything needed, including cost of hardware, cost of software, cost of new personnel, cost of training, etc. Then, you need to calculate the financial savings the new system will enable; e.g., reduce staff by 1/3, save five hours a day. Sometimes, the benefits are intangible, however, e.g., compete with our major competitor.

Once it has been determined that the project is feasible, a project plan that plots out the course for the entire systems development effort is created—i.e., budget, resources, schedule, etc. The next step, then, is to start the actual analytical part of systems development, for which we need to collect some information.

Information-Gathering Channels

One of the first things to do when starting a new project is to gather information. Your job will be to understand everything about the department and the proposed system that is to be automated. If you are to merely modify an existing system, you will already be halfway there. In this case, you will have to review all of the system documentation, the system itself, and the end users to ferret out the changed requirements.

How will you make sense out of a department and its processes when you don't know anything about it? One of the things you can do is to act like a detective and gather up every piece of documentation you can find. When I built the FOCUS system, I scrounged around and managed to find policy manuals and memos that got me part of the way toward understanding what these people did for a living. Other sources of information include reports used for decision making, performance reports, records, data-capture forms, organization Web sites, competitors' Web sites, and archived data.

However, a passive review is seldom enough. The next step is to be a bit more active and direct. The first thing you can do is interview end users. For our FOCUS project, although I had already created a project team consisting of tech people and end users, I decided that it would be worthwhile to interview a representative sampling of people working in different jobs, all "touching" the process to be automated.

You can't interview someone without preparation. This preparation consists of, first, understanding all you can about the job and the person to be interviewed, and then, preparing a set of questions for that person. Sometimes, an interview may be insufficient to meet your needs. The subject may not be able to articulate what he or she does. The next step, then, is to observe the person at work.

I've done much work in the artificial intelligence arena, where observation is a large part of the systems analysis process. One of the case histories that people in the field often talk about is concerning the building of a tax expert system. At one end of a large table sat a junior accountant with a number of tax books piled in front of him. At the other end sat some of the most senior tax accountants at the firm, with nothing in front of them. In the middle sat the systems analyst, armed with a video recorder and a script that contained a problem and a set of questions. The task at hand was for the junior accountant to work through the problem, guided by the experts. The experts relied on just their knowledge and experience. Thus, they were able to assist the junior accountant in solving the problem, while the video camera recorded the entire process.

Observation can only be done selectively—a few people at the most. A technique that will allow you to survey a large number of people at one time is the questionnaire. Building a questionnaire requires some skill. There are generally two types of questionnaires, open-ended and closed. The following list gives examples of both:

Open-ended

1. What are the most frequent problems you encounter in buying books from a bookstore?_____
2. Of the problems listed above, which is the most troublesome one?_____

Closed

1. The tool is used as part of program development cycle to improve quality
   1 2 3 4 5 (circle appropriate response, where 5 is the highest score)

A good questionnaire will be one that has a combination of both types of questions (hybrid). It's also important to ensure that you format the questionnaire for easy readability (lots of white space and even spacing), put all the important questions first (in case they don't finish the survey), and vary the type of questions so that they don't just circle the 5's or 1's all the way down the page.

Diagramming or Modeling the System

There are a wide variety of techniques that can be used to describe a problem and its solution diagrammatically, and a wide variety of tools that can be used to draw these diagrams. One of the diagrammatic techniques is flowcharting and the tool of choice is Microsoft Visio, as shown in Figure E.1.

One of the most practical tools is the DFD (data flow diagram). A DFD is quite logical, clear, and helpful when building systems—even Web-based systems. All inputs, outputs, and processes are recorded in a hierarchical manner. The first DFD, referred to as DFD 0, is often a view of the system from a high-level perspective. A child DFD is much more detailed. Figure E.2 is a snippet from a real online test system. It is a rather complicated system that allows people to take tests online. This particular DFD shows the data flow through the log-in process. The rectangular boxes (e.g., D5) are the data stores. Note that D5 is an online cookie and D1, on the other hand, is a real database. D1 is a relational database (RDB) and this is one particular table in it. The databases and their corresponding tables are defined in a data dictionary. The square box is the entity (i.e., test taker) and can be a person, place, or thing. The other boxes are process boxes. Process 1.1 is the process for Get Name. There will be a related child DFD labeled 1.1 Get Name. This child DFD will also appear in a process dictionary, which will contain a detailed specification for how to program this procedure.

Other modeling tools include the following:

Entity relationship diagram (ERD): An ERD is a database model that describes the attributes of entities and the relationships between them. An entity is a file (table). Today, ER models are often created graphically, and software converts the graphical representations of the tables into the SQL (Structured Query Language) code required to create the data structures in the database, as shown in Figure E.3.

State transition diagram (STD): An STD describes how a system behaves in response to external events. Figure E.4 depicts an STD for a system that accepts complaints from citizens regarding potholes and its response to these complaints.

Data Dictionary: A data dictionary is a highly organized listing of all data elements that pertain to the system. This listing contains some very specific information, as shown in Figure E.5. It should be noted that there are many variations in the formats of data dictionaries.

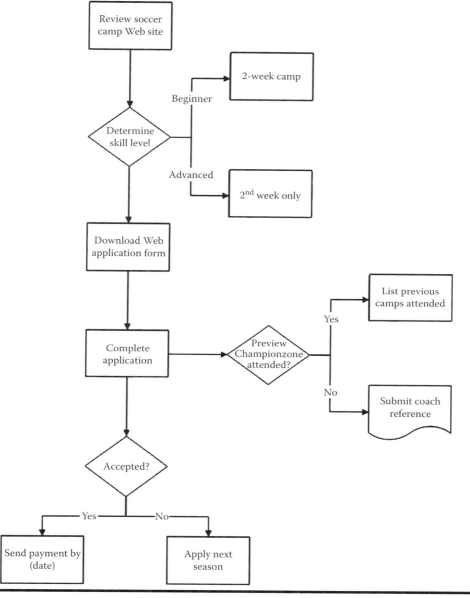

Figure E.1   A flowchart created using Microsoft Visio.

Process Specification (PSPEC): The PSPEC describes the "what, when, where, and how" of the program in technical terms. It describes just how the process works and serves to connect the DFD to the data dictionary. It uses pseudocode (sometimes called Structured English or Program Definition Language—PDL) to explain the requirements for programming the process to the programmer. An example is shown as follows:

Process #1

Name Log-on

Number: 1

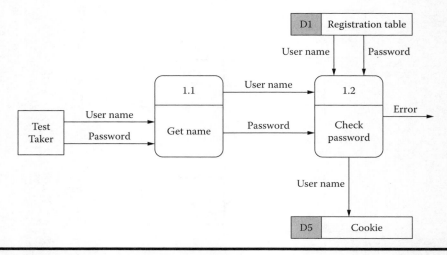

Figure E.2   A data flow diagram (DFD) from an online test system.

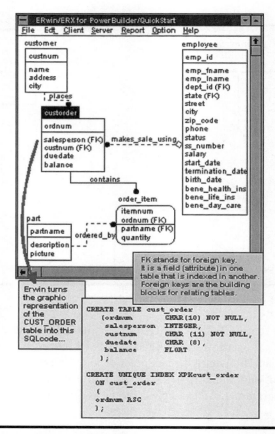

Figure E.3   An entity relationship diagram (ERD).

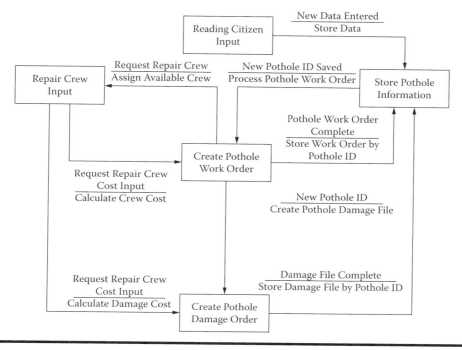

Figure E.4   A state transition diagram (STD) for a system that accepts complaints from citizens regarding potholes.

Name: Log-on

Description: Registered test takers will log on to their account with their username and password through this process. Once they register, they will be able to take the test.

Input data: Username from the test taker, password from the test taker, username from the Registration table, password from the Registration table

Output data: Username to the cookie

Type of process: Validation

Process logic:

    Get username and password from the user

    If correct then

        Allow the user to take the test

    else

        Produce an error

    endif

Other ways of representing process logic are as follows:

  a. A decision table

  b. A decision tree

  c. A mathematical formula

  d. Any combination of the above

Name:	Pothole
Aliases:	None
Where used/How used:	Pothole information is the main input (Pothole Submission) and output (Fixed Pothole Data) of the whole system (see level 0 of the ERD).
Content Description:	
Pothole ID = Ten digit number Address = Sixty Characters City = Thirty Characters State = Two Characters Zip = Nine Characters Location = Ten Characters District = One digit number Repair Priority = Two digit number Repair Crew ID = Two digit number Repair Time = Hours or Days Status = Five Characters Material Cost = Dollar amount Total Cost = Dollar amount Description = Two Hundred and Fifty Characters	
Supplementary Description:	
Location possible values: "curb", "middle", "left side", "right side" District possible values: North = 1, South = 2, East = 3, West = 4 Repair Priority possible values = 1 to 10 Status possible values: "Open" or "Closed"	

Figure E.5   An example of a data dictionary.

Class diagrams: Analysts working on an OO (object-oriented system) will utilize OO tools and diagrammatic techniques. One of these techniques is a class diagram that is drawn using UML (Unified Modeling Language), as shown in Figure E.6.

Developmental Methodologies

The Software Engineering Institute (SEI), which is part of Carnegie Mellon located in Pittsburgh, Pennsylvania, is famous for having developed for a framework that describes software process maturity. A summary of the five phases of software process maturity is as follows:

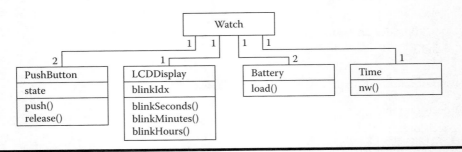

Figure E.6   A class diagram that is drawn using Unified Modeling Language (UML).

Stage 1: Initial, which is characterized by processes:
  - That are ad hoc.
  - That have little formalization.
  - That have tools informally applied.
Key actions to get to next step:
  - Initiate rigorous project management, management oversight, and QA.
Stage 2: Repeatable, which is characterized by processes:
  - That have achieved stability with a repeatable level of statistical control.
Key actions to get to next step:
  - Establish a process group.
  - Establish a software development process architecture.
  - Introduce software engineering methods and technology.
Stage 3: Defined, which is characterized by processes:
  - That have achieved a foundation for major and continuing progress.
Key actions to get to next step:
  - Establish a basic set of process managements to identify quality and cost parameters.
  - Establish a process database.
  - Gather and maintain process data.
  - Assess relative quality of each product and inform management.
Stage 4: Managed, which is characterized by processes:
  - That show substantial quality improvements.
  - That are coupled with comprehensive process measurement.
Key actions to get to next step:
  - Support automatic gathering of process data.
  - Use data to analyze and modify the process.
Stage 5: Optimized, which is characterized by processes:
  - That demonstrate major quality and quantity improvements.
Key actions to get to next step:
  - Continue improvement and optimization of the process.

Companies that have achieved a Stage 2 process maturity or higher make use of methodologies to ensure that the company does achieve a repeatable level of quality and productivity. There are many methodologies available for use. Some of these are vendor driven; i.e., they are used in conjunction with a software toolset.

In general, methodologies can be categorized as follows (it should be noted that a methodology can be used in conjunction with another methodology):

Systems development life cycle (SDLC): This is a phased, structured approach to systems development. The phases include requirements feasibility, analysis, systems design, coding, testing, implementation, and postimplementation testing. Variations of these stated phases are possible. Usually, phases are executed sequentially, although there is some potential for overlap. This is the methodology that is used most often in industry.

Iterative (prototyping) model: Most often, this approach is used to replace several of the phases in the SDLC. In the SDLC approach, the "time to market" can be several months (sometimes years). During this time, requirements (scope) may change and the final deliverable, therefore, might become obsolete. To prevent this from happening, it is a good idea to try and compress the development cycle, shortening the time to market, and providing interim results to the end user. The iterative model consists of three steps: (1) listen to customer, (2) build or revise a mock-up, (3) the customer test-drives the mock-up; then, return to the first step.

Rapid application development (RAD): This is a type of iterative model. The key word here is *rapid*. Development teams try to get a first pass of the system out to the end user within 60–90 days. To accomplish this, the normal seven-step SDLC is compressed into the following steps: business modeling, data modeling, process modeling, application generation, and testing and turnover. Note the term *application generation*. RAD makes use of application generators, formerly called CASE (computer-assisted software engineering) tools.

Incremental model: The four main phases of SDLC are analysis, design, coding, and testing. If we break a business problem into chunks (or increments), we can use an overlapping, phased approach to software development. For example, we can start the analysis of Increment 1 in January, Increment 2 in June, and Increment 3 in September. Just when Increment 3 starts up, we will be at the testing stage of Increment 1 and coding stage of Increment 2.

Joint application development (JAD): JAD is more of a technique than a complete methodology. It can be utilized as part of any of the other methodologies discussed here. In this technique, one or more end users are "folded" into the software development team. Instead of an adversarial software developer–end-user dynamic, the effect is to have the continued, uninterrupted attention of the persons who will ultimately be using the system.

Reverse engineering: This technique is used to first understand a system from its code, generate documentation based on that code, and then make desired changes to the system. Competitive software companies often try to reverse-engineer their competitors' software.

Reengineering: Business goals change over time. Software must also change to be consistent with these goals. Instead of building a system from scratch, the goal of reengineering is to retrofit an existing system to new business functionality.

Object-oriented (OO) methods: Object-oriented analysis (OOA), object-oriented design (OOD), and object-oriented programming (OOP) are very different from what has been already discussed. In fact, you will need to learn a whole new vocabulary as well as new diagramming techniques.

Systems Design

Most of the models that have been discussed earlier fall under the structured rubric (except for the OO model). The requirements document—or SRS—is written for a broad audience and reflects this structured technique. Usually, it is provided not only to IT staff but to the end users as well. In this way, the end users are able to review what they have asked for as well as the general architecture of the system. Once approved, the system must be designed. The system specification, here called the SDS (Systems Design Specification), contains a fine level of detail—enough detail to allow programmers to code the entire system. This means that the SDS must contain the following:

a. Information on all processes
b. Information on all data
c. Information about the architecture

You have to begin somewhere. That "somewhere" is usually the highest level of a design. There are three logical ways to approach this:

Abstraction: This permits you to concentrate at some level of generalization without regard to irrelevant low-level details. Abstraction is the high-level design or logical design.

Stepwise refinement: This is a successive decomposition, or refinement, of the specifications. In other words, you move from the high level to the detailed, from the logical to the physical.

Modularity: This means that you can identify a good design when you see a compartmentalization of data and function.

If you look at the DFD in Figure E.2., you will observe that the DFD is not the first in the series. The very first DFD would have been DFD 0, which is equivalent to the high level of detail that it is recommended to begin from. Here (at DFD 0) you can see the logical components of the system. Beneath the "0" level, the DFD begins to get more detailed and more physical. At these lower (or child) levels we start specifying files and processes.

The design document that you create will rarely look the same from one organization to another. Each organization has its own template, its own standard diagramming tool (e.g., Microsoft Visio versus SmartDraw), and its own diagramming format (e.g., flowcharts versus UML versus DFD).

When the requirements document is high level, the specification is much more detailed. It is, after all, a programming specification. For the most part, the specification document for the testing system that was discussed earlier included (1) a general description of the system, (2) its users, (3) its constraints (e.g., must run on a PC), (4) the DFDs or other format, (5) the data dictionary, (6) the process dictionary, and (g) a chart (Gantt) showing the tasks that need to be done. The purpose of this specification (usually called a *spec* by those in the field) is to give the programmers a manual they can code from. If it is a good spec, the programmers will not need to come back to you time after time to get additional information.

Design Strategies

Designing a system involves making many decisions. For example, in creating an online testing system, I had to answer the following questions:

1. What platform should the testing software run on? PC, Internet, or both?
2. If it was going to run on the Internet, should it be compatible with all browsers or just with a specific one?
3. What kind of programming language should be used? Should the client use VBScript or JavaScript? Should all of the process be on the back end? If so, which language should be used—Perl or Java?
4. What kinds of servers do I need? Do I run Microsoft NT, UNIX, or Linux? Do I need an E-commerce server? How about a RealMedia server?
5. What kind of network am I going to use? A VPN (virtual private network), Internet, intranet, or LAN?

There were hundreds of other questions that I had to answer before we were able to proceed. Answering these questions required much research. For example, if you were going to design a medical claims processing system, you would probably decide in favor of using an optical scanning system to process the thousands of medical claims that come in every day. There are many vendors of optical scanning equipment. Part of your job would be to make a list of the vendors, meet with them, and then perhaps test one or two of the competitive products.

Essentially, the job of a systems analyst here is to be an explorer—go out and hunt down the best combination of technologies to create the most cost-effective system.

Doing this may require a combination of strategies:

1. Program the whole project in-house.
2. Find out if there is a software package that you can buy and use.
3. Let someone else program it (outsource).
4. A combination of any of these items in any order.

Object-Oriented Methodologies

OO systems development follows the same pattern as structured systems development. First, you must analyze your system (OOA). Next, you design the system using OOD. Finally, you code the system using OOP techniques and languages (e.g., C++, Java).

OO techniques may have some similarity with traditional techniques, but the concept of OO is radically different from what most development people are used to. This methodology revolves around the concept of an object. An object is a representation of any information that must be understood by the software. Some examples of objects:

- External entities: printer, user, sensor
- Things: reports, displays
- Occurrences or events: alarm, interrupt
- Roles: manager, engineer, salesperson
- Organizational unit: team, division
- Places: manufacturing floor
- Structures: employee record

Therefore, an object can be any person, place, or thing.

One of the important features of OO is the reusability of its objects. A well-coded object is often thought of as a "black box." What this means is that the programmer should be able to "glue together" several objects to create a working system. He or she need not know much about any of these objects. Do you remember playing with Lego blocks as a child? It was easy to create structures such as bridges and buildings. That was because each of the blocks was easily connected to all other blocks. The same principle applies to objects (see "Encapsulation" in OO definitions).

Some OO definitions are as follows:

Class: In object technology, a user-defined data type that defines a collection of objects which share the same characteristics. An object, or class member, is one instance of the class. Concrete classes are designed to be instantiated. Abstract classes are designed to pass on characteristics through inheritance.

Object: A self-contained module of data and its associated processing. Objects are the software building blocks of object technology.

Polymorphism: In object technology, the ability of a generalized request (message) to produce different results based on the object that it is sent to.

Inheritance: In object technology, the ability of one class of objects to inherit properties from a higher class.

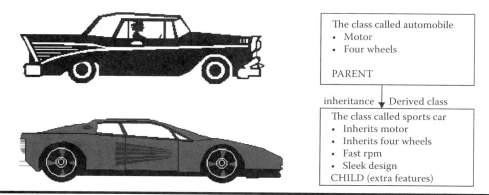

The class called automobile
- Motor
- Four wheels

PARENT

inheritance ↓ Derived class

The class called sports car
- Inherits motor
- Inherits four wheels
- Fast rpm
- Sleek design
CHILD (extra features)

Figure E.7   The depiction of a class called "automobile."

Encapsulation: In object technology, making the data and processing (methods) within the object private, which allows internal implementation of the object to be modified without requiring any change to the application that uses it. This is also known as *information hiding.*

Figure E.7 depicts a class called "automobile." This class has several common attributes. One is that it has a motor. Another is the fact that an automobile has four wheels. In an OO system, you can create derived classes from this "parent" class. The figure also depicts a derived class called "sports car" which is represented by a shiny red sports car. It also inherits a motor and four wheels from the parent class. But in this derived class, we have some additional attributes: increased rpm and sleek design. Therefore, the sports car is the "child" of the parent class named automobile. So, we can say "every convertible is an automobile, but not every automobile is a convertible."

To develop an OO application, one must define classes. If you know anything at all about OO programming languages such as C++, you will have observed that all variables within a program are defined as some "type" of data. For example, in C and C++, a number is defined as a type called "integer." So, when we define a class in a programming language, it is defined as a type of class.

```
// Program to demonstrate a very simple example of a class called
DayOfYear.
#include <iostream.h>
// This is where we define our class. We will call it DayOfYear
// It is a public class. This means that there are no restrictions
// on use. There are also private classes.
// The class DayOfYear consists of two pieces of data: month and day, and
// one function named output ( )
class DayOfYear
{
public:
 void output ( );
 int month;
 int day;
};
```

Designing OO systems requires the use of different modeling and definitional techniques that take into account the concept of classes and objects. UML is an emerging standard for modeling

OO software. Figure E.6 shows a sample class diagrammed using UML. Contained within a typical OO design specification are numerous diagrams (models):

- Class diagrams
- Object models
- Package diagrams that show how the classes are grouped together
- Collaboration diagrams that show how the classes "collaborate" or work with one another

Testing

When you tie many programs together, you have a system. It is not uncommon for a system to have thousands of lines of code (KLOC). All of this code must be tested. The very first level of testing is at the programmer's desk. Here, he or she employs whatever tools are available to ensure that everything works as it should.

Figure E.8 shows what a Visual Basic (VB) debugger looks like. A debugger, for those who don't know the derivation of the term, is a program that helps eliminate "bugs" from a program. In IT, bug is an error, but the term originated from an incident connected with one of the first computers in the early 1950s. A real bug crawled into the computer, and it stopped working. Ever since, we use the term *debugging* to describe the process of ridding a program of its faults.

The debugger will only run if your code "compiles and links" first. When you compile a program, it goes through a syntax checker. This syntax checker checks for obvious errors (e.g., referencing a variable that doesn't exist).

When a group of programmers work together, their PM might think it a good idea to hold a "walkthrough." This is when the team gets together and examines the code, as a group, to find flaws and discuss better ways to do things. Usually, this doesn't happen. One reason is that programmers don't like to have a walkthrough and another is that it is very time consuming.

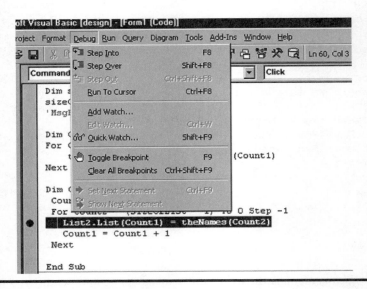

Figure E.8 Visual Basic's (VB's) debugger.

The testing that a programmer does at his own desk, can be considered a unit testing—testing a unit of work (a program). When several programs have to interact, you may need to perform integration testing. This is a test to determine if the separate parts of the system work well together. For example, let's say Program 1 creates a file that contains a student file. Program 2 processes that student file. If Program 1 makes a mistake and creates the student file incorrectly, then Program 2 will not work.

A system test checks the complete system—soup to nuts. All of the inputs, all of the outputs, and everything in between are checked. If there is an existing system, a parallel test is done. "Parallel" is a good term for this type of testing because you run both systems in parallel and then check the results for similarities and differences.

Finally, acceptance testing is done. This means that you run a test, the end user agrees (or disagrees) with it, and finally, approves (or disapproves) it.

In any case, testing requires a lot of work, involving many people, including the end users and a QA department. QA staff spend all their time writing testing scripts (i.e., a list of things to test for), and then running those scripts. If they find an error, they send a report to the programmer, who then fixes it.

QA usually uses testing tools to assist with this massive job. These tools assist with the creation of scripts, and then automatically run those scripts. This is especially helpful when doing stress testing—testing to see how well the system works when many people use it at the same time.

Testing is normally not performed in a vacuum. An analyst or manager prepares a test plan that details exactly what must be tested and by whom. The test plan contains the testing schedule as well as intricate details on what must be tested. These details are called *test cases* and form the basis for the test scripts that are used by the programmer or QA staff member, usually in conjunction with a testing tool.

A sample test case, which would appear in a test plan, is as follows. This would then be turned into a script for use by the testers.

1.1.1 Test Case: Accounting: Payment
    1.1.1.1 Description
The purpose of this test is to determine if a representative of the service care provider can enter a payment receipt within the accounting subsystem.
    1.1.1.2 Required Stubs/Drivers
The accounting subsystem will be invoked with particular attention to the Payment class.
    1.1.1.3 Test Steps
        1. The service care provider must successfully log into the system.
        2. The service care provider must invoke the Accounting user interface to enter the payment receipt.
        3. The service care provider must enter a payment receipt and press the button to commit the transaction.
    1.1.1.4 Expected Results
Test Success
        1. A subsequent query indicates the customer's balance reflecting the recent payment.
        2. A successful message is displayed.
Test Failure
        1. The customer's balance does not reflect the payment receipt.
        2. The customer's balance reflects an incorrect amount that is a result of faulty logic within the program.

Standards and Metrics

When you build a house, there are standards that you must adhere to. Otherwise, the home owner's lamp won't plug into the electrical outlet. The size of the outlet is consistent with a standard that is used throughout the building industry. Those who travel know that one must carry an adapter because a hair dryer brought from the United States may not plug into foreign electrical outlets. This is because many standards in America are different from the standards in other countries.

Standards are an important fact of life. Without them we would be living in chaos. This is especially true in the IT industry. The American National Standards Institute (ANSI; www.ansi.org), which is located in New York, was founded in 1918 to coordinate the development of U.S. voluntary national standards in both the private and public sectors. It is the U.S. member body to the International Organization for Standardization (ISO) and International Electrotechnical Commission (IEC). Information technology standards pertain to programming languages, electronic data interchange (EDI), telecommunications, and physical properties of diskettes, cartridges, and magnetic tapes. The Institute of Electrical and Electronics Engineers (IEEE; www.ieee.org) is another membership organization that develops standards.

For example, IEEE 1284 is an IEEE standard for an enhanced parallel port that is compatible with the Centronics port commonly used on PCs. Instead of just data, it can send addresses, allowing individual components in a multifunctional device (printer, scanner, fax, etc.) to be addressed independently. IEEE 1284 also defines the required cable type that increases distance to 32 feet.

Your company might well adhere to ISO 9000 and 9001. As I mentioned earlier, ANSI is the U.S. member body to ISO, a Geneva-based organization that sets international standards. (ISO 9000 is a family of standards and guidelines for quality in the manufacturing and service industries from the International Standards Association. ISO 9000 defines the criteria for what should be measured. ISO 9001 covers design and development. ISO 9002 covers production, installation, and service, and ISO 9003 covers final testing and inspection.)

If you implement quality standards in your organization, you need to have a way to measure whether or not those standards are being adhered to. In IT, we use metrics (measurements). The most prevalent metric used is lines of code, which is the number of lines of code a programmer can program in an hour.

A controlled development and maintenance program is essential to bring down the cost associated with an SDLC. The control mechanism can be implemented by first setting up specific goals and then selecting the right set of metrics for measurement against those goals. Goals need to be tangible and balanced, or they will be considered unachievable. Intermediate targets are needed to monitor the progress of the project and ensure that it is on the right track. Project data collection and analysis should also be part of the control mechanism.

A four-step procedure is outlined to establish targets and means for assessment. The procedure is not focused on any particular set of metrics; rather, metrics should be selected on the basis of goals. This procedure is suitable to set up goals for all the project deliverables or for any partial product created in the software life cycle. The four steps are described in the text, as follows:

1. Define measurable goals: The project goals establishment process is similar to the development process for project deliverables. Software projects usually start with abstract problem concepts, and the final project deliverables are obtained by continuously partitioning and refining the problem into tangible and manageable pieces. Final quantified goals can be transformed from initial intangible goals by following the same divide-and-conquer method for software deliverables. Three sources of information are helpful in establishing the targets:
   - Historical data under the assumptions that data is available, development environment is stable, and projects are similar in terms of type, size, and complexity.
   - Synthetic data such as modeling results, is useful if models used are calibrated to the specific development environment.
   - Expert opinions.
2. Maintain balanced goals: The measurable goals are usually established on the basis of the following four factors—cost, schedule, effort, and quality. It is feasible to achieve just a single goal, but it is always a challenge to deliver a project with the minimum staff and resources on time and within budget. It needs to be kept in mind that trade-off is always involved, and all issues should be addressed to reach a set of balanced goals.
3. Set up intermediate goals: A project should never be measured at its endpoint only. Checkpoints should be set up to provide confidence that the project is running on course. The common practice involves setting up quantifiable targets for each phase, measuring the actual values against the targets, and establishing a plan to make corrections for any deviations. All four earlier-mentioned factors (cost, schedule, effort, quality) should be broken down into phases or activities for setting up intermediate targets. Measurements for cost and effort can be divided into machine and human resources according to the software life-cycle phase so that expenditures can be monitored, to ensure that the project is running within budget. Schedules should always be defined in terms of milestones or checkpoints to ensure that intermediate products will be evaluated and final product can be delivered on time. The quality of intermediate products should always be measured to guarantee that the final deliverable will meet its target goal.
4. Establish the means of assessment: This activity involves two aspects—data collection and data analysis. Based on the project characteristics such as size, complexity, level of control, etc., a decision should be made in terms of whether a manual or an automated data collection process should be used. If a nonautomated process is applied, then the availability of the collection medium at the right time should be emphasized. The following two types of data analyses should be considered:
   - Project analysis—This type of analysis, consisting of checkpoint analysis and continuous analysis (trend analysis), is concerned with verifying whether the intermediate targets are being met, to ensure that the project is on the right track.
   - Component analysis—This type of analysis concentrates on the finer level of detail of the end product, and is concerned with identifying those components in the product that may require special attention and action. The complete process includes deciding on the set of measures to be analyzed, identifying the components detected as anomalous using measured data, finding out the root cause of the anomalies, and taking corrective actions.

Installation

When you have a very small system, you can just put it online (direct). If your system is larger, then there are several ways to approach the system installation (implementation). If you are going to replace an existing system, then you can install the new system in parallel mode. This means that you run both systems simultaneously for a period of time. Each day the end users check the outputs, and when they feel comfortable, retire the old system.

Many companies use multiple servers with the same system running on each server. A good way to approach system installation is to install it on a single server first, see how it runs, and then install it on another server. This is called a *phased approach*.

Documentation

One day, all the programmers who wrote the original system will leave. If documentation is inadequate, the new programmers will not understand how to work on the system. I recently worked on a foreign project (Internet gambling) where the programmer did not have any documentation at all. The system was written using C++ and ASP. There were hundreds of programs, and it was almost impossible to figure out which program ran first. So, system documentation is necessary.

It is also critical to have some documentation for the end users. You may have seen the manuals that come with software that runs on your PC. When you use Microsoft Visio, you are the end user of this software and will need a manual to use the software effectively. So, if you write a system you will also need to write a manual for your end users.

Finally, you will need to train your end users to use the system. When I worked for the New York Stock Exchange, we brought in a tool that permitted our end users to use a 4th Generation Language (4GL) to run their own queries against the system's database. We needed to train these end users to use the 4GL productively. Instead of writing and teaching a course ourselves, we hired an expert who did it for us (outsourcing).

Maintenance

Many years ago I worked with a PL who wanted to play with a new toy. At the time, databases were just coming into vogue and the PL decided to create a database for a new system. The problem was that this particular system didn't need this particular database. The system was written, but because of the horrid choice of database it never ran well. In fact, it "bombed" out all the time.

After a year of problems, management decided that the system needed to be fixed. And fix it we did. This fixing is called *corrective maintenance*—modifying an existing system so that it works correctly. There are many reasons why maintenance is done.

One reason we're all familiar with is security and viruses. Systems people frequently make modifications to software because of problems such as these. The casino gaming programmers mentioned in Reference B had to suspend programming new features into the system to eliminate the "Code Red" worm. This is an example for *preventive maintenance*.

Most often, the reason for maintenance is to simply improve the system. Casino end users deciding to add a new game to the system, adding a new data field to a database, or requiring a new report would be examples of *maintenance for improvement*.

Some organizations have two types of programmers. One type usually works on new software and the other is stuck with maintenance. This does not happen often because maintenance programmers are usually an unhappy lot and, consequently, their turnover rate is quite high.

All systems need to be managed. One cannot make changes to a system willy-nilly. The way to control what happens to a system is to regularly hold meetings with end users and develop a prioritized list of changes and additions they want made. Occasionally, a request for change may come in from a person who is not on the end-user committee. To handle these requests, system personnel usually make use of a standard change request form. This form contains information such as desired change, reason for change, screen shots of the existing screen that needs to be changed (if applicable), and more, depending on the organization. Usually these changes have to be authorized by the end user's management before it can be sent to the computer department.

Once the change request comes to the computer department, if it's simple and there's some spare time, the modification is scheduled immediately. Usually, however, it is added to a prioritized list of things to do. Once it reaches the top of the list, the same SDLC steps used during development are used during maintenance. In other words, you need to determine whether the modification is feasible, determine its cost, develop a specification, etc.

Training

Once the system has been installed, the end users will require some training. There are numerous ways to achieve this, from in-house training to CAI (computer-assisted instruction).

Once the end users have been trained, they will need support on a day-to-day basis. First, as already discussed, they will need a manual to look up answers to the questions. Some systems do not use paper manuals. Instead, everything is embedded in a Help file. If the manuals prove insufficient, then the company might want to do what most companies are doing now—fund and staff a help desk. Sometimes, people in end-user departments rely on a person (within their department) who has become quite an expert at using the system. This person is usually referred to as the resident expert.

Conclusion

In this reference, we have covered a broad array of systems development issues and methodologies. We started the "grand tour" by discussing the SDLC that identifies the different steps IT team members take when developing a computer system, using the traditional structured approach. These steps include, but are not limited to, feasibility study, analysis, design, testing, and implementation.

It is of utmost importance that an IT team use a methodology to build a system. Although systems can certainly be built without using such a methodology, the resulting systems are usually flawed, inefficient, and too expensive to maintain.

References

Keyes, J. (2002) *Software Engineering Handbook*. New York: Auerbach.

Links

http://www.extremeprogramming.org/ Extreme programming introduction.
http://www.itmweb.com/bench.htm IT metrics and benchmarks.
http://www.ambysoft.com/unifiedprocess/agileUP.html The Agile Unified Process.
http://www-306.ibm.com/software/awdtools/rup The Rational Unified Process.
http://www.swebok.org/htmlformat.html Software Engineering Body of Knowledge.

Reference F: The Feasibility Study and Cost–Benefit Analysis

A feasibility study is a detailed assessment of the need, value, and practicality of a proposed enterprise, such as systems development. Simply stated, it is used to prove that a project is either practical or impractical. The ultimate deliverable is a report that discusses the feasibility of a technical solution, and provides the basis for the steering committee to decide whether it is worth accepting any of the suggestions.

What Is a Feasibility Study?

At the beginning of every project, it is often difficult to determine if the project will be successful or not, if the cost of the project will be reasonable with respect to the requirements of building a certain software, or if the project will be profitable in the long run.

In general, a feasibility study should include the following information:

1. Brief description of proposed system and characteristics
2. Brief description of the business need for the proposed system
3. A cost–benefit analysis
4. Estimates, schedules, and reports

In developing the feasibility study there is a need for considerable research into the business as well as technical viability of the proposed system.

Feasibility Study Categories

There are actually three categories of feasibility, which are described in the following subsections.

Financial Feasibility

A systems development project should be economically feasible and should provide good value to the organization. The benefits should outweigh the costs of completing the project. The financial

247

feasibility also includes the time, budget, and staff resources used during all the stages of the project through completion.

A feasibility study will determine if the proposed budget is enough to fund the project to completion. When finances are being discussed, time considerations must also be factored in. Saving time and enhancing user convenience have always been major concerns when companies develop products. Companies want to make sure that services rendered are timely. No end user wants to wait for a long time to receive service or use a product, however good it is, if another similar product is immediately available.

The following are the key risk issues:

1. The length of the project's payback times: The shorter the payback time, the lower the risk.
2. The length of the project's development time: The shorter the development time, the less likely it is that objectives, users, and development personnel will change; consequently, the lower the risk.
3. The magnitude of the changes made to estimates: The smaller the changes made in cost, benefit, and life-cycle estimates, the greater the confidence that you will achieve the expected result.

Technical Feasibility

It should be practical to develop a computer system. Also, the system should be easy to maintain. It is important that the necessary expertise be available to analyze, design, code, install, operate, and maintain the system. Technical feasibility addresses the possibility and desirability of a computer solution in the problem area. Assessments can be made on the basis of many factors, such as knowledge of current and emerging technical solutions, availability of technical personnel on staff, working knowledge of technical staff, capacity of the proposed system to meet requirements, and capacity of the proposed system to meet performance requirements.

The process of developing new technology must take into account the current technology. Will today's technology be able to sustain what we plan to develop? How realistic is the project? Do we have the knowledge and tools needed to accomplish the job? Technology is getting more and more advanced with each passing day, and somehow we need to know if our objectives can be realized. It is not enough to note if the product in development is technologically feasible, we also have to make sure that it is at par with or more advanced than the technology in use today.

The following are the key risk issues:

1. Project staff skills and clarity of project design requirements: Technical risk is reduced where similar problems have been solved, or where the design requirements are understandable to all project participants.
2. Proven and accepted equipment and software: Tried and tested hardware and software components carry lower risk. Projects that are novel or break new ground carry higher risk.
3. Project complexity: A project that requires a high degree of technical skills and experience will have a higher associated risk than a less-sophisticated one that can be handled by less specialized people.

Organizational or Operational Feasibility

A systems development project should meet the needs and expectations of the organization. It is important that the system be made operational and that it be accepted by the user. The following requirements should be taken into consideration in determining if the system is operationally feasible: staff resistance or receptiveness to change, management support for a new system, nature or level of user involvement, direct and indirect impact of new system on current work practices, anticipated performance and outcome of the new system compared to the old system, and viability of development and implementation schedule. The following issues should also be addressed:

1. Does the organization to which the information system is to be supplied have a history of acceptance of information technology, or has past introduction led to conflict?
2. Will personnel within the organization be able to operate the new technology?
3. Is the organizational structure compatible with the proposed information system?

The following are the key risk issues:

1. User acceptance: The more strongly users support the project, the lower the risk of failure.
2. Changes to organizational policies and structure: The more a project influences changes to relationships within an organization or modifies existing policies, the greater the risk.
3. Changes to method of operation, practices, and procedures: The more a project necessitates major changes or modifications to standard operating procedures in an organization, the greater the risk of failure.

Organizational feasibility, depending on the scope of the software to be developed, might require the following analyses, particularly if the software being developed is a product that will be introduced to the marketplace:

Competitive analysis: Competitive analysis refers to the study of the current trends and different brand names available in today's market to enforce competitive advantage in product development.

New product development analysis: New product development is a key factor in feasibility studies; it studies the need and uniqueness of a product, justifying further study, development, and subsequent launching.

Performance tracking analysis: Performance tracking evaluates how well a product will perform technically and financially with regard to its features and requirements.

Scheduling the Feasibility Study

Creating a schedule for the feasibility study is very important in that it puts into perspective the amount of time required, the people involved, the potential consumers, and the competition that will provide the relevant information. Tasks include selecting a team, assigning appropriate tasks to each team member, and estimating the amount of time required to finish each task. Some of the scheduling tools that can be utilized are diagrams showing relevant work scheduling in relation to the tasks required to finish the feasibility study. Some tools use a task list (Table F.1), a Gantt chart (Figure F.1), or a PERT (program evaluation review technique) diagram (Figure F.2; a network of nodes and arrows that are evaluated to determine the project's critical activities). Precedence of activities is important in determining the length of the project when using a PERT diagram.

Table F.1 Task List

Feasibility Study Tasks	Detailed Activity	Weeks Required
Data Gathering	Conduct Interviews	3
	Administer Questionnaires	4
	Read Company Reports	4
	Introduce Prototype	5
	Observe Reactions to Prototype	3
Data Flow and Decision Analysis	Analyze Data Flow	8
Proposal Preparation	Perform Cost–Benefit Analysis	3
	Prepare Proposal	2
	Present Proposal	2

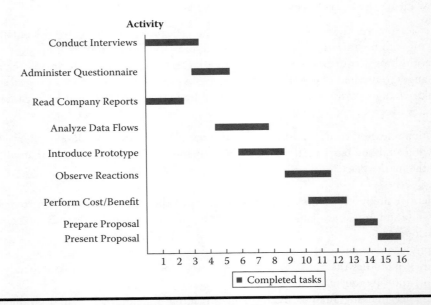

Figure F.1   A two-dimensional Gantt chart: Figuring the time schedule with respect to the related activity may also be accomplished using a Gantt chart.

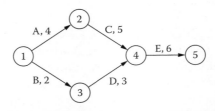

Figure F.2   A PERT (program evaluation review technique) diagram.

		YR 1	YR 2	YR 3	YR 4	YR 5
Int Rate		10.00%				
NPV		$1,450,582.94				
IRR		103%				
Payback Payback manually calculated		2.0yrs				

Assumptions	EXPENSES	YR 1	YR 2	YR 3	YR 4	YR 5
	IT Related					
Initial Hardware plus additional yearly capacity	Hardware	$304,000	$50,000	$50,000	$50,000	$50,000
Solution Software and licensing costs for upgrades	Software	$111,000				
Project related design and implementation costs	People	$90,000				
Training, policies and procedures	Training/Materials	$250,000				
Costs associated with potential unknown factors	Variance	$75,000				
	User Related					
	Hardware					
	Software					
Human Resources for the Project	People	$300,000				
Training for developers on application rollback	Training/Materials	$10,000				
	Lost Opportunity					
	Total	$1,140,000	$50,000	$50,000	$50,000	$50,000
	BENEFITS					
	IT Related					
Gains achieved from buying less servers	Hardware	$83,300	$83,300	$83,300	$83,300	$83,300
	Software	$0				
1 man less spent Managing Storage	People	$50,000	$50,000	$50,000	$50,000	$50,000
Gains from more efficient use of storage	Productivity Gains	$75,000	$100,000	$125,000	$150,000	$175,000
	User Related					
	Hardware	$0				
	Software	$0				
Improved development efficiency, based on company growth	People	$150,000	$175,000	$200,000	$225,000	$250,000
Improved profit margins on projects, based on company growth	Productivity Gains	$200,000	$225,000	$250,000	$275,000	$300,000
	Total	$558,300	$633,300	$708,300	$783,300	$858,300
	Total PMT	($581,700)	$583,300	$658,300	$733,300	$808,300

Figure F.3   Comparison of expected benefits to expenses.

The Feasibility Study Process

There is a specific process that a feasibility study should follow. The study should analyze the proposed project and produce a written description, define and document possible types of systems, and develop a statement regarding the probable types of systems. The feasibility study should analyze the costs of similar systems, produce a rough estimate of the system size, costs, and schedules, and define the benefits of the system. It should produce an estimate of the next stage of the life cycle. Analysis of the current system is necessary to establish feasibility of a future technical system. This will provide justification for the functions that the new system will perform. Finally, a report should be written, containing suggestions, findings, and information about necessary resources.

A feasibility report will be written and submitted to management, containing all relevant information including financial expenses and expected benefits, as shown in Figure F.3. On the basis of this report, management will determine the future of the project. Much of the information will come from the analyst and the systems investigation. The report should include information on the feasibility of the project, the principal work areas for the project, any needs for specialist staff that may be required at later stages, possible improvements or potential savings, costs and benefits, as well as recommendations. Charts and diagrams related to the project, such as Gantt and PERT charts, should be included in the feasibility report. Obviously, the project cannot proceed until the feasibility report has been accepted.

Determining Feasibility

A proposal may be regarded feasible if it satisfies the three criteria we've discussed at length earlier: financial, technical, and operational. Scheduling and legal issues must also be considered. It is possible to proceed with the project even if one or more of these criteria fail to be met. For example, management may find that it is not possible to proceed with the project at one point in time, but may find that the project can commence at a later date. Another option would be for management to make amendments to the proposed agenda and agree to proceed upon those conditions. Conversely, a project that may have been determined feasible may later be determined infeasible because of changes in circumstances.

Other Considerations

With many kinds of projects, costs and benefits are usually the main concerns. There are, however, other concerns that should also be considered. Project timeframe is a consideration that should be addressed in the feasibility study. Realistic estimates should be made, detailing staff resources and time required to complete the different phases of the project.

In dealing with the project, it is also important to consider all legal or regulatory issues that may occur throughout the feasibility study, or during any stage of the project. It may be wise to conduct a preliminary investigation of any obligations, or regulatory or legal issues prior to commencement of the initial project stages.

Stages of Feasibility Study

The stages of a feasibility study include the following, as shown in Figure F.4:

1. Define project scope
2. Activity analysis
3. Needs analysis
4. Conceptual modeling
5. Use case modeling
6. Identify nonfunctional requirements
7. Identify options
8. Select options
9. Plan acquisition strategy
10. Develop business case
11. Package the feasibility study

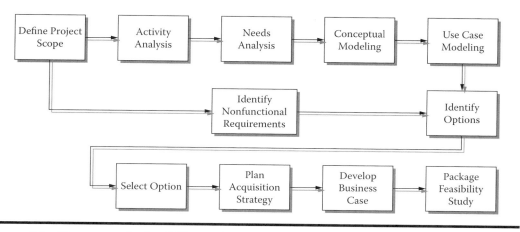

Figure F.4   The stages of a feasibility study.

Cost–Benefit Analysis

One of the major deliverables of the feasibility study is the cost–benefit analysis. In this document, the organizational, financial, and technical aspects of creating the software are put into a dollars and cents format.

The purpose of this document is to determine whether the costs exceed the benefits of the new or modified system. Costs associated with a computer project can be categorized as follows:

1. Systems analysis and design
2. Purchase of hardware
3. Software costs
4. Training costs
5. Installation costs
6. Conversion and changeover costs
7. Redundancy costs
8. Operating costs, including people costs

Many specific costs are subcategorized within these categories, such as analyst calculations of total cost of project, alternatives to purchasing hardware, the staff needed to train users, maintenance costs for hardware and software, costs of power and paper, and costs associated with personnel to operate the new system. The following is a more detailed list:

Equipment: Includes disk drives, computers, telecommunications, tape drives, printers, facsimiles, voice and data networks, terminals, modems, data encryption devices, and physical firewalls (leased or purchased).

Software: Includes application programs, operating systems, diagnostic programs, utility programs, commercial off-the-shelf (COTS) software such as word processors and graphics programs, database management software, communications software, and server software (leased or purchased).

Commercial services: Includes teleprocessing, cell phones, voice mail, online processing, Internet access, packet switching, data entry, and legal services.

Support services: Includes systems analysis and design, programming, training, planning, project management, facilities management, and network support.

Supplies: Includes tapes, paper, pens, pencils, CD-ROMs, etc.

Personnel: Includes the salary and benefits for all staff involved. Benefits are usually calculated at a rate of 30 percent of the base salary.

It is important that the benefits outweigh the costs. Some of the benefits cannot necessarily be measured; nevertheless, they should be taken into consideration. Some of those benefits are intangible, such as savings in labor costs, benefits due to faster processing, better decision making, better customer service, and error reduction. When dealing with both benefits and costs, it may be difficult to determine either in advance.

Cost information can be obtained from the following:

1. Experiences from the past: Old documents and information will be useful in getting some ideas about the cost of software, hardware, and each service. Invoices of expenses incurred on resources purchased for prior projects are particularly useful.
2. Costs from market: It's also important to get the current market price for your software system.
3. Publishing: Business and trade publications, and the Internet are other sources of price information, as well as product functionality.
4. Personal experience: End users and system staff might have relevant information on costs and product feature sets.

Conclusion

The primary goal of the feasibility study is to evaluate the risks and benefits, and the potential of a proposed project. We also know that the study should aid in producing a solid plan for the research stage and the stages to follow, so that the project will be given careful consideration and be properly funded. According to Burch, a feasibility study will help you make informed and transparent decisions at crucial points during the developmental process, to determine whether proceeding with a particular course of action is operationally, economically, and technically viable. It should provide a means of minimizing risks, clarifying issues and expectations, and improving the decision-making process for the ensuing project stages.

Reference G: Project Plan Outline

Project Deds—The Dog e-Dating System ID—PRJ01

Approval Record

Department	Printed Name	Signature	Role	Date

August 2007

Document Information

Document Name	Document Type	Doc. ID
Document2	Project Plan Outline	PRJ01

Document Creation Information

Date	Created By	Comments	# Pages
2007-08-07	Sample	Document Creation	1

Document Revision History

Ver #	Update Description	Updated by	Date
0.1	First Draft		08-07-07
0.2	Project Estimates		08-15-07
0.3	Project Schedule and Staff Organization		08-22-07
0.4	Risk Mitigation and Management Plan		08-28-07
0.5	Tracking and Control Mechanism		09-10-07

Table of Contents

1.   Goals and Objectives

1.1.   Project Name

This project plan serves as a coordinating tool, planning aid and communication device to identify and convey the key elements of Dog e-Dating System (DeDS) project. The development effort will be performed entirely within the organization without the participation of outside parties.

Project Title: DeDS—The Dog e-Dating System
Sponsor: Sample
Organization Name: Sample
E-mail: email@domain.com
Phone: +1

1.2. Business Goals and Objectives

The primary business goal of the company is to gain a market share of 20 percent on the online DeDS by the end of the first year, corresponding to a 32 percent increase on current yearly net revenue. Additionally, it will serve as a promoting vehicle for partnerships agreements, and as an advertisement medium for pet stores that will increase the net revenue by 8 percent by the end of the first year. The market share should rise to 30 percent at the end of the second year, representing 48 percent of yearly net revenue and partnerships, and advertisement revenues should represent 20 percent of our net revenue.

The goal of the project is to create a platform that enables the fulfillment of the business objectives, by creating an interactive online system that registers information from customers, and potential customers which supports matching of eligible dogs for breeding based on different searchable criteria.

1.3. Scope

As a result of the limited gene pool due to continuous inbreeding, deleterious genes become widespread and the breed loses vigor. Apart from natural causes, most of the time this is due to a paucity of options or lack of knowledge of the breeder. The ultimate results of this continuous inbreeding are terminal lack of vigor and probable extinction of the breed. As the gene pool shrinks, fertility decreases, abnormalities increase (common examples are the bulldog and German shepherd), and mortality rates rise. On the other hand, selective breeding also have risks as a number of breeds now exhibit hereditary defects due to the overuse of a particular "typey" stud that was later found to carry a gene detrimental to health.

The DeDS provides a secure and informative source for selective breeding, allowing their customers to preserve or improve breed purity. When subscribing to DeDS, users will provide their contact information and relevant information about their dog. The system will perform an initial classification, and analyze and report potential matches based on client criteria or professional tips.

The system will promote business transactions between users, professional services and products from our partners, and a permission marketing database for personalized advertisement. These three areas will generate the revenue of the DeDS. The system will charge a 17 percent fee over the breed price on all business transactions between users, a monthly fee of $100 and an 8 percent fee on all products and services provided by partners, and $300 for an advertisement e-mail service to selected customers based on dog and contact details, purchased services and products, and transaction information.

1.4. Time and Budget Constraints

We propose the following chronogram for the implementation of the DeDS:

Tasks/Week	1	2	3	4	5	6	7	8	9	10	11	12	13	14	15	16	17	18	19	20
Planning																				
Requirements analysis																				
Specification																				
Construction																				
Test scripts																				
System tests																				
Configuration																				
Integration tests																				
Training																				
Acceptance tests																				
Production rollout																				
Technical support																				
Project management																				
Milestones	PPO			REQ SDP								TS				SDF SW			ACP	

PPO—Project Plan Outline

REQ—Requirements

SDP—Solution Design Draft

SDF—Solution Design Final

Doc—Manuals

SW—Software

TS—Test Specification

ACP—Acceptance

According to the budget defined for 2007, this project has a limited budget of $258.000. This amount should be spent according to the following plan:

Phase	Percent
Adjudication	30
After 4 weeks	10
After 8 weeks	10
After 12 weeks	20
Acceptance tests delivery	20
Acceptance	10

1.5.   *General and Technical Requirements*

The DeDS should support the following general requirements:

- User-friendly Web-based application
- Creation of user accounts with contact and dog information
- The ability to allow users to drop an existing account
- The ability to authenticate users based on username and password
- The ability to edit or delete contact and dog information
- A mechanism to query and search the database based on definable criteria and filters
- Secure e-payments
- Creation of accounts and participation of users on online forums and communities with e-mail forwarding facility
- A mechanism for users to create alerts based on searchable criteria
- Different currencies (up to four decimals)
- E-mail broadcast based on predefined criteria
- Banner advertisement based on user history, and contact or dog information
- Different tax rates
- An external interface based on standard protocols such as CORBA, APIs, SOAP (XML), or Web services
- At least 500 simultaneous users with no visible performance bottlenecks
- The ability to take advantage of multiprocessors, and run processes on multiple CPUs
- System uptime not lower than 99 percent
- HTTPS protocol as the basis for every authentication request and online payment

Currently, the infrastructure is based on Solaris 10 and Linux AS4 servers with Oracle 10g databases and Bea WebLogic 10 application server. All developments should be compatible with this requirement to avoid restrictions on technology migrations in the future.

According to our technological plan and system architecture, all systems should be based in an n-tier layer with support for the following hardware:

- Database Server
  Platform: Solaris 10 64-bit
  CPU: 4 × @850 MHz
  RAM: 8 GB
  Network Card: 1000 Mbps
  HD: 300 GB
- Application Server
  Platform: Solaris 10 64-bit
  CPU: 4 × @1000 MHz
  RAM: 16 GB
  Network Card: 1000 Mbps
  HD: 100 GB
- Presentation Layer
  Platform: Windows XP SP2/Vista 32-bit or 64-bit
  CPU: Pentium III 700 MHz (minimum)
  RAM: 256 MB SDRAM
  Graphics Card: AGP 4/8 MB SGRAM

1.6. Training and Documentation

According to our standards, all projects should deliver project and product documentation including but not limited to the following:

- Feasibility Report
- Project Plan
- System Requirements Specification
- Solution Design
- System Operator's Policies and Procedures
- User, Support, and Operations Manuals
- Test Specification

All training should be provided in specific courses with extensive use of real case scenarios. All course, project, and product documentation should be delivered both in paper and electronic format.

1.7. Installation

The participation of one system administrator or database administrator (DBA) in every new software installation hosted in the data center is mandatory. For that reason, all installations should be signed by the IT Manager, and scheduled at least four days in advance with the data center manager.

2.   Project Estimates

2.1. People Costs

a) Historical or Researched Data

This project will be developed by our internal IT staff. There is no need to recruit new employees or outsource to finish this project. The team will comprise eight IT resources and one Business Analyst from the business unit requirement team. The salaries of resources involved in the project are shown in the next section.

b) Salary Requirements

According to Table G.1, the average burdened labor rate is $57.7 per resource per hour based on the 40 percent salary per month.

2.2. Equipment Costs

a) Hardware

According to Section 1.5, the project will be implemented in two different servers with Solaris OS 10. Sun Microsystems replied to our request for proposal (RFP) with the following quotations:

Table G.1   Salary Requirements

Profession	40 Percent Salary per Month (Dollars)	Average Salary per Month (Dollars)
Program Manager	14080	10057,14
Programmer 1	10115	7225,00
Programmer 2	9875	7053,57
Programmer 3	9476	6768,57
Quality and Tests 1	8853	6323,57
Quality and Tests 2	8700	6214,29
Web Designer	9563	6830,71
Business Analyst	7718	5512,86
Technical Manager	12997	9283,57

- Application Server: $10,423
- Database Server: $12,775

Both servers include our partnership discount of 12 percent on the market price.

b)   Software

The software will be developed in Java J2EE over the Bea Weblogic application server with Oracle 10g database. Our current agreement with Bea will be extended and we need to purchase four more licenses (one per CPU) of Bea Weblogic Integrator. According to their last proposal from June this year, each license costs $5418, and there is a yearly support and maintenance fee of 20 percent over this value.

2.3.   Estimation Techniques

a)   COCOMO Cost Estimation

According to historical data in similar projects, the average number of lines of code per programmer per day in an object-oriented language is 120 with a 17 percent Brak. The estimation performed in COCOMO was based in the source lines of code (SLOC) sizing method, and considered the average burdened labor rate of $57.7 per resource per hour, provided by our budget expert. This corresponds to ($57.7 \times 8 \times 22$) $10,032 a month.

Because this is the first time that we are using COCOMO to estimate costs, the system was not calibrated with previous information.

The results of COCOMO show that the project will require 30.6 person-months of time to complete at a cost of $307,154.78.

b)   Process-Based Estimation

The team is composed of the resources listed in Table G.2. The team consists of nine resources corresponding to [9(9–1)/2] 36 interfaces. The results of the process-based analysis show that the

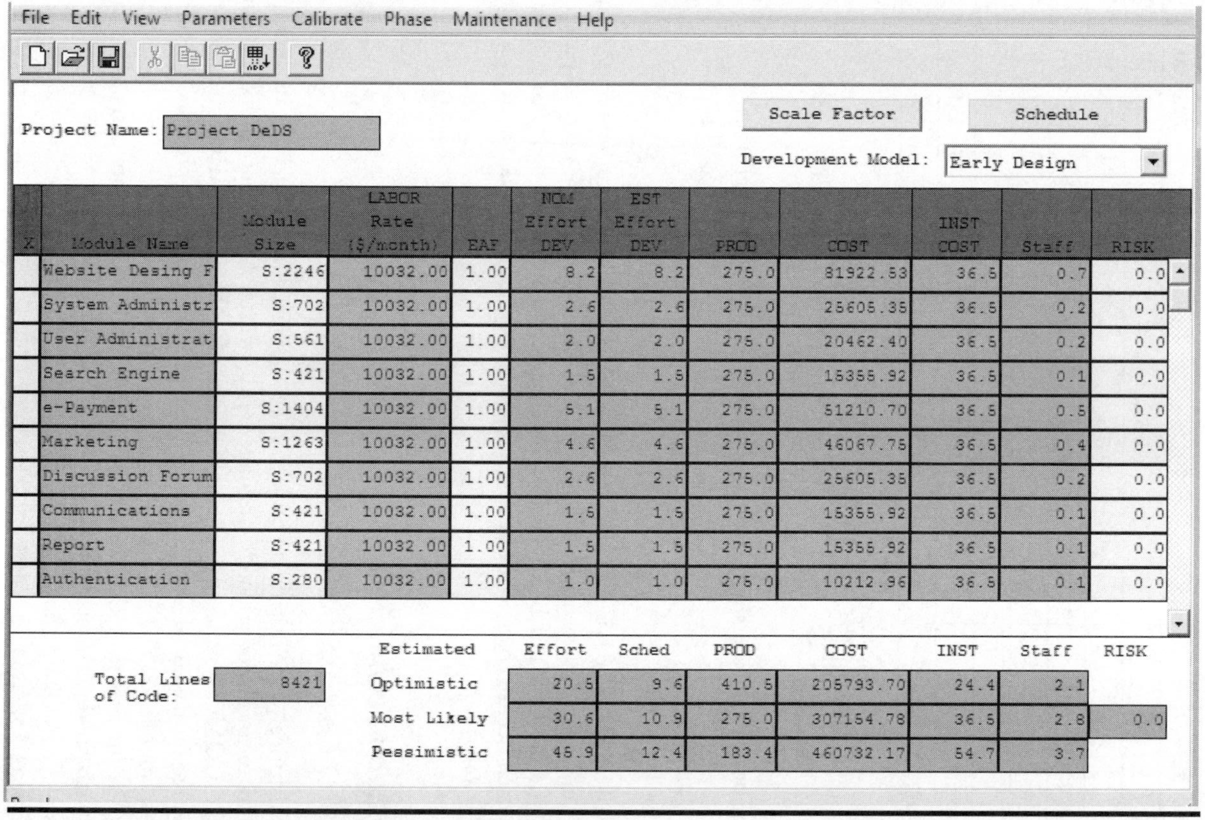

File　Edit　View　Parameters　Calibrate　Phase　Maintenance　Help

Project Name: Project DeDS

Scale Factor | Schedule

Development Model: Early Design

X	Module Name	Module Size	LABOR Rate ($/month)	EAF	NOM Effort DEV	EST Effort DEV	PROD	COST	INST COST	Staff	RISK
	Website Desing F	S:2246	10032.00	1.00	8.2	8.2	275.0	81922.53	36.5	0.7	0.0
	System Administr	S:702	10032.00	1.00	2.6	2.6	275.0	25605.35	36.5	0.2	0.0
	User Administrat	S:561	10032.00	1.00	2.0	2.0	275.0	20462.40	36.5	0.2	0.0
	Search Engine	S:421	10032.00	1.00	1.5	1.5	275.0	15355.92	36.5	0.1	0.0
	e-Payment	S:1404	10032.00	1.00	5.1	5.1	275.0	51210.70	36.5	0.5	0.0
	Marketing	S:1263	10032.00	1.00	4.6	4.6	275.0	46067.75	36.5	0.4	0.0
	Discussion Forum	S:702	10032.00	1.00	2.6	2.6	275.0	25605.35	36.5	0.2	0.0
	Communications	S:421	10032.00	1.00	1.5	1.5	275.0	15355.92	36.5	0.1	0.0
	Report	S:421	10032.00	1.00	1.5	1.5	275.0	15355.92	36.5	0.1	0.0
	Authentication	S:280	10032.00	1.00	1.0	1.0	275.0	10212.96	36.5	0.1	0.0

Total Lines of Code: 8421

Estimated	Effort	Sched	PROD	COST	INST	Staff	RISK
Optimistic	20.5	9.6	410.5	205793.70	24.4	2.1	
Most Likely	30.6	10.9	275.0	307154.78	36.5	2.8	
Pessimistic	45.9	12.4	183.4	460732.17	54.7	3.7	0.0

Figure G.1　COCOMO cost estimation (SLOC method).

Table G.2   Resources and Allocation

Resource	*Allocation (percentage)*
Program Manager	20
Programmer 1	100
Programmer 2	100
Programmer 3	100
Quality and Tests 1	100
Quality and Tests 2	100
Web Designer	100
Business Analyst	100
Technical Manager	20

project will require 20.24 person-months of time to complete at a cost of ($57.7 × 8 × 22 × 20.24) $205,541.24.

c)   Triangulation

Both methods provide different values with a considerable difference. Process-based estimation requires 20.24 person-months of time, and costs $205,541.24. COCOMO shows that the project will require 30.6 person-months of time to complete at a cost of $307,154.78. Even though the optimistic figures of COCOMO match those of process-based estimation with a very small variance, the fact is that there is a difference of nearly 34 percent. This is partly because the process is in a very early stage, and because of the experience of the programmers both in this technology and in similar previous projects. The speed of development will be very high, and there is the possibility of readapting some code.

Activity	Cust. Comm	Planning	Risk Analysis	Engineering		Construction Release		Customer Eval.	Totals
Task				Analysis	Design	Code	Test		
Function									
Website Design	0,45	0,05	0,02	0,34	0,42	0,45	0,5	0,14	2,82
System Administration	0,2	0,08	0,1	0,35	0,37	0,35	0,25	0,10	2
User Administration	0,2	0,08	0,05	0,25	0,55	0,45	0,25	0,12	2,15
Search Engine	0,15	0,05	0,01	0,33	0,39	0,38	0,29	0,10	1,85
e-Payment	0,35	0,05	0,07	0,35	0,41	0,39	0,44	0,11	2,52
Marketing	0,25	0,08	0,07	0,35	0,42	0,45	0,41	0,15	2,43
Discussion Forum	0,1	0,02	0,01	0,19	0,25	0,38	0,41	0,10	1,56
Communication	0,05	0,02	0,01	0,27	0,28	0,44	0,37	0,11	1,6
Report	0,2	0,05	0,04	0,35	0,4	0,36	0,33	0,15	2,08
Authentication	0,05	0,05	0,02	0,05	0,25	0,38	0,23	0,15	1,23
Total	2	0,53	0,4	2,83	3,74	4,03	3,48	1,23	20,24
% effort	9,88	2,62	1,98	13,98	18,48	19,91	17,19	6,08	100

Figure G.2   Process-based estimation.

3. Project Schedule

3.1. Project Task List

Table G.3 Project Task List

Number	Tasks	Deliverable	Dates/Days	Precedence	Milestone
T001	Project Kick-Off	Agreement/Contract	08-15-2007		
T999	Project Ends	Delivery			12-28-2007
T010	Requirement Definition and Analysis	Elaborate plan	08-15-2007		10-24-2007
T011	Produce Project Plan	Deliver plan	3		08-22-2007
T012	Produce Solution Design	Define requirements	14	T010	
T013		Final solution design	25		10-22-2007
T014		Final project plan	1		10-24-2007
T020	Develop Code	Web site	16		10-23-2007
T021		Modules	11		10-23-2007
T022	Create	Documentation	11		10-23-2007
T030	Design	Test plan	15	T013	11-14-2007
T031	Execute	System test	12	T030;T020;T021	11-14-2007
T032		Integration tests	8	T031	12-10-2007
T033	Prepare	Training	5	T022	12-05-2007
T034	Execute	Training	4	T033	12-05-2007
T035	Support	Acceptance tests	11	T034	12-21-2007
T036	Migrate	Software to production	5	T035	12-28-2007

3.2. Timeline Chart

See Figure G.3.

4. Staff Organization

4.1. Team Structure

The resources for this project are identified in Table G.4. Each resource is vital to this team and creates the necessary balance to achieve the project goals. This is a functional, structured team having all the skills and knowledge necessary to the success of the project. According to the

Project DeDS - Time Chart Outline

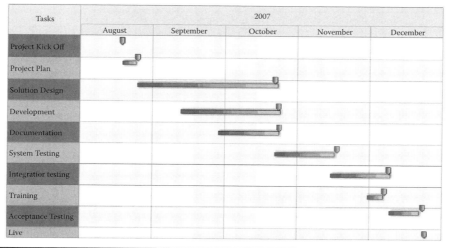

Figure G.3   Time chart.

organization chart shown in Figure G.4, the Project Manager (PM) is supported by a business analyst, and reports to the Chief Information Officer (CIO).

4.2.   *Management Reporting and Communication*

Every Monday there will be a progress meeting between the Program Manager, Quality Manager, Technical Manager, and Marketing Manager to provide feedback on project performance. Every quarter, the Program Manager will report to the steering committee the project performance and major issues concerning project development. All change requests and new requirements will be

Table G.4   Team Structure

Resource	Resource Role
Pedro	Program Manager
Paul	Programmer
Kate	Programmer
John	Programmer
Bill	Quality and Tests
Karl	Quality and Tests
Roy	Web Designer
Greg	Business Analyst
Simon	Marketing Manager
Jane	Technical Manager

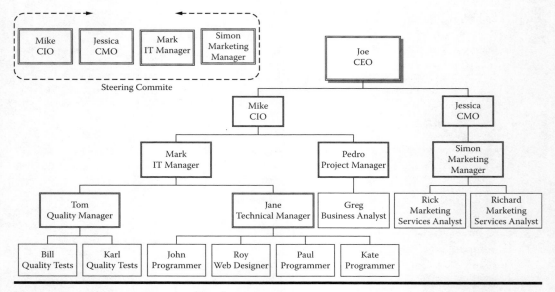

Figure G.4   Company organization chart.

approved in this forum. The Program Manager will present a revised version of the Project Plan (Gantt chart) with the impact of the new requirements or changes for the evaluation of the steering committee.

5.   Risk Management

5.1.   Project Risks

This software will be running in our data center and will be exposed to the public network through port 80 and port 81 for authentication. It is necessary to ensure that a private LAN will host this service and to isolate it from the remaining applications hosted in the data center. Additionally, it is necessary to implement rules in the firewall between the red network (exposed to the outside world) and the green network (data center VLANS) to allow connectivity between the application and the database server.

It is necessary to perform stress tests on the load-balancing Alteons, and ensure that the failsafe solution based on cluster redundancy is working. It is expected that a high volume of data will be stored in the database. To avoid performance bottlenecks in the application, it is necessary to guarantee that the DBAs suggest the required maintenance plans regarding reorganization of indexes and support activities to preserve the database performance as it grows.

According to the information uncovered in our analysis, we identified four risk areas:

1. Project Risk: Risks associated with budget, scheduling, and resources.
2. Technical Risks: Risks associated with solution design, application stress, failover, redundancy, data integrity.
3. Business Risks: Risks associated with lack of senior support, marketing failure, missing the time to market because of offers from competitors.
4. Security Risks: Risks associated with secure customer information, online payments, outside world's access to a server in our data center, etc.

These risks have been further expanded to the following categories:

- **Business Impact Risk (BU):** Product does not meet the customer requests or no longer meets the overall business strategy.
- **Financial (FI):** Budgetary requirements, creditor and debtor management, and general account management concerns.
- **Organizational (OI):** Internal requirements, and cultural and structural issues are included.
- **Compliance/Legal (CL):** Legal requirements, regulation, standard codes, and contractual requirements are included.
- **Equipment (EI):** Equipment utilized in the project (includes their maintenance and upgradation).
- **Security (SI):** Overall security of the solution and information.
- **Customers Risk (CU):** Lack of customer involvement in the project.
- **Development Risk (DR):** Risks associated with bugs in the code and delays associated with development issues.
- **Staff Size and Experience Risk (ST):** The experience and knowledge of the people involved in the project as well as the number and quantum of resources.
- **Technology Risk (TR):** The complexity associated with the design of the system.

5.2.   Risk Table

The following table lists the risks associated with the project, according to the categories described in Section 5.1. Each risk has an estimated probability based on the team's previous experience, historical data, and its impact on the development process.

Risk	Category	Probability (percent)	Impact
Change of requirements	OI	90	2
Lack of user involvement	CU	40	2
Lack of management involvement	CU	30	2
Poor acceptance by end users (product)	BU	15	2
Limited budget	FI	45	1
Inexperienced project team	ST	10	2
Fraud on payment server	SI	10	1
Customer information security hacked	SI	30	2
Delay in equipment delivery	EI	30	2
Poor estimation on load balance solution	TR	35	3
Data center security violated due to "Pin Holes"	SI	20	1
Not enough storage	EI	30	2
Staff leaving the project team	ST	10	2

Impact values: 1 = catastrophic; 2 = critical; 3 = marginal; and 4 = negligible.

5.3. Risk Mitigation, Monitoring, and Management Strategy

For each of the risk events, there is an associated contingency plan to avoid, mitigate, accept, or transfer the risk.

Risk Event	Change of requirements
Risk ID	OI-1
Risk Response Action	Acceptance
Description	Customer will change requirements during the project life cycle, requesting the team to readapt already developed code, create new functionalities, and perform new system and integration tests. The project has a small buffer to accommodate change requests and new requirements. One of the programmers is being used at 30 percent only
Assigned To	Pedro
Date	08/29/2007

Risk Event	Lack of user involvement
Risk ID	CU-1
Risk Response Action	Transfer
Description	Report lack of user involvement to the responsible functional manager and to project sponsors. Reflect the lack of participation on project schedules and stress that point on progress meetings.
Assigned To	Pedro
Date	08/29/2007

Risk Event	Lack of management involvement
Risk ID	CU-2
Risk Response Action	Mitigate
Description	Communicate the impact of AWOL Project sponsors in the project success.
Assigned To	Pedro
Date	08/29/2007

Risk Event	Limited budget
Risk ID	FI-1
Risk Response Action	Avoid
Description	Any change that implies a budget change needs to be approved by the steering committee.
Assigned To	Pedro
Date	08/29/2007

Risk Event	Poor acceptance by the customers
Risk ID	BU-1
Risk Response Action	Mitigate
Description	Evaluate through user feedback the reason for the poor acceptance. Depending on users responses, reformulate offer with Marketing, and if necessary, design more features.
Assigned To	Simon
Date	08/29/2007

Risk Event	Inexperienced project team
Risk ID	ST-1
Risk Response Action	Avoid
Description	All managers assigned to this project have several years of experience allowing them to supervise more inexperienced resources and avoid totally their lack experience or knowledge.
Assigned To	Pedro
Date	08/29/2007

Risk Event	Fraud on payment server
Risk ID	SI-1
Risk Response Action	Avoid
Description	The secure payment server will be based in an outsourced service with minimum development from our side. Before going live, our partner runs several tests to test compliance with their safety standards.
Assigned To	Pedro
Date	08/29/2007

Risk Event	Customer information security hacked
Risk ID	SI-2
Risk Response Action	Mitigate
Description	All customer information will be encrypted using a 256-bit Advanced Encryption Standard (AES) key.
Assigned To	Jane
Date	08/29/2007

Risk Event	Delay in equipment delivery
Risk ID	EI-1
Risk Response Action	Mitigate
Description	A temporary server with similar capacity can be used for a period of 1 month.
Assigned To	Jane
Date	08/29/2007

Risk Event	Poor estimation on load balance
Risk ID	TR-1
Risk Response Action	Avoid
Description	Stress tests will be executed on the load balancers to test their performance in several stress scenarios.
Assigned To	Jane
Date	08/29/2007

Risk Event	Data center security violated due to "Pin Holes"
Risk ID	SI-3
Risk Response Action	Mitigate
Description	A security team will be hired to find security violations in our system and to recommend defensive measures. Additionally, system administrators will analyze machine logs for suspicious requests.
Assigned To	Pedro
Date	08/29/2007

Risk Event	Not enough storage
Risk ID	SI-3
Risk Response Action	Mitigate
Description	Storage was bought to cover marketing expectations for the first year plus 30 percent
Assigned To	Jane
Date	08/29/2007

Risk Event	Staff leaving the project
Risk ID	SI-3
Risk Response Action	Mitigate
Description	The program manager will maintain a close relationship with all team members to spot signs that might indicate their wish to leave the project.
Assigned To	Pedro
Date	08/29/2007

6. Tracking and Control Mechanisms

Control means comparing where we are to where we were supposed to be, so that corrective actions can be employed to set right deviations from target. In our project, we will use a Tracking Gantt chart to monitor planned project activities against actual performance. This process occurs every week on Mondays during the project team meeting. The first part of the meeting will review the issue log, and establish priorities and corrective actions for each issue. All actions will be classified as Red, Yellow, or Green depending on the impact severity on the project plan. The second part of the meeting will focus on identifying and mitigating potential problems, and reducing the probability of occurrence. If any impact on the original plan in terms of schedule, budget, or resources is identified and it cannot be absorbed with current reserves, it will be documented and a replanned version of the project will be made and submitted to the steering committee for approval. Replanning without impact on final constraints will be approved directly by the PM on project team meetings. All outputs of the project team meeting will be made available to the relevant stakeholders via e-mail with the subject: Project Review Week x. To avoid delays in solving issues, communication status on future actions or identification of new issues should be reported as soon as possible either formally or informally to the PM.

6.1. Quality Assurance and Control

Software Quality Assurance (SQA) is defined as a planned and systematic approach to the evaluation of the quality of and adherence to software product standards, processes, and procedures. It ensures that standards and procedures are established, and are followed throughout the project life cycle by monitoring and auditing agreed standards.

In the DeDS project, the standards and procedures described in the following subsections will be adopted:

6.1.1. Documentation

All documentation respects the internal standards in their specific form and content. The approved standards are the following:

- IEEE 829: Software Test Documentation
- IEEE 1016: Recommended Practice for Software Design Descriptions
- IEEE 1063: Software Users Documentation

- BS ISO/IE 6592: Information Technology guidelines for the documentation of computer-based applications systems

6.1.2. Code Standards

This project will be developed using the Java programming language. All restrictions on the use of the language features, structures, style conventions, rules for data structures, interfaces, internal code documentation or comments, filenames, file organization, indentation, declarations, statements, naming conventions, and programming practices follow the code conventions for Java programming language recommended by Sun available at http://java.sun.com/docs/codeconv/

6.1.3. Procedures

The following procedures will be adopted:

- IEEE 1074: Standard for Developing Software Life-Cycle Processes
- ISO/IEC 12207: Information Technology—Software Life-Cycle Processes

6.1.4. Software Quality Assurance Activities

The following activities will be audited by the Q&A team:

- Process monitoring, to ensure that all steps documented in the procedure are carried out
- Configuration Management monitoring
- Baseline development and control
- Configuration Control against associated documentation
- Software authentication
- Software performance against specification
- Approved changes to the baseline
- Test procedures (software requirements with test plans)
- Accuracy and completion of test reports
- Regression testing, to ensure that nonconformances have been corrected before delivery
- Adherence to design standards
- Placement of approved design under Configuration Management
- Conformance with approved design standards
- Inclusion of allocated modules in the detail design
- Resolution of all action items
- Readiness for testing of all deliverables
- Certification that testing is complete and software documentation is ready to be delivered
- Participation in the test readiness review, and completion of all action items

6.2. *Change Management and Control*

The change management process is essential to proactively identify modifications in a project. All change requests will be delivered by the requestor to the Program Manager. The Program Manager will keep a log of all requests received. All change requests will be tracked by the Program Manager through a Change Request Log.

Reference H: Glossary

A

activity: An element of work performed during the course of a project. An activity normally has an expected duration, cost, and resource requirements and results in a deliverable or handoff to another activity. In this way, the activity is tied back to the work breakdown structure (WBS). Activities are often subdivided into tasks.

activity-based budget: A budgeting concept based on the goods and services produced by an organization for its customers, rather than the traditional cost-based budget that is based on requests from cost centers. Activities are processes that consume resources, such as time and money, to produce a given output.

actual cost (AC): The total costs incurred that must relate to whatever cost was budgeted within the planned value and earned value—which can sometimes be direct labor hours alone, direct costs alone, or all costs including indirect costs—in accomplishing work during a given time period. See also earned value.

actual cost of work performed (ACWP): The term has been replaced by the term actual cost.

administrative closure: The process of generating, gathering, and disseminating information to formalize phase or project completion.

assumptions: The factors that (for planning purposes) are considered to be true, real, or certain. Assumptions affect all aspects of project planning and are part of the progressive elaboration of the project. Project teams frequently identify, document, and validate assumptions as part of their planning process. They generally involve a degree of risk.

B

baseline: The original approved plan (for a project, a work package, or an activity) with or without approved scope changes. It is usually used with a modifier (e.g., cost baseline, schedule baseline, performance measurement baseline). Also called baseline plan.

budget at completion (BAC): The sum of the total budgets for a project.

budgeted cost of work performed (BCWP): The term has been replaced by the term earned value.

budgeted cost of work scheduled (BCWS): The term has been replaced by the term planned value.

business case: A structured proposal for business improvement that functions as a decision package for organizational decision makers. It may contain the goals of the project and how those goals support the goals of the enterprise. Other sections may include a cost–benefit analysis, a requirements analysis, and a make-or-buy analysis. A business case usually includes a comprehensive fiscal analysis and estimate.

business requirements: These are requirements that refer to business functions of the project, such as project management, financial management, or change management, and how the project will satisfy the business mission of the customer. See also customer requirements.

buy-in: Usually refers to securing a personal or organizational agreement with project goals or management methods. Buy-in from senior management or functional departments may be necessary to accomplish many aspects of an enterprise project.

C

capital programming: An integrated process within a company for planning, budgeting, procurement, and management of the company's portfolio of capital assets to achieve the company's strategic goals and objectives with the lowest life-cycle cost and least risk.

capital project (investment): The acquisition of a capital asset and the management of that asset through its life cycle, after the initial acquisition. Capital projects (investments) may consist of several useful segments.

change control: The processes, procedures, and responsibilities for identifying, evaluating, and managing change. Integration is achieved by assessing a potential change's impact on all relevant aspects of a project, primarily scope, cost, schedule, risk, and quality. Change control involves implementing process-change requests and the systematic tracking of change assessment and implementation.

change management: The process of implementing change control. Change management is the active involvement of project management in monitoring and controlling the change control process.

change control management plan: *See integrated change control management plan.*

closeout: The last phase of a project. Closeout involves closing contracts, archiving records, completing project administrative tasks, and conducting final project reviews.

communications management: *See project communications.*

communications management plan: The plan that describes how the various types of project information are distributed, reviewed, updated, and filed.

concept definition: A phase of a project in which the initial business case (based on a business need) is tested and the viability of the proposed solution and approach is explored. During the concept definition phase, the project is "initiated," or "chartered," and the project sponsor, business sponsor, or project manager is given authority to proceed with the project.

configuration management (CM): Any documented procedure used to apply technical and administrative direction and surveillance to identify and document the functional and physical characteristics of an item or system, control any changes to those characteristics, record and report the change and its implementation status, and audit the items and system to verify their conformance to requirements.

constraint: An applicable restriction that will affect the performance of the project. A constraint is any factor that affects when an activity can be scheduled.

contingencies: *See reserve and contingency planning.*

contingency planning: The development of a management plan that identifies alternative strategies to be used to ensure the project's success even if specified risk events occur.

contingency reserve: The amount of money or time needed above the estimate to reduce the risk of overruns of the project objectives to a level acceptable to the organization.

contract: A mutually binding agreement that obligates the seller to provide the specified product and obligates the buyer to pay for it.

contract administration: The process of managing the relationship with the seller.

contract closeout: Completion and settlement of the contract, including resolution of any open items.

control: The process of comparing actual performance with planned performance, analyzing variances, evaluating possible alternatives, and taking appropriate corrective action as needed.

control charts: A graphic display of the results, over time and against established control limits, of a process. They are used to determine if the process is "in control" or in need of adjustment.

corrective action: Changes made to bring the expected future performance of the project in line with the plan.

cost baseline: The process of freezing cost estimates and budgets. When a baseline is established, the change control process is implemented and performance is measured against the baselined cost data.

cost budgeting: The process of allocating the overall cost estimates to individual project activities.

cost control: The process of controlling changes to the project budget.

cost estimating: The process of developing an approximation (estimate) of the cost of the resources needed to complete project activities.

cost management: The process of monitoring project cost data to determine performance and variance from the planned cost targets/estimates.

cost management plan: A plan that describes the process for implementing change control over cost estimates and the project time-phased cost baseline. The plan includes the steps taken when the performance measurement system identifies major or minor cost variances.

cost of quality: The costs incurred to ensure quality. The cost of quality includes quality planning, quality control, quality assurance, and rework.

cost performance index (CPI): The cost-efficiency ratio of earned value (EV) to actual cost (AC; i.e., CPI = EV/AC). CPI is often used to predict the magnitude of a possible cost overrun, using the following formula: BAC/CPI = projected cost at completion, where BAC is the budget at completion.

cost variance (CV): Any difference between the budgeted cost of an activity and the actual cost (AC) of that activity. In earned value (EV), CV = EV – AC.

crashing: The process of taking action to decrease the total project duration after analyzing a number of alternatives to determine how to get the maximum duration compression at the least cost.

critical activity: Any activity on a critical path. Most commonly determined by using the critical path method. Although some activities are "critical," in the dictionary sense, without being on the critical path, this meaning is seldom used in the project context.

critical path: The series of activities that determines the duration of the project. In a deterministic model, the critical path is usually defined as those activities with float less than or equal to a specified value, often zero. It is the longest path through the project. *See critical path method.*

critical path method (CPM): A network analysis technique used to predict project duration by analyzing which sequence of activities (which path) has the least amount of scheduling flexibility (the least amount of float). Early dates are calculated by means of a "forward pass," using a specified start date. Late dates are calculated by means of a "backward pass," starting from a specified completion date (usually, the forward pass' calculated project early finish date).

critical success factors: The factors that define how progress and outcomes will be measured on a project—sometimes called "objectives." Some typical critical success factors include functionality, quality, time, and cost.

current finish date: The current estimate of the point in time when an activity will be completed.

current start date: The current estimate of the point in time when an activity will begin.

customer: Generally, the organization that receives and becomes the final owner of the project output. The customer can be either internal or external to the organization developing the project output.

customer approval: The formal process of receiving written acceptance of the project output.

customer requirements: The requirements that enumerate and state the customer needs that the project output will satisfy. Requirements typically start with the phrase "The system shall ….."

D

data date (DD): The date at which, or up to which, the project's reporting system has provided actual status and accomplishments. Also called "as of date."

deliverable: Any measurable, tangible, verifiable outcome, result, or item that must be produced to complete a project or part of a project. Often used more narrowly in reference to an external deliverable, which is a deliverable that is subject to approval by the project sponsor or customer.

dependency: The logical relationship between and among tasks of a project's WBS, which can be graphically depicted on a network. May also refer to dependencies among projects.

deployment process: *See also system deployment.*

duration (DU): The number of work periods (not including holidays or other nonworking periods) required to complete an activity or other project element. Usually expressed as work days or work weeks. Sometimes incorrectly equated with elapsed time. *See also effort.*

duration compression: The process of shortening the project schedule without reducing the project scope. Duration compression is not always possible and often entails an increase in project cost.

E

early finish date (EF): In the critical path method, the earliest possible point in time by which the uncompleted portions of an activity (or the project) can be finished, depending on the network logic and any schedule constraints. Early finish dates can change as the project progresses and changes are made to the project pan.

earned value (EV): The physical work accomplished plus the authorized budget for this work. It is the sum of the approved cost estimates (may include overhead allocation) for activities (or portions of activities) completed during a given period (usually project-to-date). Previously called the budgeted cost of work performed (BCWP) for an activity or group of activities.

earned value management (EVM): A method for integrating scope, schedule, and resources, and for measuring project performance. It compares the amount of work that was planned with what was actually earned and what was actually spent to determine if cost and schedule performance are as planned.

effort: The number of labor units required to complete an activity or other project element. Usually expressed as staff hours, staff days, or staff weeks. It should not be confused with duration.

element: One of the parts, substances, or principles that make up a compound or complex whole.

estimate: An assessment of the likely quantitative result. Usually applied to project costs and durations, and should always include some indication of accuracy (e.g., ±x percent). Usually used with a modifier (e.g., preliminary, conceptual, and feasibility). Some application areas have specific modifiers that imply particular accuracy ranges (e.g., order-of-magnitude estimate, budget estimate, and definitive estimate in engineering and construction projects).

estimate at completion (EAC): The expected total cost of an activity, a group of activities, or of the project when the defined scope of work has been completed. Most techniques for forecasting EAC include some adjustment of the original cost estimate, based on project performance to date.

F

final performance report: A report developed during the closeout phase of the project to capture the final variance from baselined scope, cost, and schedule.

finish date: A point in time associated with an activity's completion. Usually qualified by one of the following: actual, planned, estimated, scheduled, early, late, baseline, target, or current.

float: The amount of time that an activity may be delayed from its early start without delaying the project finish date. Float is a mathematical calculation and can change as the project progresses and changes are made to the project plan. Also called slack, total float, and path float.

functional manager: A manager responsible for activities in a specialized department or function (e.g., engineering, manufacturing, and marketing).

H

human resource management: The processes employed to organize the efforts of the personnel assigned to the project. Human resource management includes organizational planning, staff acquisition, and team development.

I

impact assessment: The process of evaluating project risks and performance variances to determine the effect on project disciplines such as scope, cost, and schedule.

impact probability chart: A probability chart that rates risks on the cost effect a risk occurrence will generate on the project budget. It can be expressed as follows: very high (above 81 percent), high (60–80 percent), probable (40–79 percent), low (20–39 percent), and very low (below 19 percent).

information collection and distribution: The process of making needed information available to project shareholders.

initiation: Approving the Project Sponsor, Business Sponsor, or Project Manager to begin the next phase in the project life cycle.

integrated change control: The process of coordinating changes across the entire project.

integrated change control management plan: A plan that establishes the processes, procedures, and responsibilities for identifying, evaluating, and managing change. Integration is achieved by assessing a potential change's impact on all relevant aspects of a project, primarily, scope, cost, schedule, risk, and quality.

integrated project team (IPT): A multidisciplinary team lead by a project manager, responsible and accountable for planning, budgeting, procurement, and life-cycle management of the investment to achieve its cost, schedule, and performance goals. Team skills include budgetary, financial, capital planning, procurement, user, program, value management, earned value management, and other staff skills, as appropriate.

L

lessons learned: The documented learning gained from the process of executing the project. Lessons learned may be identified at any point. This is also considered a project record.

life cycle: The entire useful life of a product or service, usually divided into sequential phases that include initiation, development, execution, operation, maintenance, and disposal or termination.

life-cycle costs: The overall estimated cost for a particular program alternative over the period corresponding to the life of the program, including direct and indirect initial investment (nonrecurring) costs plus any periodic or continuing (recurring) costs for operation and maintenance.

life-cycle costing: The concept of including acquisition, operating, and disposal costs when evaluating various alternatives.

M

major acquisition: A capital project (investment) that requires special management attention because of its (1) importance to a company's mission, (2) high development, operating, or maintenance costs; (3) high risk, (4) high return, or (5) significant role in the administration of a company's programs, finances, property, or other resources.

management plan: *See project management plan.*

master schedule: A summary-level schedule that identifies the major activities and key milestones.

milestone: A significant event in the project, usually completion of a major deliverable.

milestone reviews: Decision points in the life cycle at which the project/system is presented to stakeholders and approved (or disapproved) to move forward to the next step in the process.

mitigation: *See risk mitigation.*

monitoring: The capture, analysis, and reporting of project performance, usually as compared to plan.

N

network analysis: The process of identifying early and late start and finish dates for the uncompleted portions of project activities. See also critical path method, program evaluation and review technique, and graphical evaluation and review technique.

O

operational (steady state): An asset or part of an asset that has been delivered and is performing its mission.

organizational breakdown structure (OBS): A depiction of the project organization arranged so as to relate work packages to organizational units.

organizational planning: The process of identifying, documenting, and assigning project roles, responsibilities, and reporting relationships.

P

performance criteria: A variety of standards used to evaluate variances from the scope, scheduled, and cost baselines. Examples could include scheduled activities that are one week late, cost increases that exceed 10 percent of the budget, or the addition of a work breakdown structure (WBS) work package.

performance reporting: The process of collecting and disseminating performance information. This includes status reporting, progress measurement, and forecasting.

PERT chart: The term is commonly used to refer to a project network diagram. See program evaluation and review technique for the traditional definition of PERT.

planned value (PV): The cumulative budgeted value of the project for work scheduled to date. PV is calculated by applying the scheduled percentage of completion against the cost budget.

planning: The process of preparing, developing, or acquiring the information you will use to design the investment; assess the benefits, risks, and risk-adjusted life-cycle costs of alternative solutions; and establish realistic cost, schedule, and performance goals, for the selected alternative, before either proceeding to full acquisition of the capital project (investment) or useful segment, or terminating the investment. Planning must progress to the point where you are ready to commit to achieving specific goals for the completion of the acquisition before proceeding to the acquisition phase. Information-gathering activities may include market research of available solutions, architectural drawings, geological studies, engineering and design studies, and prototypes. Planning is a useful segment of a capital project (investment). Depending on the nature of the investment, one or more planning segments may be necessary.

PMBOK: The Project Management Body of Knowledge Guide published by the Project Management Institute. This document represents project management best practices.

PMBOK map/mapping: The process of coordinating organizational project management functions with the functional processes and knowledge area activities described in the PMBOK.

policy and governance: Formal written standards that control the operational functions of a major enterprise.

postimplementation report: A report that documents project status and performance, following the post-implementation review.

postimplementation review: The last of the IT milestone reviews. Conducted at a time when an assessment of the operation of the project output is practical. Determines open project activities and ensures that major project requirements are satisfied.

procurement management: *See project procurement management.*

procurement management plan: A plan that describes the project procurement processes such as solicitation planning, solicitation, source selection, and contract administration. Includes the tools and techniques and outputs from each procurement process.

program: A group of related projects managed in a coordinated way. Programs usually include an element of ongoing work.

program evaluation and review technique (PERT): An event-oriented network analysis technique used to estimate project duration when there is uncertainty in the individual activity duration estimates. PERT applies the critical path method, using durations that are computed by a weighted average of optimistic, pessimistic, and most likely duration estimates. It computes the standard deviation of the completion date from those of the path's activity durations.

project: A temporary endeavor undertaken to create a unique product, service, or result.

project assumptions: *See assumptions.*

project authority: Generally, a senior organizational executive who approves project mission and cost planning. In some cases, the project authority and project sponsor may be the same executive.

project budget: The estimated costs, over time, for each project work breakdown structure (WBS) element.

project charter: A formal document issued by senior management that provides the project manager with the authority to apply organizational resources to project activities.

project closeout: *See closeout.*

project constraints: *See constraint.*

project control: The act of monitoring and measuring variances from the project plan. Implementation of the integrated change control process establishes control over project activities.

project communications: The process that ensures the generation, collection, dissemination, and storage of project information. Project communications includes communications planning, information distribution, performance reporting, and administrative closure.

project initiation: *See initiation.*

project life cycle: A collection of generally sequential project phases whose names and numbers are determined by the control needs of the organization or organizations involved in the project.

project management: The application of knowledge, skills, tools, and techniques to project activities to meet the project requirements.

project management information system (PMIS): A system that facilitates project information flow within an organization.

project management office (PMO): The body at the enterprise, administration, or project level that provides project managers with standards, tools, and techniques. The PMO maintains project metrics, and in most cases monitors and consolidates project cost reporting.

project management plan: A management summary document that states the essentials of a project in terms of its objectives, justification, and how the objectives are to be achieved. It describes how major activities of the project management function are to be accomplished (project execution) and the methods of overall project control. The project management plan includes the subsidiary plans covering the project management knowledge areas.

project management process: Overlapping activities occurring at varying intensities throughout each phase of the project.

project management software: A class of computer applications specifically designed to assist planning and controlling of project costs and schedules.

project management team: The members of the project team who are directly involved in project management activities. On some smaller projects, the project management team may include all of the project team members.

project manager (PM): The individual responsible for managing a project.

project master schedule: A detailed schedule (based on project milestones and deliverables) that integrates all aspects of the project. The project master schedule uses the work breakdown structure (WBS).

project performance reports: *See performance reporting.*

project phase: A collection of logically related project activities, usually culminating in the completion of a major deliverable.

project management plan development: The process of integrating and coordinating all project plans to create a consistent, coherent document.

project management plan execution: The process of carrying out the project plan by performing the activities included therein.

project planning: The development and maintenance of the project plan.

project procurement management: A subset of project management that includes the processes required to obtain goods and services from outside the organization to attain the project scope. It consists of procurement planning, solicitation planning, solicitation, source selection, contract administration, and contract closeout.

project procurement management plan: *See procurement management plan.*

project quality management: A subset of project management that includes the processes required to ensure that the project will satisfy the needs for which it was undertaken. It consists of quality planning, quality assurance, and quality control.

project schedule: The planned dates for performing activities and meeting milestones.

project scope: The extent of work that must be done to deliver a product with the specified features and functions.

project scope management: A subset of project management that describes the processes required to ensure that the project includes all of the work required, and only the work required, to complete it successfully. It consists of initiation, scope planning, scope definition, scope verification, and scope change control.

project sponsor: An executive-level person or organization that champions the project goals. In some cases, but not all, the project sponsor may control the financial resources for the project.

project status report: The report that details the current and upcoming activities on the project. It can also describe performance related to project scope, schedule, and cost.

project team members: The people who report either directly or indirectly to the project manager.

project team resources: Generally, the term refers to personnel assigned to the project team. It may include skill descriptions and availability.

project time management: A subset of project management that describes the processes required to ensure timely completion of the project. It consists of activity definition, activity sequencing, activity duration estimating, schedule development, and schedule control.

Q

qualitative risk analysis: A qualitative analysis of risks and conditions that prioritizes their effects on the project objectives. It involves assessing the probability and impact project risks and using methods such as the probability and impact matrix to classify risks into categories of high, moderate, and low for prioritized risk response planning.

quality assurance (QA): The process of evaluating overall project performance on a regular basis to provide confidence that the project will satisfy the relevant quality standards. It may also refer to the organizational unit that is assigned responsibility for quality assurance.

quality control (QC): The process of monitoring specific project results to determine if they comply with relevant quality standards and identifying ways to eliminate causes of unsatisfactory performance. It may also refer to the organizational unit that is assigned responsibility for quality control.

quality management: A function that determines and implements the quality policies, plans, procedures, specifications, and requirements and encompasses the subfunctions of quality assurance (managerial) and quality control (technical).

quality management plan: A plan that addresses what will be measured, how it will be measured, the responsibilities for those activities, and how quality improvement will be implemented during the course of the project.

quality planning: The process of identifying which quality standards are relevant to the project and determining how to apply them.

quantitative risk analysis: Analysis that measures the probability and consequences of risks and estimates their implications for project objectives. Risks are characterized by probability distributions of possible outcomes. This process uses quantitative techniques such as simulation and decision tree analysis.

R

reserve: A provision in the project plan to mitigate cost or schedule risk. Often used with a modifier (e.g., management reserve, contingency reserve) to provide further detail on what types of risk are meant to be mitigated. The specific meaning of the modified term varies by application area.

resource: People, equipment, and materials used to accomplish activities.

rework: Action taken to bring a defective or nonconforming item into compliance with requirements or specifications.

risk: An uncertain event or condition that if it occurs, has a positive or negative effect on a project's objectives.

risk category: A class of potential risk reflecting technical, project management, organizational, or external sources.

risk containment plan: A document detailing all identified risks, including description, cause, probability of occurrence, impacts on objectives, proposed responses, owners, and current status. Also referred to as risk response plan.

risk event: A discrete occurrence that may affect the project for better or worse.

risk identification: The process of determining which risk events might affect the project and documenting their characteristics.

risk management: The art and science of identifying, analyzing, and responding to risk factors throughout the life of a project and in the best interests of its objectives.

risk management plan: A plan that documents how risk management processes will be carried out during the project. This is an output of risk management planning.

risk mitigation: A process that seeks to reduce the probability or impact of a risk to below an acceptable threshold.

risk monitoring and control: The process of monitoring residual risks, identifying new risks, executing risk reduction plans, and evaluating their effectiveness throughout the project life cycle.

risk response plan: *See risk containment plan.*

S

schedule baseline: *See baseline*

schedule control: The process of controlling changes to the project schedule.

schedule critical path: Activities or tasks in a project schedule that will either shorten or lengthen the total duration of the project if the duration of the activities or tasks changes.

schedule dependency: The linking of tasks in a project schedule in order of execution or implementation. Example: task must be completed before task B.

schedule development: The process of analyzing activity sequences, activity durations, and resource requirements to create the project schedule.

schedule management: A function that updates the project master schedule and compares progress with the baseline schedule. Changes to the project schedule are managed through the integrated change control plan.

schedule performance: The process of comparing the project master schedule with the baseline schedule to determine slippage or changes in scope.

schedule performance index (SPI): The schedule efficiency ratio of earned value (EV) accomplished against the planned value (PV). The SPI describes what portion of the planned schedule was actually accomplished. SPI is calculated as SPI = EV/PV.

schedule variance (SV): Any difference between the scheduled completion of an activity and the actual completion of that activity. In earned value, SV = EV − PV where PV is the planned value.

scope: The products and services to be provided by a project. *See project scope and product scope.*

scope change: Any change to the project scope. A scope change almost always requires an adjustment to the project cost or schedule.

scope change control: The process of controlling changes to project scope.

scope creep: Any change to the project scope (products and services described by the project) that happens incrementally and is hard to recognize.

scope definition: The process of subdividing the major deliverables into smaller, more manageable components to provide better control.

scope management: *See integrated change control.*

scope planning: The process of progressively elaborating the work of the project, which includes developing a written scope statement that includes the project justification, the major deliverables, and the project objectives.

scope statement: A document that provides a basis for making future project decisions and for confirming or developing a common understanding of project scope among the stakeholders. As the project progresses, the scope statement may need to be revised or refined to reflect approved changes to the scope of the project.

scope verification: Formalizing acceptance of the project scope.

simulation: This uses a project model that translates the uncertainties specified at a detailed level into their potential impact on objectives that are expressed at the level of the total project. Project simulations use computer models (e.g., Monte Carlo technique) and estimates of risk at a detailed level.

solicitation: The process of obtaining quotations, bids, offers, or proposals, as appropriate.

source selection: The process of choosing from among potential vendors.

sponsor: *See project sponsor.*

staff acquisition: The process of getting needed human resources assigned to and working on the project.

stakeholder: An individual or organization that is actively involved in the project or whose interests may be positively or negatively affected as a result of project execution or project completion. They may also exert influence over the project and its results.

start date: A point in time associated with an activity's start, usually qualified by one of the following: actual, planned, estimated, scheduled, early, late, target, baseline, or current.

statement of work (SOW): A narrative description of products or services to be supplied under contract.

system development: A project life-cycle phase encompassing the design, integration, and demonstration of the project output. Generally follows the planning phase and is usually accomplished in conjunction with the execution and control process groups.

systems development life cycle: A life cycle that varies by project output. For example, in the construction, the systems development life cycle could be described as feasibility, planning, design, construction, and turnover. For software development, a spiral (the life cycle repeats until complete) process is employed: requirements identification, systems design, build and rebuild, and evaluation.

system development methodology: The type of methodology to be used in a system development project, e.g., Rational Unified Process, spiral development, iterative development, information engineering methodology, or rapid application development methodology.

system operation: The phase in the system life cycle where the system is in use and ongoing activities such as regular maintenance and improvement are under way.

system prototype: A developmental model that is used for testing in an operational environment. Typically built to be modified into the production model.

T

task: A generic term for work that is not included in the work breakdown structure (WBS), but potentially could represent a further decomposition of work by the individuals responsible for that work. Also, the lowest level of effort on a project.

triggers: Sometimes called risk symptoms or warning signs, these are indications that a risk has occurred or is about to occur. Triggers may be discovered in the risk identification process and are watched in the risk monitoring and control process.

U

user: Usually, a member of the customer's organization. The person or organization that will operate the project's output.

V

variance: Any divergence from the plan. For example, if the schedule falls behind, it is said to have negative variance. A variance is typically expressed in explicit terms, such as a $200,000 overrun. Variance can also be expressed as an index; for example, a schedule performance index of 0.89 would mean the schedule is 11 percent behind the baseline plan (schedule).

W

work activities: Sometimes called tasks, these are generally the project events or efforts that make up a schedule. Activities have a duration (time), consume resources, and in most cases, are dependent or result from other activities.

work activity durations: The amount of time it takes to accomplish the work. Can be expressed in hours, day, weeks, or months.

work breakdown structure (WBS): A deliverable-oriented grouping of project elements that organizes and defines the total scope of the project. Each descending level represents an increasingly detailed definition of a project work.

work breakdown structure (WBS) baseline: The process of freezing the WBS to measure the effect of change. When the WBS is baselined, change control is applied and change is assessed against other aspects of the project, such as cost and schedule.

work package: A deliverable at the lowest level of the work breakdown structure (WBS), where that deliverable may be assigned to another project manager to plan and execute. This may be accomplished through the use of a subproject where the work package may be further decomposed into activities.

Source: VA IT Project Management Handbook. Retrieved from http://www.ocio.usda.gov/p_mgnt/.

INDEX

Index